GENE ACTION

Second Edition

Philip E. Hartman
Sigmund R. Suskind

The Johns Hopkins University

D1363847

PRENTICE-HALL, INC.   *Englewood Cliffs, New Jersey*

FOUNDATIONS OF MODERN GENETICS SERIES
Sigmund R. Suskind and Philip E. Hartman, editors

© *Copyright 1965, 1969*
by PRENTICE-HALL, INC.
Englewood Cliffs, New Jersey
All rights reserved. No part of this
book may be reproduced in any form
or by any means without permission in
writing from the publishers.

Printed in the United States of America
P–13–347542–5
C–13–347559–X

Library of Congress Catalog Card Number:
69–10439

Current printing (last digit) :
12 11 10 9 8 7 6 5 4 3 2

PRENTICE-HALL INTERNATIONAL, INC., *London*
PRENTICE-HALL OF AUSTRALIA, PTY., LTD., *Sydney*
PRENTICE-HALL OF CANADA, LTD., *Toronto*
PRENTICE-HALL OF INDIA PRIVATE LTD., *New Delhi*
PRENTICE-HALL OF JAPAN, INC., *Tokyo*

PRENTICE-HALL FOUNDATIONS OF MODERN *Genetics* SERIES

Sigmund R. Suskind and Philip E. Hartman, Editors

AGRICULTURAL GENETICS
James L. Brewbaker

GENE ACTION, Second Edition
Philip E. Hartman and Sigmund R. Suskind

EXTRACHROMOSOMAL INHERITANCE
John L. Jinks

DEVELOPMENTAL GENETICS*
Clement Markert and Heinrich Ursprung

HUMAN GENETICS, Second Edition
Victor A. McKusick

POPULATION GENETICS AND EVOLUTION
Lawrence E. Mettler and Thomas G. Gregg

THE MECHANICS OF INHERITANCE, Second Edition
Franklin W. Stahl

CYTOGENETICS
Carl P. Swanson, Timothy Merz, and William J. Young

*Published jointly in Prentice-Hall's *Foundations of Developmental Biology Series.*

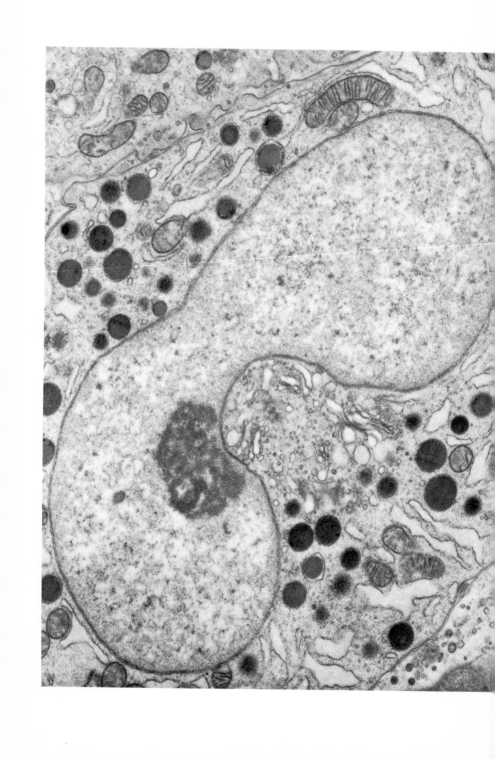

To David M. Bonner,

with our warm affection and respect

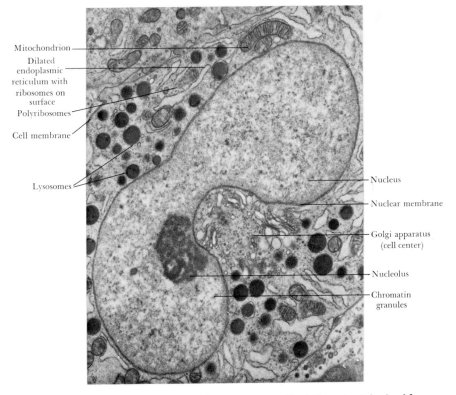

Mitochondrion

Dilated
endoplasmic
reticulum with
ribosomes on
surface

Polyribosomes

Cell membrane

Lysosomes

Nucleus

Nuclear membrane

Golgi apparatus
(cell center)

Nucleolus

Chromatin
granules

FRONTISPIECE. *Electron micrograph of bone marrow cell of the rat, stained with lead. Photograph courtesy of Dr. Leon P. Weiss, Department of Anatomy, The Johns Hopkins University School of Medicine. Magnification on page ii:36,125 ×. Reproduced above in reduced size with identifying labels.*

Foundations of Modern Genetics

The books in this series are intended to lead the alert reader directly into the exciting research literature of modern genetics. The forefront of genetic research draws heavily on concepts and tools of chemistry, physics, and mathematics. Because of this, the principles of genetics are presented here together with discussions of other relevant scientific areas. We hope this approach will encourage a fuller comprehension of the principles of genetics and, equally important, of the types of experiments that led to their formulation. The experimental method compels the questions: What is the *evidence* for this concept? What are its *limitations*? What are its *applications*?

Genetics today is penetrating increasingly into new areas of biology. Its rapidly expanding methodology is enabling research workers to find answers to questions that it was futile to ask only a short while ago. Even more provocative studies now underway are raising new, heretofore unimagined questions.

The design of the individual short volumes of the Prentice-Hall Foundations of Modern Genetics Series permits stimulating, selective, and detailed treatments of each of the various aspects of the broad field of genetics. This facilitates more authoritative presentations of the material and simplifies the revisions necessary to keep abreast of a rapidly moving field. Each volume has its own individual focus and personality while at the same time overlapping with other volumes in the Series sufficiently to allow ready transition. Collectively, the Series, now complete, covers the main areas of contemporary genetic thought, serving as a thorough, up-to-date textbook of genetics—and, we hope, pointing the reader toward experiments even more penetrating than those described.

SIGMUND R. SUSKIND
PHILIP E. HARTMAN

Contents

Chemical Order
amid Biological Diversity

We are confronted by an amazing diversity of organisms in the world about us and by a variety of cell types within a single complex organism. Clearly, this complexity must have its basis at the intracellular and molecular level. How can we begin to unravel and resolve such seemingly complicated problems?

Part of biological diversity stems from inheritance, part from interaction of the organism with its environment. To understand the mechanisms that provide a cell with its features or phenotype, we must question the nature of cell heredity and of gene action.

Fortunately, there is order in biology just as there is in chemistry, physics, and mathematics. The taxonomist classifies various organisms into groups whose members have overlapping features, the cytologist labels classes of cell structures (frontispiece), the chemist groups molecules of similar structure, and so on. Knowledge allows the rational assortment of information into orderly arrays, which continue to expose the secrets of nature. The chemical story of the cell is the synthesis of small molecules and their union to form specific classes of macromolecules. Only recently have we gained knowledge concerning the structures of the giant molecules in cells that largely control the cell's form and activities. These macromolecules are polymers, and knowledge of their structure and function has offered us a unique probe into basic biological processes. In *The Mechanics of Inheritance,* a companion volume in this series, Franklin W. Stahl presents the evidence that the genetic material of many organisms is composed of deoxyribonucleic acid (DNA). DNA molecules are giant linear polymers usually containing four different smaller molecules repeated many times: adenine, thymine, guanine, and cytosine. These four chemical building blocks share some common structural features and represent the four letters in the nucleic acid genetic code, A, T, G, and C. *The Mechanics of Inheritance* is concerned with the structure and replication of DNA and its accurate partitioning to progeny. In this book we focus on mechanisms through which the genetic information determines the specific characteristics of cells and organisms.

Our approach will be simple and direct. Gene action is equated with protein formation and function. It will be assumed that these are the basic processes from which all other consequences arise. Chapter 2 considers the structure of proteins and some of the methods used to study these large molecules.

Watson-Crick Base Pairing

How does the protein-synthesizing machinery read and translate the nucleic acid code into an accurate positioning of each amino acid during formation of the polypeptide chain of the protein? Recall the rules of specific base pairing (Watson-Crick pairing) in double-stranded DNA: the purine adenine pairs with the pyrimidine thymine and the purine guanine pairs with the pyrimidine cytosine (Fig. 1.1). Stahl's *The Mechanics of Inheritance* presents the evidence for the existence of these hydrogen-bonded purine-pyrimidine base pairs in DNA and stresses their importance in DNA replication.

Just as guanine pairs with cytosine in the two strands of the DNA double helix, so can a guanine in a DNA strand pair with a cytosine in a ribonucleic acid (RNA) strand (and vice versa). Similarly, the adenine of DNA can pair with the uracil in RNA, the thymine in DNA with the adenine in RNA. Thus, RNA contains uracil instead of the thymine found in DNA, and these two bases have similar base-pairing properties. The basic hydrogen-bonding rules that apply to these DNA-RNA hybrid molecules are essentially those that apply to the two strands of DNA itself. Two RNA strands of complementary base sequence also can form a duplex structure by similar rules, forming the purine-pyrimidine base pairs A:U and G:C.

These base-pairing rules provide a mechanism that is extremely important in the determination of the amino acid sequence of a polypeptide chain (Fig. 1.2). Most likely the base sequence in only one strand of the DNA duplex serves as master template for the enzymatic synthesis of a messenger RNA (mRNA) complementary

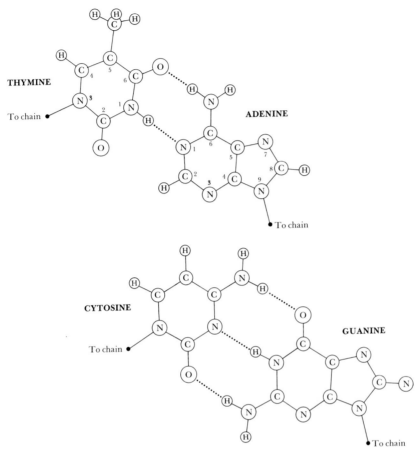

FIG. 1.1. *The Watson-Crick base pairs in DNA: adenine-thymine and guanine-cytosine.*

copy. The information contained in the specific, inherited sequence of bases in the DNA thereby is built into a messenger ribonucleic acid copy. This is called *transcription* of genetic information.

This chemical information in the mRNA then can be *translated* into an amino acid sequence. During translation, small ribonucleic acids called *transfer RNAs* (tRNA) become oriented along the mRNA. This occurs on subcellular particles called *ribosomes*. The ribosomes serve to orient the different components in some crucial manner. Each tRNA molecule has an amino acid attached to it. The ordering of the small tRNA molecules along the long, linear mRNA chain again is due to Watson-Crick base pairing and similar complementary sequences on

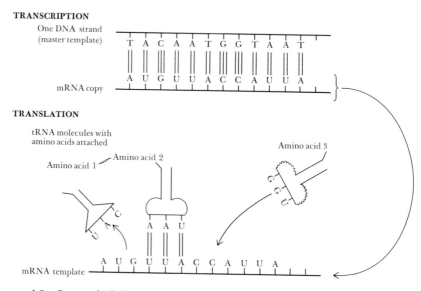

FIG. 1.2. *Some principal steps in protein biosynthesis and the important roles base pairing plays in the process.*

the mRNA and the various tRNA molecules (Fig. 1.2). During the enzyme-mediated translation step, the individual amino acids that are covalently bound to each tRNA type now become ordered in a specific sequence in the growing polypeptide chain. The amino acids are successively linked in linear sequence by peptide bonds and detached from their tRNA molecules. In the process, a string of amino acids, a *polypeptide chain,* is formed. The sequence of amino acids in the polypeptide chain represents the primary structure of the protein.

The nature of the interactions which permit accurate transcription and translation during protein synthesis are only partially understood.

In the process, the four-letter genetic code in the DNA has been transcribed to an mRNA intermediate and this mRNA sequence translated into a specific polypeptide sequence containing the 20 different amino acids. Chapter 6 introduces the subject of protein synthesis, and later chapters examine various aspects of this process.

Colinearity of Gene and Polypeptide Chain

Note the exquisite simplicity of the above system (Fig. 1.2). A specific sequence of components (bases) in one segment of a linear macromolecule (DNA) has specified ultimately the sequence of components (amino acids) in another macromolecule (protein) of totally different chemical composition. The two molecules are *colinear* (parallel) structures. An alteration in the structure of the template DNA leads to a concomitant alteration in the same relative position along a specific protein product.

Figure 1.3 illustrates the principle of colinearity of gene and polypeptide chain. An alteration in the DNA is a mutation, inherited as the master template is inherited. The mutation results in a change in the sequence or number of bases in the DNA. This change is copied in mRNA and thence translated as an amino acid sequence different from the normal amino acid sequence. The polypeptide chain subsequently folds into one or more chemically feasible forms. The final configuration of the mutant protein may be similar to the normal protein and thus ultimately lead to a phenotype that is only quantitatively different from the normal. Or, the final configuration of the protein may be drastically altered, in which case a more drastic phenotype ultimately results. The kind and position in the chain of the qualitative amino acid change determine the quantitative effect on the phenotype. Aspects of this situation are discussed in Chap. 3. What we are interested in here is the location of the amino acid change in the polypeptide chain itself and the location of the genetic change in the DNA. The amino acid change and its absolute position in the chain

FIG. 1.3. *Colinearity between gene and polypeptide chain. The highly schematic diagram pictures the normal (wild-type) and three different mutant genes and their products. A qualitative change in the gene elicits a qualitative change in the messenger RNA and in the amino acid sequence of the polypeptide chain. Owing to differences in patterns of folding, the activities of the final protein products may be altered qualitatively or quantitatively. The bottom of the diagram shows two colinear structures inferred from genetic and from chemical experiments. One is a genetic map, determined from recombination tests, and the second is a map of the polypeptide chain indicating the locations of the alterations in each of the three mutants.*

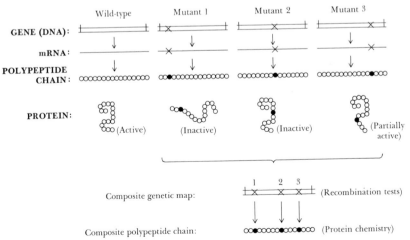

can be determined by the methods of protein chemistry, as outlined in Chap. 2. The position of the genetic alteration in the DNA can be determined by recombination tests between mutants of different origin. Through the combined efforts of these different disciplines we can determine that the two structures are colinear. The linear sequence of nucleotides in the gene, and subsequently in the mRNA, specifies the linear sequence of amino acids in the protein. You might think about the importance and the significance of the idea of colinearity, and the evidence for it, as you read the chapters that follow.

Throughout transcription and translation numerous enzyme-catalyzed reactions play an important role. How are these and other biochemical processes of the cell integrated and controlled? For example, what forms of regulation are exerted on the biosynthesis of small molecules and of macromolecules? Biological systems are highly ordered and balanced. We can learn about their function through careful study of normal metabolism as well as by disruption of this orderliness by specific mutation or by sudden environmental modification. Some of these facets of gene action will be examined once the basic plan of protein biosynthesis has been described and some critical experimental methodology has been introduced. You will find that most of the systems we discuss are microbial; it is these model, easily manipulated test-tube systems that so far have shed most light on the subjects with which we are concerned.

But first, in Chaps. 2 and 3 we shall consider some of the basic chemistry of protein structure and the evidence for genetic control of this structure. Firm grounding in these subjects is essential to comprehension and enjoyment of our subsequent discussions of gene action and its control.

References, Including Extensive Introductions to Microbial and Biochemical Genetics

Modern review or symposium articles on genetical subjects form excellent supplements to the contents of this book. Particularly good sources are: *Advances in Genetics, Progress in Nucleic Acid Research and Molecular Biology, Advances in Virus Research, Annual Review of Microbiology, Annual Review of Biochemistry, Annual Review of Genetics,* and *Cold Spring Harbor Symposia on Quantitative Biology.*

The current literature in gene action is scattered among many journals. The subject indexes of *Biological Abstracts* and of *Chemical Abstracts* form good starting places, assisting in location of material. Many good articles in genetics are to be found in: *Genetics, Genetical Research, Journal of Bacteriology, Journal of Molecular Biology, Mutation Research, Proceedings of the National Academy of Science U.S., Japanese Journal of Genetics, Molecular and General Genetics* (formerly *Zeitschrift für Vererbungslehre*), *Biochemical Genetics.*

Adams, M. H., *Bacteriophages*. New York: John Wiley & Sons, Inc. (Inter-science Division) , 1959.

Burdette, W. J., ed., *Methodology in Basic Genetics*. San Francisco: Holden-Day, Inc., 1963.

Fincham, J. R. S., and P. R. Day, *Fungal Genetics*. Philadelphia: F. A. Davis Co., 1963.

Hayes, W., *Genetics of Bacteria and Their Viruses*, 2nd ed. New York: John Wiley & Sons, Inc., 1969.

Jacob, F., and E. L. Wollman, *Sexuality and the Genetics of Bacteria*. New York: Academic Press, Inc., 1961.

Peters, J. A., *Classic Papers in Genetics*. Englewood Cliffs, N.J.: Prentice-Hall, Inc., 1959. An annotated collection of important original literature in genetics that gives an excellent view of the evolution of concepts concerning genes and how they act.

Stent, G. S., *Molecular Biology of Bacterial Viruses*. San Francisco: W. H. Freeman and Company, 1963.

Taylor, J. H., *Selected Papers on Molecular Genetics*. New York: Academic Press, Inc., 1965. A collection of reprints of 55 important papers in biochemical genetics, including a number on the functioning of genetic material.

Wagner, R. P., and H. K. Mitchell, *Genetics and Metabolism*, 2nd ed. New York: John Wiley & Sons, Inc., 1964. An excellent textbook on biochemical genetics, including many aspects of gene action.

NOTE: Other volumes in this series are cited in each chapter to which they pertain. We recommend that you consult them for important background information and for discussions related to many topics in this book.

The legends to many of our figures contain references to the source of the material explicitly detailed therein. These sources generally are good starting points where you may find more information concerning the topic under discussion. In the interests of conserving space, they are not cited again under the references at the ends of chapters, although it would be appropriate to do so in most cases.

Two

Protein Structure

Proteins are an important class of molecules, essential to cell structure and cell function. The proteins with catalytic activities, enzymes, are largely responsible for determining the phenotype or properties of a cell in a particular environment. The total hereditary material of the cell, the genotype, dictates which kinds of protein the cell can potentially produce. Most gene action can be attributed to a mechanism by which individual genes dictate the structures of individual kinds of proteins. We want to understand how the genetic material governs the structure and consequently the activities of proteins and how the environment influences the expression of this genetic potentiality.

Proteins are immensely versatile macromolecules. Built into the structure of proteins is information that instructs them in "what to do" (catalytic activity), "where to go" in the cell (intracellular organization), and "when and how to perform" (control of function through interactions with other proteins, small activators, or inhibitors). The basic, *primary* structure of a protein is relatively simple and consists of one or more linear chains of small building blocks, amino acids, held together by covalent bonds called *peptide bonds*. This linear structure, the polypeptide chain, often assumes a helical shape to give what is called the *secondary structure*. This, in turn can fold in specific fashions to give the three-dimensional or *tertiary structure* of the protein molecule. Finally, some proteins are built of subunits of identical or different types of polypeptide chains. These subunits interact with one another in a highly specific manner to form the *quaternary structure* of the protein. The permissible conformations, and subsequently the biological activity of the protein in a given environment, are specified primarily by the sequence of amino acids in the polypeptide chain. In these folded, specifically oriented configurations of the protein lie many of the secrets of gene action. This chapter summarizes some aspects of protein structure that are essential to later discussions of protein biosynthesis and how mutations in the genetic material influence protein structure and biological activity.

Primary Structure: *The Amino Acid Sequence*

The *primary structure* of a protein refers to the sequence of small, nitrogen-containing compounds called *amino acids,* which are the building blocks of the protein molecule. In the general structure for an ionized amino acid shown in Fig. 2.1, R stands for side chains that are different for each amino acid. R can be as simple as a hydrogen atom (H) or a methyl group (CH_3), or it can be a more complex structure. The first carbon is part of the acidic carboxyl group (COO^-). The second carbon (printed in bold type), to which is attached a basic ammonium group (NH_3^+), is called the α *carbon.* Amino acids are amphoteric electrolytes: they can act either as acids or as bases. The amino acid in Fig. 2.1 is in the zwitterion, or dipolar, form. In acid solutions, the ionization of the carboxyl group is suppressed, and the molecule possesses a positive charge; in basic solutions, the molecule loses a proton from the amino group and thus carries a negative charge. The net charge of the protein, determined by the charge of the individual R groups, is responsible for the electrolytic properties of the molecule, so that proteins, as well as their constituent amino acids, are amphoteric molecules.

The α carbon of most amino acids is joined by covalent bonds to four different groups. The exception is glycine, in which R is a hydrogen atom. Thus, except in glycine, the α carbon is asymmetric. Because of this asymmetry, the amino acid molecule can assume two alternative optical configurations or isomers, the D isomer and the L

FIG. 2.1. *General formula for an amino acid.*

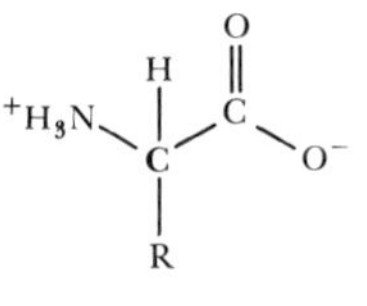

FIG. 2.2.   *Amino acids found in proteins.*

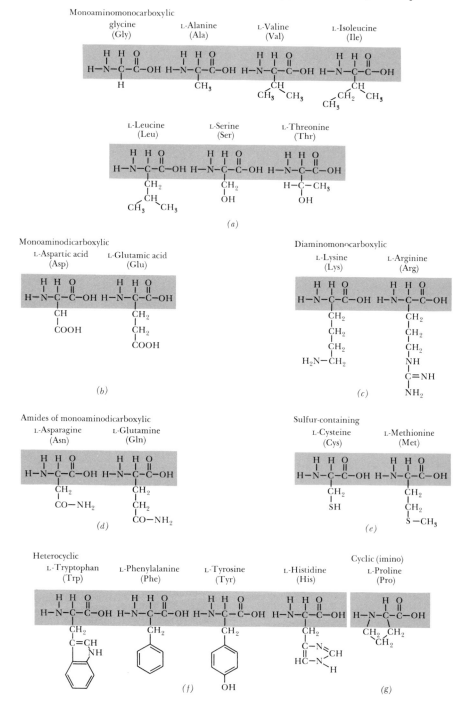

isomer. This optical activity refers to the ability of amino acids or certain derivatives in solution to rotate a plane of polarized light to the right or to the left.

Although many different amino acids have been isolated from various plants and animals, only 20 of the L isomers are found in most proteins. The nearly universal use of only 20 amino acids for the synthesis of widely different proteins is one of nature's enigmatic rules. We can only argue, teleologically, that during the course of evolution other amino acids may have been tried, tested, and found to present either no advantage or a disadvantage to organisms.

Formulas for these 20 amino acids are depicted in Fig. 2.2. The abbreviations given in the figure are standard nomenclature, agreed upon by chemists and increasingly utilized by geneticists.

Proteins vary widely in amino acid content. Different types of proteins within an organism may have very different amounts of a particular amino acid. Some amino acids are numerous in one protein but rare in others. Other amino acids, for example tryptophan, are entirely absent in certain proteins. In most cases, however, a single protein contains all 20 of the amino acids.

The molecular weights of the amino acids in proteins average about 110. The molecular weight of a protein is approximately equal to the total of the molecular weights of its component amino acids if we neglect the water molecules that are mainly associated with the protein in solution. Proteins generally have molecular weights between 12,000 and 90,000. Still larger proteins are known; however, most of these probably are dimers or higher multimers containing smaller polypeptide chains as subunits.

The amino acids are linked by a covalent bond termed a *peptide bond* (one type of amide linkage) between the amino group of one amino acid and the carboxyl group of an adjacent amino acid. A pair of amino acids linked in this manner is called a *dipeptide*. A group of three is called a *tripeptide,* and so on. The general structure of a *polypeptide chain* is shown in Fig. 2.3. The peptide bonds, indicated by bold type, provide the backbone of the protein and are responsible for important facets of its molecular organization. The amino acid side chains (R in Fig. 2.3 and the unshadowed areas in Fig. 2.2) also play important roles in protein structure and function.

FIG. 2.3. *A polypeptide chain consisting of an N-terminal amino acid (on the left), a number (n) of centrally located amino acids, and a C-terminal amino acid (on the right).*

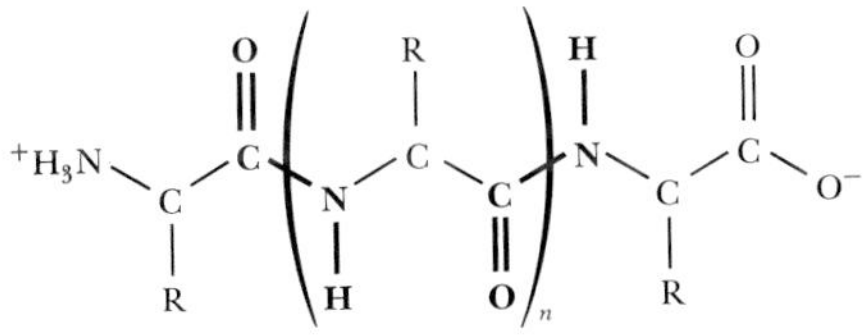

The terminal amino acid with the free amino group in the poly-peptide chain is called the *N-terminal amino acid.* The terminal amino acid with the free carboxyl group is called the *C-terminal amino acid.* Each amino acid in the chain is termed a *residue.* In numbering the amino acids in an extended polypeptide chain, convention dictates that the N-terminal residue be number 1 and that the C-terminal residue be the final number in the sequence. When the sequence of amino acids in a peptide is described, the C-terminal residue is mentioned last. For example, a tripeptide with an N-terminal glycine linked to an alanine that is linked to a C-terminal histidine is referred to as glycyl-L-alanyl-L-histidine and is abbreviated Gly-Ala-His. If the sequence of amino acids in such a tripeptide is not known, the abbreviation would be (Gly,Ala,His), the parentheses and commas denoting that only the composition of the tripeptide is known.

We can consider that a single protein species produced by genetically identical cells has a definite composition. For example, the "A protein" portion of the enzyme tryptophan synthetase from the bacterium *Escherichia coli* has been extracted, purified, and shown to contain 267 amino acid residues. Each amino acid is represented a certain number of times. Such an analysis is garnered from an examination of a large collection of A protein molecules. Since this population of molecules appears homogeneous by chemical and physical criteria, one may extrapolate the results of analyses on populations of molecules to individual molecules. When this protein is analyzed for amino acid composition, a definite number of each type of amino acid is found. The same results are found for different batches of the A protein. In addition, the *sequence* of amino acids along the linear polypeptide chain may be considered to be unique and constant in a single protein species. This stability of amino acid composition and sequence remains as long as no genetic change occurs. As an example of amino acid composition and sequence, the detailed primary structure of the tryptophan synthetase A protein is shown in Fig. 2.4.

The first and most crucial requirement in studies of protein structure is the complete purification of the protein from crude cell extracts. Wisdom in the selection of the organism as well as the protein is very important, because substantial quantities of the pure protein are needed for thorough analysis. Although we cannot yet be absolutely certain that the pure isolated proteins and the proteins in their native

FIG. 2.4. *Primary structure of the tryptophan synthetase A protein of the bacterium* Escherichia coli. *Some places where the protein is split by various treatments are indicated. The amino acid sequence in the polypeptide chain has been determined by methods described in the text. Sequence drawn from C. Yanofsky, G. R. Drapeau, J. R. Guest, and B. C. Carlton,* Proc. Natl. Acad. Sci. U.S., 57 *(1967), 296, and J. R. Guest, G. R. Drapeau, B. C. Carlton, and C. Yanofsky,* J. Biol. Chem., 242 *(1967), 5442.*

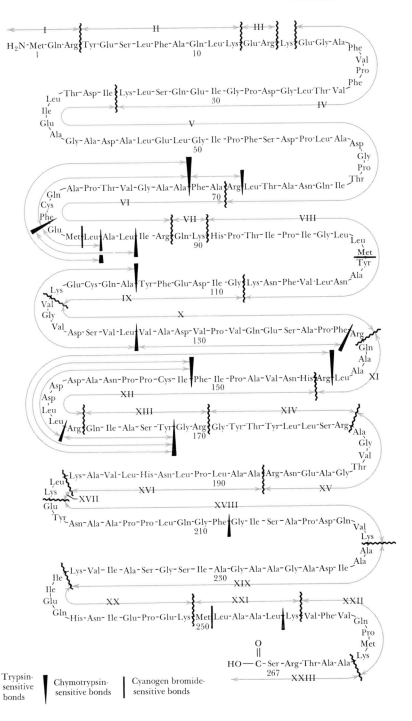

Trypsin-sensitive bonds
Chymotrypsin-sensitive bonds
Cyanogen bromide-sensitive bonds

state in the cell are identical in all respects, the methods of modern biochemistry do provide us with considerable reassurance that this is often so.

DETERMINING THE SEQUENCE

The sequence of amino acids cannot be determined directly at the present time in long, unfragmented polypeptide chains. As discussed below, the chemical methods of sequentially removing single amino acid residues from a polypeptide have limitations that increase with the length of the polypeptide chain. For example, the treatments occasionally break some of the internal peptide bonds, and the attack on all the molecules of a protein population is not entirely synchronous or complete. Therefore, ordinarily the protein is initially cut into short peptide segments that are more uniformly susceptible to treatment. These highly refined chemical and enzymatic procedures have evolved from approaches first introduced by Nobel-prize winner Frederick Sanger in the 1940s.

Fragmentation of the polypeptide chain. To fragment the polypeptide chains of a population of identical protein molecules, the breakages must be obtained at the same specific positions in each of the chains. Only in this manner can a yield of fragments of homogeneous composition be produced. Several chemicals can be used to accomplish this. For example, cyanogen bromide in slightly acidic solution cleaves the peptide bond between methionine and the next amino acid, yielding peptide fragments, one with a new N-terminal amino acid and one with a C-terminal homoserine (Fig. 2.5). Another useful chemical is the oxidizing agent *N*-bromosuccinimide, which often breaks the polypeptide chain adjacent to tryptophan residues.

The proteolytic enzyme trypsin specifically splits polypeptide chains at the carboxyl side of arginine and lysine residues (shown by wavy lines in Fig. 2.4). Trypsin does not act in cases where proline is the immediately succeeding residue. The peptides released by trypsin (tryptic peptides) are indicated by Roman numerals, numbering from the N-terminal end to the C-terminal end of the original polypeptide chain. The production of a mixture of the two types of tryptic peptides can be avoided by pretreating the protein with carbon disulfide. This compound chemically protects the lysine residues from the action of trypsin, and thus tryptic hydrolysis occurs only at the arginine sites.

Another widely used enzyme is chymotrypsin, which most effectively hydrolyzes peptide bonds adjacent to the aromatic amino acids tryptophan, phenylalanine, and tyrosine. Chymotrypsin hydrolyzes other peptide bonds more slowly, for example, following leucine residues at the points indicated in Fig. 2.4. The hydrolysis is blocked if a proline residue is next to the aromatic amino acid or if the aromatic amino acid

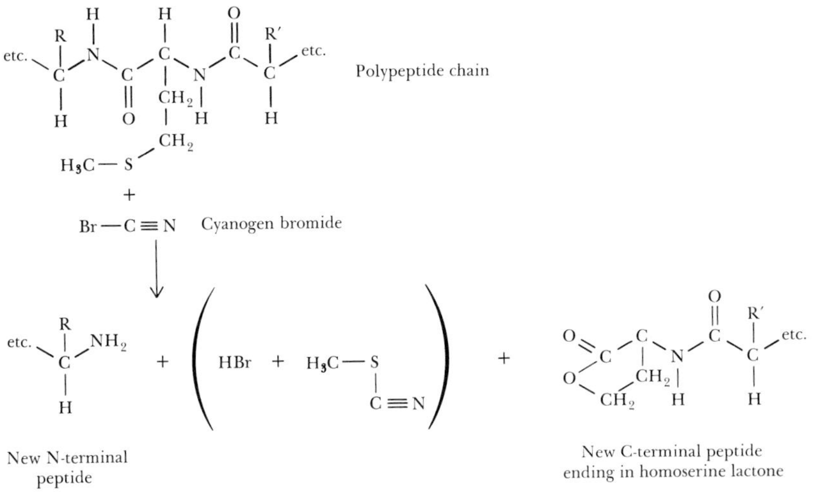

FIG. 2.5. *Chemical treatment that specifically breaks polypeptide chains into fragments at methionyl residues.*

is N-terminal. Other proteolytic enzymes also may be used—pepsin, subtilisin, papain, or Nagarse (bacterial Al protease), for example.

Isolation and characterization of peptides. As can be seen in Fig. 2.4, treatment of a protein can produce a mixture of peptides of different amino acid composition. Before the individual peptides can be analyzed, they must be separated.

The methods for separation take advantage of the different sizes and solubilities of the various peptide fragments, as well as of their different net charge (number and type of charged amino acid residues). Separation and purification can be achieved by passing the protein digest through a glass column filled with an ion-exchange resin. Such a resin has a higher affinity for some charged groups than it has for others; thus it retards the passage through the column of some peptides to a greater extent than it does others. Peptides also may be separated on the basis of their differential solubilities in certain solvents by a process called countercurrent distribution.

A mixture of peptides also can be separated by the *"fingerprint"* technique. Figure 2.6 shows a fingerprint of peptides obtained from a digest of normal tryptophan synthetase A protein. A small drop of the protein hydrolysate was placed at a spot (labeled "origin" in the figure) on one edge of a sheet of filter paper. A suitable solvent was allowed to flow through this spot and across the paper, moving different peptides different distances, depending on the solubilities of the peptides in the solvent used. This first step is known as *chromatography*. The paper was then turned 90° and placed in a second buffered solvent,

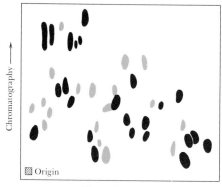

Chromatography ⟶

Origin

Electrophoresis ⟶

FIG. 2.6. *Fingerprint of peptide fragments obtained after tryptic and chymotryptic digestion of wild-type* E. coli *tryptophan synthetase A protein. The intensity of the staining of a spot is influenced by the quantity and composition of the peptide. See the text for details. Drawn from D. R. Helinski and C. Yanofsky, Proc. Natl. Acad. Sci. U.S., 48 (1962), 173, and J. R. Guest and C. Yanofsky, J. Biol. Chem., 240 (1965), 679.*

and a high-voltage electric current was run through the solution. Because the peptides differed in net charge, they migrated at different rates. This step is called *electrophoresis*. The combination of the two procedures conveniently separates the different peptides. When suitably stained, the peptides are seen at different spots on the paper. The behavior of peptides in these separation methods gives some idea of their size and content of charged amino acids and also provides some hints as to their composition.

In Figure 2.6 the paper was sprayed with a dye, ninhydrin, which revealed the distribution of the peptides. This dye forms colored complexes (yellowish to yellowish-gray to blue) with free α-amino acids and also reacts with peptides. To obtain more information about the amino acid composition of the peptides, other color reagents can be used, each of which reacts with and thus reveals only those peptides that contain histidine, arginine, or tyrosine residues. The protein also may be selectively labeled with a radioisotope by allowing synthesis to occur in cells exposed to a specific radioactive amino acid before extraction and purification of the protein. Superimposition of a stained fingerprint and photographic film exposed to a fingerprint made from radioactive protein can aid in localizing particular amino acids in certain peptides.

Frequently, the proteolytic enzymes are used sequentially. Thus trypsin can be used first to produce tryptic peptides; these peptides may be isolated and then exposed to chymotrypsin. The chymotryptic peptides may be separated and, when necessary, further degraded with papain (Fig. 2.7).

Sequencing the amino acids in peptides. After the peptides have been isolated, they can be analyzed for their individual content and sequence of amino acids. Exopeptidases are useful in this analysis. Exopeptidases split off amino acids one at a time from one of the ends of the peptide, aminopeptidase from the amino end and carboxypeptidase from the carboxy end. The sequence and nature of the amino acids composing the peptide influence the enzymatic release of free amino acids. For example, the specificity of aminopeptidase disallows release of a "masked" N-terminal amino acid; no N-terminal amino acid is found after treatment of some proteins of higher organisms and the viruses that parasitize them since acetylserine, a substituted amino acid, occupies the first position in these proteins. As a further example of how structure affects enzymatic digestion, we may observe the unique bonding in the polypeptide chain at proline residues (see Fig. 2.2). When proline becomes the N-terminal residue during diges-

FIG. 2.7. *Tryptic peptide VI, isolated from tryptophan synthetase A protein of E. coli, includes residues 70 through 88 of the protein (consult Fig. 2.4). The Cys residue has been oxidized and is thus referred to as CySO₃H. To determine the sequence of amino acids in this peptide, 19 amino acids long, the peptide was subjected to digestion first with chymotrypsin and the smaller peptide fragments isolated (top diagram). One of these, labeled TP VI C1, was further digested with papain and its digest products isolated (center diagram). The composition of each resultant peptide was analyzed. Sequence analyses were performed on each peptide including the original tryptic peptide. These data led to construction of the sequence of the 19 amino acids as shown at the bottom of the diagram. Similar studies with many other peptide fragments led to the proposal for the complete primary structure of the protein as shown in Fig. 2.4. Papain peptide C1Pa5 was isolated as a minor component during purification of C1Pa1 and C1Pa3. After J. R. Guest and C. Yanofsky, J. Biol. Chem., 241 (1966), 1.*

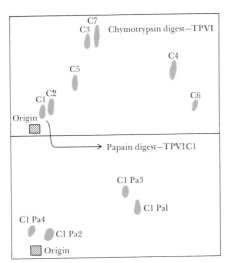

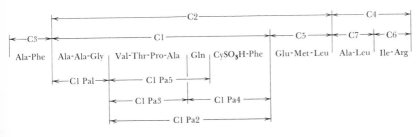

tion, the enzyme leucine aminopeptidase is usually unable to hydrolyze further. This configurational specificity also affects hydrolysis of C-terminal amino acids by carboxypeptidase A. There are additional substrate restrictions for these enzymes; leucine aminopeptidase fails to release amino acid from tryptic peptide XII of the tryptophan synthetase A protein (Fig. 2.4), which contains an N-terminal histidine followed by asparagine.

A chemical method superior to the use of aminopeptidase for the stepwise degradation from the N-terminal end utilizes phenylisothiocyanate (PTC), as depicted in Fig. 2.8. The N-terminal amino acid reacts with PTC in step 1. Treatment with acid splits off the derivative phenylthiohydantoin amino acid. As in the case when exopeptidases are used in sequencing, the split product can be separated and identified or the composition of the residual peptide can be determined. A portion of the residual peptide can be reutilized for the determination of

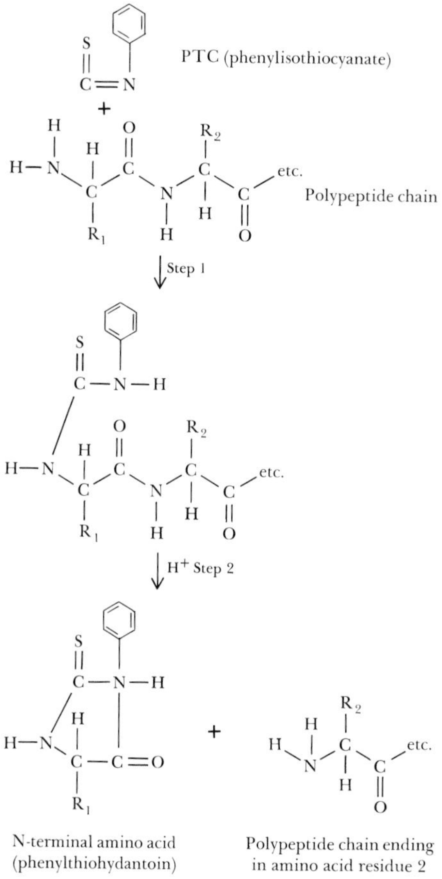

FIG. 2.8. *Edman PTC method for the determination of N-terminal amino acid residues in peptides.*

N-terminal amino acid (phenylthiohydantoin)

Polypeptide chain ending in amino acid residue 2

	Composition of residual peptide (residues present per peptide)						
	Val	Thr	Pro	Ala	Glu	CySO$_3$H	Phe
TP VI C1 Pa2	1.01	0.89	0.94	1.13	1.16	1.00	1.00
Edman, cycle 1 (83%)	**0.19**	0.86	1.05	1.08	1.12	0.89	1.04
cycle 2 (78%)	0	**0.21**	1.02	0.93	1.13	1.04	0.93
cycle 3 (99%)	0	0.13	**0.35**	1.05	1.12	0.95	0.92
cycle 4 (91%)	0	0	0.31	**0.34**	1.15	0.96	0.87

FIG. 2.9. *Edman degradation of a peptide obtained from* E. coli *tryptophan synthetase A protein. The peptide is peptide TP VI C1 Pa2, marked off at the lowest portion of Fig. 2.7; it includes residues 75 through 81 in the primary structure of the A protein shown in Fig 2.4. During the isolation and processing of the peptide, the Gln at position 79 had been converted to Glu and Cys to cysteic acid* (CySO$_3$H). *The composition of the residual peptide was determined after each cycle of the Edman degradation. The percentage recovery is indicated in parentheses for each step. The data show the degree of synchrony in the hydrolysis and provide an indication of the precision of the technique. From J. R. Guest and C. Yanofsky, J. Biol. Chem., 241 (1966), 1.*

the second amino acid in the sequence (now the N-terminal amino acid). This recycling can proceed several times, as indicated in Fig. 2.9. By quantitating the recoveries, the order of several amino acids along the N-terminal portion of the peptide can be determined. Recently, a highly florescent compound, "dansyl" (5-dimethylamino-1-naphthalene sulfonyl chloride), has been employed to identify N-terminal amino acids in polypeptides. The sample is reacted with dansyl, hydrolyzed, and the dansylated amino acids are separated chromatographically and identified by comparing them to known danysl-amino acid standards.

In general, "fingerprints" are used primarily to monitor the number and distribution of peptides obtained following a particular treatment. Most recent separations of peptides for subsequent analysis employ glass columns containing various polystyrene ion-exchange resins. The determination of the amino acid composition of the peptides is rapidly performed by a semiautomated procedure using commercial ion-exchange instruments called amino acid analyzers.

Putting the pieces together. To determine the order of the amino acids in the entire chain, the order of the peptides in the chain must be established. A simple example of the usefulness of overlapping sequence can be visualized by attempting to spell a 10-letter word correctly, given only sequences of three, four, or five letters at a time. If there is some overlap of letters within the groups, it becomes possible to put the pieces together to form the intact word. The overlapping in some small peptides is shown in Fig. 2.7; these overlaps, along with sequence data on critical parts of the peptides, allow the determination of a unique sequence of amino acids for tryptic peptide VI. Similar reasoning is applied toward placement of the tryptic peptides in the linear order shown in Fig. 2.4. For example, a cysteine-containing chymotryptic peptide overlaps the ends of tryptic peptides IX and X. If we assume that the amino acids are arranged linearly and not in a hodgepodge, amino acid composition data alone tell us that this chymotryptic peptide must contain portions of tryptic peptides IX and X. A large body of data, in which Figs. 2.7 and 2.9 represent only a small sample, gives us confidence in assuming polypeptide chains are linear, not branched, structures.

MODIFICATIONS IN PRIMARY STRUCTURE

Some proteins contain amino acids that are not listed among the "magic 20" shown in Fig. 2.2. Some of these, for example formylmethionine and acetylserine, contain masked amino groups and appear only at the N-terminal end of the polypeptide chain. At least formylmethionine plays an important role in genetic punctuation and will be discussed in Chapter 9. Hydroxyproline is found in large amounts in a connective-tissue protein, collagen, and in certain plant proteins. Hydroxylysine also is present in collagen and in the enzymes trypsin and chymotrypsin. N-Methyllysine is found in the proteins composing the flagella of some bacterial species but in no other proteins in these organisms. Work with radioactive tracers shows that hydroxyproline arises from proline as a result of modification after its incorporation into collagen. Less exacting studies on bacteria indicate that methylation of lysine occurs after lysine has been incorporated into the polypeptide chain.

Other proteins contain accessory groups that are believed to be added to the amino acid side chains after synthesis of the polypeptide. Various carbohydrate moieties are attached, often through covalent bonds, to the side chains of amino acids in certain proteins. In the enzyme cytochrome c, the heme group is bound through union of two of its vinyl side chains to two cysteinyl residues of the polypeptide chain.

We know very little about how these modifications in primary structure are accomplished in the cell. Much remains to be done in this important area of research, for the mechanisms underlying these modifications are sure to have important bearing on concepts of gene action and metabolic control.

Secondary Structure: Helix Formation

Physical measurements demonstrate that a protein is neither a long, extended, two-dimensional chain nor simply a randomly coiled structure. Rather, some portions of the polypeptide chain are neatly coiled (ordered) and others are neatly folded but remain uncoiled (disordered).

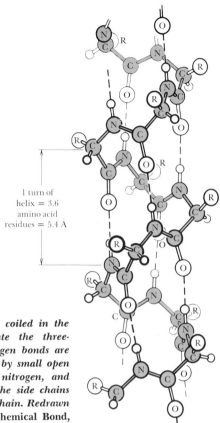

1 turn of
helix = 3.6
amino acid
residues = 5.4 A

FIG. 2.10. *Portion of a polypeptide chain coiled in the α-helical configuration, drawn to indicate the three-dimensional structure of the helix. Hydrogen bonds are indicated by dashed lines, hydrogen atoms by small open circles. C, N, and O represent carbon, nitrogen, and oxygen atoms, respectively; R stands for the side chains of the amino acids composing the peptide chain. Redrawn from Linus Pauling,* The Nature of the Chemical Bond, *3rd ed., Ithaca, N.Y.: Cornell University Press, 1960.*

The ordered regions of many proteins have the secondary structure proposed in the 1950s by Linus Pauling and his coworkers—a definite geometric arrangement of individual polypeptide chains stabilized by a variety of noncovalent bonds. The secondary structure found in the ordered regions of most proteins (the compact, or globular, proteins) is a helical coil called an α helix. Details of the structure of the α helix are shown in Fig. 2.10. Such a helical structure meets certain essential, restrictive physicochemical requirements. The α helix allows maximum intrahelical hydrogen-bond formation (dashed lines in Fig. 2.10) between the C=O and H−N linkages, which stabilizes the structure in the helical form. The extent of hydrogen bonding can be observed by noting the changes in the ultraviolet absorption of the protein solution when the protein is in a helical, as opposed to an uncoiled, form. In addition, optical rotation measurements give an estimate of the proportion of the protein molecule that exists in the α-helical configuration in solution.

In aqueous solution, proteins hydrogen-bond with water molecules, and, in the process, an exchange of hydrogen atoms takes place between the water and the protein. Using deuterium water (deuterium is a heavy hydrogen isotope), one can measure the availability for exchange with water of particular hydrogen atoms along the polypeptide chain. Hydrogen atoms that are hydrogen-bonded within the structure of the protein (for example, the hydrogen bonds of the α helix) have a greatly decreased capacity for deuterium exchange. All these methods indicate that some globular proteins may be almost completely in a helical configuration, while others are ordered over as little as 20 percent of their length.

The most convincing evidence for the presence of the α helix comes from X-ray diffraction studies on protein crystals. X rays are diffracted by the planes of a crystalline structure of a substance. Because the atomic structure of each crystalline substance is unique, different molecules give different X-ray diffraction patterns. Such patterns from protein crystals can reveal their molecular arrangement. Nobel-prize winners J. C. Kendrew and M. F. Perutz have developed X-ray diffraction methods that allow resolution of protein structure at the 2-Å level. From the dimensions given in Fig. 2.10, one can see that this resolution is sufficient to probe the structure of the α helix; indeed, even the positions of the individual amino acids can be discerned. X-ray diffraction will ultimately allow confirmation of the structures of proteins previously analyzed by chemical amino acid–sequencing methods. Of very great importance is the fact that current X-ray diffraction methods are contributing to our knowledge of the tertiary structure of proteins.

Tertiary Structure: Folding of the Chain

Figure 2.11 depicts the three-dimensional structure of a myoglobin molecule. The long, linear polypeptide chain (primary structure) exhibits helical regions (secondary structure) indicated by the letters. The molecule is folded at particular positions to give the precisely twisted three-dimensional structure shown (tertiary structure).

We are just beginning to understand how tertiary structure is achieved and the types of forces by which tertiary structure is maintained. Our knowledge of these forces comes from studies involving the disruption (denaturation) of the complex configuration of the protein and its restoration (renaturation) to a native configuration. Some of the forces that cause and maintain the folded configuration are results of various types of interactions of amino acid side chains. Also, in three-dimensional models constructed from X-ray diffraction patterns, one can determine which amino acid side chains in one segment of the polypeptide chain are in juxtaposition with amino acid side chains of another portion of the polypeptide chain.

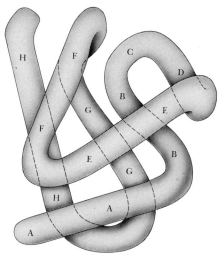

FIG. 2.11. *Schematic representation of the three-dimensional structure of a myoglobin molecule. Myoglobin is an oxygen-binding heme protein found in muscle tissue. The letters refer to helical portions of the chain; these are separated by nonhelical segments. For descriptions of methods used to elucidate this structure, consult J. C. Kendrew, Sci. Am., 205 (Dec. 1961), 96; and Science, 139 (1963), 1259; R. E. Dickerson, in The Proteins, Vol. II, 2nd ed., H. Neurath, ed., New York: Academic Press, Inc., 1964, p. 505.*

Hydrogen bonding between C=O and H−N groups within the helical structure of the polypeptide is a major stabilizing force in maintaining secondary structure. However, the bond angles necessary for rotation of the molecule into the helix are restricted at proline residues: the cyclical nature of the proline residue (see Fig. 2.2) dictates that the two carbons nearest the imino peptide bond remain coplanar with the atoms comprising the bond. These two carbons of the proline ring, by protruding, sterically block formation of the α-helical configuration. Therefore, in the vicinity of proline residues, the polypeptide chain is unable to form an α helix and is forced to twist or bend. X-ray diffraction shows that all the bends in polypeptide chains cannot be accounted for simply by the occurrence of proline residues. There must be other forces that overcome the tendency for the formation of the α helix and that permit the protein to assume other configurations.

One of the strong stabilizing forces in tertiary protein structure is the disulfide bond, shown at the top of Fig. 2.12. The disulfide bond (−S−S−) is a covalent linkage formed by the oxidation of the sulfhydryl groups (−SH) of two cysteine residues. Reexamination of Fig. 2.2 will demonstrate that cysteine is the only amino acid with an exposed sulfhydryl group found in proteins. In a native protein containing several cysteine residues, only certain pairs interact to form disulfide bridges at specific places in the molecule. Such bridges may be broken by chemical reduction (−S−S− → −SH + −SH) or by oxidation of the cystine residues to cysteic acid residues (−S−S− → $2SO_3H$).

Although disulfide bridges are important in stabilizing the protein in its native configuration, other forces contribute strongly to the proper folding of the polypeptide into a three-dimensional protein molecule. This is strikingly illustrated by the following type of experi-

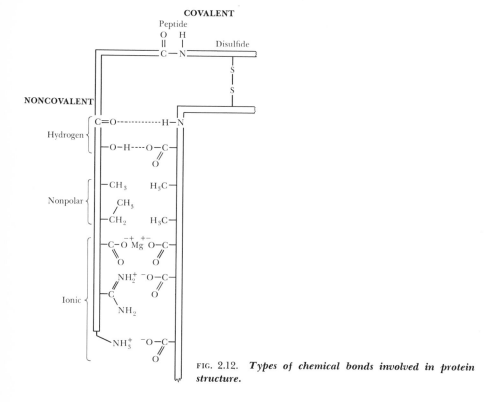

FIG. 2.12.   *Types of chemical bonds involved in protein structure.*

ment, which has been performed with several enzymes. The disulfide bridges of the native protein are chemically reduced. The protein is then allowed to reoxidize slowly in very dilute solution. During this slow reoxidation, the disulfide bonds reform and interchange, until ultimately the native protein configuration is again attained.

One of these other forces is the hydrogen bond. Hydrogen bonding, depicted in Fig. 2.12, may take place between the C=O and H−N of nearby peptide bonds of an α helix (compare Fig. 2.10) or between C=O and H−N that are in different segments of the polypeptide chain, thereby contributing to the overall folding process. Hydrogen bonds may also form between amino acid side chains—between a tyrosine hydroxyl (−OH) and a carboxyl (C=O) of glutamic acid, for example.

OH

Although these amino acid residues may be far removed from each other in the linear sequence of the polypeptide chain, their affinities for the sharing of the hydrogen atom bring them into proximity in the folded protein.

Other weak-bonding forces are considered to play important roles in the association of different segments within the polypeptide chain. Nonpolar amino acid side chains are attracted by hydrophobic (water-excluding) interactions, just as oil droplets tend to coalesce in water. As Fig. 2.12 shows, the hydrates that are formed may be either alike or mixed. Evidence for a role of nonpolar side chains in protein structure stems from several observations. Urea, an effective denaturant in high concentrations, also disrupts hydrates of nonpolar compounds. Addition of extra nonpolar side chains to proteins (methylation of $-NH_2$ to $-N(CH_3)_2$, for example) stabilizes them.

Finally, various types of ionic bonds may help to form and maintain the folded protein configuration. Divalent cations such as magnesium ion (see Fig. 2.12) may form electrostatic bonds with two acidic side chains. And basic and acidic groups of the constituent amino acids may also interact, as shown at the bottom of the figure.

Quaternary Structure: Protein-Protein Interactions

Although some proteins are composed of a single polypeptide chain, others consist of two or more interacting chains, which may be identical or different in primary structure. This specific association of subunits into a complex macromolecule is referred to as the quaternary structure. The aggregate is referred to as a multimer to distinguish it from polymers, which are usually built of covalently bound, oft-repeating subunits. The same forces involved in forming and maintaining tertiary structure are involved in interactions of several polypeptide chains to form a quaternary structure: disulfide bridges, hydrogen bonds, nonpolar bonds (hydrophobic), and electrostatic bonds. As is the case in tertiary structure, various combinations of these bonds are used by different species of proteins in maintaining quaternary structure.

Protein-protein interactions are very common in biological systems. They serve a number of functions. They allow the construction of large aggregates built of identical protein subunits, as in the case of the capsids or "protein coats" that protect the nucleic acids of virus particles from destruction. Since, as we shall see in Chapter 3, each polypeptide chain requires its individual genetic message, protein repetition allows the formation of a relatively large structure from a genetic element of minimal size, that is, conservation of genetic information. In addition, protein-protein interactions of a highly specific and selective nature allow the construction in the cell of multifunctional enzyme complexes. Protein-protein interactions also afford opportunities for increasing or decreasing the rates of enzyme-catalyzed reactions.

A well-studied example of interaction of protein subunits in a virus particle may be found in tobacco mosaic virus (TMV). TMV particles are rodlike, tubular structures about 3,000 Å long and 180 Å in diameter, with a molecular weight of about 40 million. The tube is constructed of a single RNA molecule 30,000 Å long that is coiled about the central axis of the particle. The RNA molecule is embedded in a protein matrix (the coat) that stabilizes the RNA, protecting it

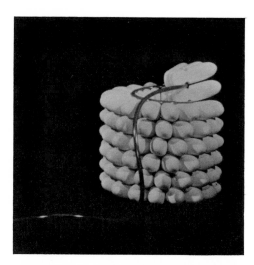

FIG. 2.13. (a) *Model depicting the helical arrangement of some of the protein molecules (white) and the RNA (long gray structure) in a TMV particle. From* H. *Fraenkel-Conrat,* Design and Function at the Threshold of Life: The Viruses, *New York: Academic Press, Inc., 1963.* (b) *Electron micrograph of a partially disrupted rod of TMV showing periodicity along the axis. Structures, interpreted as being individual polypeptides, are visible. From* J. *Nagington and* R. W. *Horne,* Virology, 15 *(1961), 348; photograph courtesy of* R. W. *Horne and* P. *Wildy.* Magnification 720,000×.

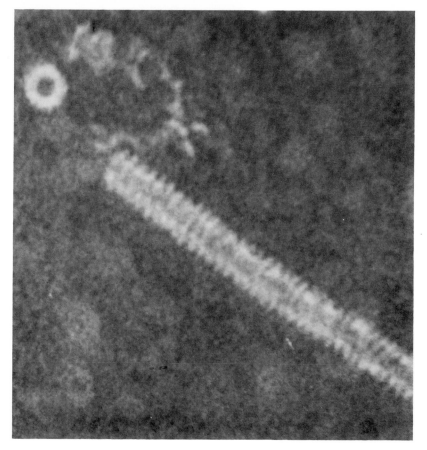

from disruption by changes in the enzymatic and physical conditions of the environment (Fig. 2.13).

The subunits of the protein matrix have been seen in the electron microscope, and their arrangement in crystals of the virus has been studied by X-ray diffraction methods. The intact particles have been treated with carboxypeptidase, and the C-terminal threonine residues have been quantitatively recovered. Approximately 2,200 threonine residues are released per virus particle, indicating that the protein consists of about 2,200 polypeptide chains, all of which could be identical. The fingerprint profile of the tryptic peptides of the protein also has been used to establish the presence and identity of the polypeptide chain subunits.

Mild acid or alkali separates the RNA from the protein and fragments the protein into a number of packets of polypeptide chains. These packets readily reassociate to form long rods when the pH is returned to neutrality. The reconstituted rods have essentially the same structure as the protein of the initial virus rods except that, in the absence of the RNA, they form in heterogeneous lengths. They are less stable to denaturing agents than are the normal-length reaggregates formed in the presence of RNA. The last three amino acids at the C-terminal end, Pro-Ala-Thr, are not required for reaggregation and binding; they can be removed from the intact virus without noticeable effect on the stability of the rods. The polypeptide chains constituting a packet cannot be completely dissociated from one another and reaggregated into rods except under very special conditions. Many treatments that completely dissociate the polypeptide chains lead to irreversible denaturation of the protein.

These observations suggest that the orderly and specific quaternary structure of the protein depends upon critical interactions between the polypeptide chain subunits. Only when the specific tertiary structure is attained and the proper environmental conditions are provided can the appropriate interactions occur. The specific quaternary structure depends mainly on protein-protein interactions, but the limitation on rod length imposed by the presence of TMV RNA shows that accessory substances also may be involved. All evidence at present supports the view that the primary structure of the protein, which dictates the limitations of secondary and tertiary structure, also delineates the correct quaternary structure necessary for the biological activity of the molecule. Because of the specific structure of the folded polypeptide chain, only certain segments of it will be available to take part in protein-protein interactions. In TMV protein, the N-terminal portion of the molecule is suspected of playing a particular role in protein-protein interactions, for the N-terminal peptide tends to form aggregates of high molecular weight in vitro even when separated from the rest of the chain.

Examples of the interactions of nonidentical protein subunits are to be found in the hemoglobin molecule (Fig. 2.14), in the *E. coli* pyruvate dehydrogenase complex (Fig. 2.15), and in the active forms

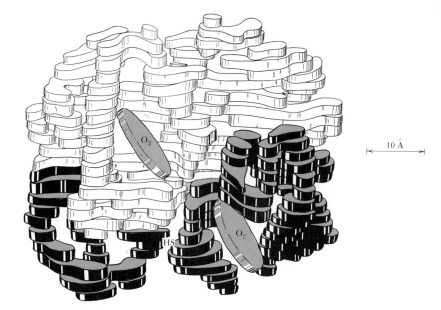

FIG. 2.14. *Interaction of four polypeptide chains to constitute the hemoglobin molecule. Hemoglobin is an oxygen-binding blood protein. Each of the chains is folded approximately as is the myglobin molecule depicted in Fig. 2.11. The two α chains (white) are alike in primary structure, as are the two β chains (black). The α and β chains differ slightly from each other, for the structure of each type of chain is dictated by a different gene. The heme groups, associated in the binding of oxygen, are shown as gray disks. Redrawn from M. F. Perutz, Science, 140 (1963), 863; See also H. Muirhead, J. M. Cox, L. Mazzarella, and M. F. Perutz, J. Mol. Biol., 28 (1967), 117.*

FIG. 2.15. (a) *Electron micrograph showing various orientations of the* E. coli *pyruvate dehydrogenase complex (×300,000).* (b) *Selected individual images of the complex (×600,000).* (c–e) *Interpretative model of the complex viewed down a fourfold axis* (c), *a threefold axis* (d), *and a twofold axis* (e). *The entire complex has a molecular weight of about 4 million and catalyzes the overall reaction: pyruvate + CoA + NAD+ ⟶ acetyl CoA + CO₂ + NADH + H+. Actually, the overall reaction proceeds in five consecutive seps involving enzyme-bound intermediates. The complex consists of three enzymes, pyruvate dehydrogenase, dihydrolipoyl transacetylase, and a flavoprotein, dihydrolipoyl dehydrogenase. The transacetylase component consists of 24 identical polypeptide chains of molecular weight about 40,000 each, which are organized into a cube. The 24 molecules of pyruvate dehydrogenase (black spheres; molecular weight of about 90,000 each), and 24 molecules of flavo-*

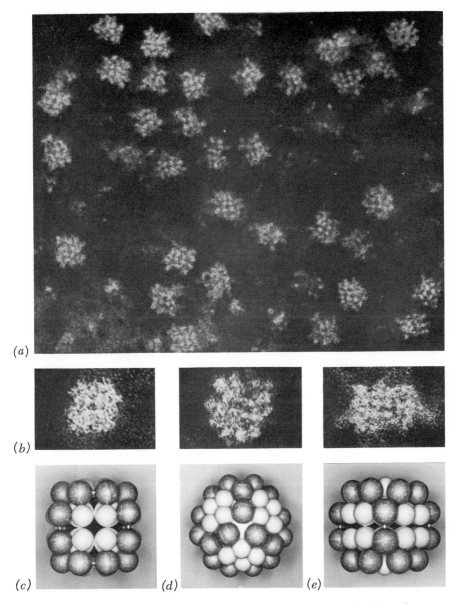

protein (white spheres; molecular weight of about 55,000 each) are thought to be distributed in a regular manner along the edges of the transacetylase cube. After L. J. Reed and R. M. Oliver, in Structure, Function and Evolution in Proteins: Brookhaven Symp. Biol., 21 (*1968*).

POLYPEPTIDE:

ACTIVE FORM:

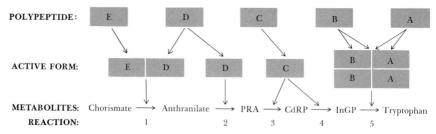

METABOLITES: Chorismate ⟶ Anthranilate ⟶ PRA ⟶ CdRP ⟶ InGP ⟶ Tryptophan
REACTION: 1   2   3   4   5

FIG. 2.16. *Abbreviated diagram of proteins effective in tryptophan biosynthesis in E. coli. Five classes of polypeptide chains, labeled A through E, are involved in the five enzymatic steps that convert chorismate to tryptophan. The polypeptide chains participating in reactions 1 (polypeptides E and D) and 5 (polypeptides A and B) are inactive or only very weakly active in these reactions when isolated; full activity in these reactions is exhibited only by the specific protein aggregates. Polypeptide D is normally found entirely complexed with E, but polypeptide D is equally active in reaction 2 whether free or in the complex. Consult the text and Chap. 3 for further descriptions of this system. Drawn after J. Ito and C. Yanofsky, J. Biol. Chem., 241 (1966), 4112, and M. E. Goldberg, T. E. Creighton, R. L. Baldwin, and C. Yanofsky, J. Mol. Biol., 21 (1966), 71.*

of two enzymes involved in tryptophan biosynthesis (Fig. 2.16). These systems show us the importance of quaternary structure in cell metabolism and in cell organization. They suggest that the orderly and specific quaternary structure of a protein must depend upon critical interactions between the component subunits. Accessory substances may play a role in these interactions. For example, strict limitations on rod length are imposed by the presence of TMV RNA; in its absence the rods are not uniform in length as they are in its presence. All evidence at present supports the view that the primary structure of the protein, which dictates the limitations of secondary and tertiary structure, also delineates the correct quaternary structure necessary for the biological activity of the molecule.

Protein Configuration and Activity

Cellular metabolism requires that proteins interact with molecules other than proteins. In some cases these interactions can affect the tertiary structure of the protein. Indeed, an enzyme achieves its catalytic activity by binding the substrate to itself at a specific region called the active center. Enzymatic activity may be inhibited by the binding of small molecules (1) at the active center of the enzyme, so that the reaction with substrate is blocked (isosteric effects); or (2) at other positions in the protein molecule, so that its tertiary structure is changed and its affinity for substrate is subsequently altered (allosteric effects; see the discussion of feedback inhibition in Chap. 5). You will no doubt encounter this critical relationship between protein configuration and biological activity in many aspects of modern biology: in studies on the mechanism of action of hormones, the nature of the specificity of antigen and antibody reactions, and the structure and organization of multicomponent enzyme systems, to name a few.

Chapter 3 reviews evidence that mutations affect the primary structure of proteins. From the discussion above, we already can make several predictions as to how changes in primary structure might affect certain properties of protein molecules. We might expect that substitutions of amino acids in the polypeptide could drastically affect secondary, tertiary, and even quaternary structure, thereby modifying the activity, stability, total charge, and immunological properties of the protein molecule. The extent of the change in properties should depend not only upon the site of the substitution but also upon the type of amino acid substituted. For example, replacement of a glutamic acid (with a negatively charged side chain) by a lysine (with a positively charged side chain) might be expected to have a much more drastic effect than would the substitution of a valine by an isoleucine residue. These suppositions lead us to believe that qualitative changes in the primary structure of proteins can lead to quantitative changes in the properties of proteins.

The increasingly convincing evidence that many aspects of the secondary and tertiary structure are a consequence of the primary structure has further implications for genetics. We consider that the folding and the configuration of native protein molecules, including their quaternary structure, are largely dictated by the interactions of critically positioned side chains of the amino acids composing the polypeptide chain. That this is universally true remains to be determined. Nevertheless, evidence from a few proteins is strong enough to allow us freedom, in terms of genetic considerations, to disregard the details of the folding process and to assume that folding occurs spontaneously and automatically once the amino acid sequence is determined. We can, therefore, now ask how mutations affect the primary structure, the subject discussed in Chap. 3.

Questions

2.1. In the library, locate an original article or a review article that gives the complete primary structure of a polypeptide chain of a natural protein (for example, ribonuclease, hemoglobin, cytochrome c, albumin, or TMV). Note the name of the protein, its source (tissue and organism), the number of polypeptide chains it contains, and the source from which you obtained your information. Copy the amino acid sequence for the first 75 residues, starting at the N-terminal end.

    (*a*) Would you find an N-terminal amino acid released from this protein by treatment with aminopeptidase?

(b) How many peptide fragments would you expect to obtain after digestion of the 75-residue portion of the polypeptide chain with trypsin? After chymotryptic digestion?

(c) Would you expect any nonpeptide products to be released by tryptic digestion? By tryptic digestion followed by chymotryptic digestion?

(d) How would you determine the sequence of amino acids in tryptic peptide I, the N-terminal tryptic peptide? Write out the sequence.

(e) Following the form of Fig. 2.1 and the structures of amino acids shown in Fig. 2.2, draw out the structure of peptide I, the N-terminal peptide, through the first four amino acid residues.

(f) Which amino acids in tryptic peptide I might play roles in determining the tertiary structure of the protein? Describe the role of each.

(g) Do any of the tryptic and chymotryptic peptides overlap in a manner that allows their unequivocal placement relative to one another solely on the basis of amino acid content (that is, lacking knowledge of the order of amino acids within the fragments)?

(h) Now, suppose that you know the N-terminal and C-terminal amino acids in each fragment. Again see how many fragments you can place in sequence.

2.2. Hemoglobin A is the normal, adult human hemoglobin, an oxygen-transporting blood protein. The hemoglobin molecule is a multimer composed of four polypeptide chains.

(a) What types of bonds do you believe might be involved in holding the four subunits of the hemoglobin protein together? What tests could you apply to differentiate some of these possibilities?

(b) Of the four polypeptide subunits of the hemoglobin A protein, two polypeptide chains are identical α chains; the other two polypeptide chains, β chains, are different in primary structure from the α chains but are identical to each other. However, many of the amino acid sequences in the α chain are similar to those in the β chain. What bearing do you think these facts might have on the evolution of these two kinds of polypeptide chains?

(c) Would you expect the α chains and the β chains to fold in identical, similar, or extremely different configurations? Why?

2.3. List the main steps in the elucidation of protein primary structure and briefly note the purpose of each step.

2.4. Select three methods currently used in studies on protein conformation. Compare them, listing some of the advantages and disadvantages of each method.

References

Anfinsen, C. B., *The Molecular Basis of Evolution.* New York: John Wiley & Sons, Inc., 1963. An inexpensive paperback edition of an excellent, simple introduction to proteins and their significance in genetics, first published in 1959.

————, "General Remarks on Protein Structure and Biosynthesis," in *Informational Macromolecules*, H. J. Vogel, V. Bryson, and J. O. Lampen, eds. New York: Academic Press, Inc., 1963. A discussion of the folding of polypeptide chains and their biosynthesis.

Bailey, J. L., *Techniques in Protein Chemistry*, 2nd ed. New York: American Elsevier Publishing Company, Inc., 1967. Accurate, concise, cookbook style outlines of methods used in separating and sequencing peptides and proteins.

Bamford, C. H., A. Elliott, and W. E. Hanby, *Synthetic Polypeptides: Preparation, Structure and Properties*. New York: Academic Press, Inc., 1956.

Chance, R. E., R. M. Ellis, and W. W. Bromer, "Porcine Proinsulin: Characterization and Amino Acid Sequence," *Science, 161* (1968), 165. The two short polypeptide chains of the hormone insulin are derived from a single-chain protein by cleavage and elimination of a connecting peptide of 33 amino acids.

Dayhoff, M. O., and R. V. Eck, *Atlas of Protein Sequence and Structure 1967–68*. Silver Spring, Md.: National Biomedical Research Foundation, 1968. Compilation of partial and complete amino acid sequences found in proteins to date.

Edgar, R. S., and W. B. Wood, "Morphogenesis of Bacteriophage T4 in Extracts of Mutant-Infected Cells," *Proc. Natl. Acad. Sci. U.S., 55* (1966), 498. First of a series of papers, from several laboratories, on the assembly in vitro of complex protein aggregates with biological activity.

Green, D. E., and O. Hechter, "Assembly of Membrane Subunits," *Proc. Natl. Acad. Sci. U.S., 53* (1965), 318. Role of proteins in organelle structure.

Harrington, W. F., R. Josephs, and D. M. Segal, "Physical Chemical Studies on Proteins and Polypeptides," *Ann. Rev. Biochem., 35* (1966), 599. A recent and critical guide to the literature on conformation of proteins and polypeptides with emphasis on stereochemistry, optical rotatory dispersion, and hydrogen-exchange studies.

Hirs, C. H. W., ed., *Enzyme Structure*, Vol. 11 of the Methods of Enzymology series, S. P. Colowick and N. O. Kaplan, eds. New York: Academic Press, Inc., 1967. More than 70 articles on amino acid analyses, cleavage of peptide chains, sequence determination, separation of peptide chains in multimers, conformational changes, and other methods used in analyses of protein structure.

Kellenberger, E., "Control Mechanisms in Bacteriophage Morphopoiesis," in *Principles of Biomolecular Organization* (Ciba Foundation Symposium). London: J. & A. Churchill Ltd., 1966, p. 192. A companion paper to that of Edgar and Wood, cited above.

Klotz, I. M., "Protein Subunits: A Table," *Science, 155* (1967), 697. A list of proteins in which subunits are held together by noncovalent bonds.

Koshland, D. E., Jr., "The Active Site and Enzyme Action," *Advan. Enzymol., 22* (1960), 45. An introduction to enzyme structure and conformation that may be expanded by consulting more recently published references cited at the ends of Chaps. 4 and 5.

Lauffer, M. A., and C. L. Stevens, "Structure of the Tobacco Mosaic Virus Particle; Polymerization of Tobacco Mosaic Virus Protein." *Advan. Virus Res., 13* (1968), 1.

McElroy, W. D., M. DeLuca, and J. Travis, "Molecular Uniformity in Biological Catalyses," *Science, 157* (1967), 150. Conformational changes in some enzymes with parallel functions are discussed. The article introduces the concept of "homosteric effects," that is, modifications of reactions of bound intermediates when a normal substrate or structurally similar molecule combines at the catalytic site.

Neurath, H., ed., *The Proteins: Composition, Structure and Function,* 2nd ed., Vols. I–IV. New York: Academic Press, Inc., 1963–1966. Critical reviews.

Phillips, D. C., "The Three-Dimensional Structure of an Enzyme Molecule," *Sci. Am. 215* (Nov. 1966), 78. A luxuriantly illustrated and well-written description of the anatomy of the enzyme lysozyme.

Stahman, M. A., ed., *Polyamino Acids, Polypeptides, and Proteins.* Madison: University of Wisconsin Press, 1962.

Subunit Structure of Proteins: Biochemical and Genetic Aspects, Brookhaven Symposia in Biology 17. Upton, N.Y.: Brookhaven National Laboratory, 1964. A series of papers on research involving proteins where subunit structure is important.

Timasheff, S. N., and M. J. Gorbunoff, "Conformation of Proteins," *Ann. Rev. Biochem., 36,* Pt. I (1967), 13. Results with various proteins reviewed by categories of methods used in the analysis.

Witkop, B., "Chemical Cleavage of Proteins," *Science, 162* (1968), 318.

Woodward, D. O., and K. D. Munkries, "Genetic Control, Function, and Assembly of a Structural Protein in *Neurospora,*" in *Organizational Biosynthesis,* H. J. Vogel, J. O. Lampen, and V. Bryson, eds. New York: Academic Press, Inc., 1967, p. 489. Role of proteins in cellular organization.

Advances in Protein Chemistry. This series of volumes contains many excellent discussions, each focused on a different aspect of protein structure and function.

Annual Review of Biochemistry. Concentrates on up to date and often critical guides emphasizing the recent literature, including selected topics in the area of protein chemistry.

Genetic Control
of Protein Structure

How do we know that the genetic material, nucleic acid, dictates the structure of proteins? What is the relation between gene and polypeptide chain? Increasingly numerous examples, from the genetics of man to the genetics of viruses, afford experimental confirmation of the determinative role of nucleic acid in specifying the structure of proteins.

The particular examples of gene-protein relationships we have selected for discussion occur in microorganisms and were chosen because the genetic analysis has progressed to an advanced state and/or detailed analysis of the specific protein is available. The reader who thoroughly understands these examples will be able to extrapolate readily to other genetic systems. Certainly, one striking outcome of the genetics of microorganisms is the satisfactory application of concepts derived therefrom to situations in higher organisms where the genetic data may be relatively limited.

Operational Definitions of the Gene

Stahl in *The Mechanics of Inheritance* describes the structure and properties of the nucleic acids, particularly DNA. Stahl presents the main evidence that DNA is the genetic material and that it is accurately replicated and passed to the progeny. He also describes how hereditary mutations occur in the DNA through alterations in the base composition or sequence in its polynucleotide chains. He discusses the use of inheritance tests for distinguishing mutant genetic sites located at different positions on a polynucleotide chain. The mechanism of redistributing genetic material is called *recombination*. If two mutations are located on separate chromosomes, they segregate randomly; if they are located on a single chromosome, or on a single nucleic acid molecule, they may separate with less than random frequency and are said to be linked. Generally, the closer the location of two mutations along a polynucleotide chain, the less frequent their separation, that is, the lower the recombination frequency between the two mutations. Two independently derived mutations that affect the same base pair in the DNA molecule never show recombination.

Finally, Stahl surveys some of the evidence that the polynucleotide chain consists of segments, each controlling the expression of a particular trait. That is, one sequence of base pairs along the polynucleotide chain affects one function, whereas another sequence along the chain affects a second function.

Mutation, recombination, function: these are the three operational methods by which genetic tests delineate the structure of the hereditary material.

All three methods arose as purely genetical procedures and originally were considered to give identical estimates of the mysterious units of heredity, the genes. Later it was discovered, by examining large numbers of progeny, that some mutations in the structure presumed to represent a single gene were separated by recombination (for example, one recombinant per 10,000 progeny). The advances in this area of fine-structure genetics were tremendously facilitated through work, in the 1950s, with microorganisms whose rare recombinants could be detected and quantitatively scored much more easily than could those of higher organisms. As a result, we now recognize the gene as a section of a polydeoxyribonucleotide chain, divisible both by mutation and recombination and concerned with a specific unitary function.

One Gene, One Polypeptide Chain

Mendel considered that a particular trait is derived from a pair of factors, one inherited from each parent, and that when the two factors differ only one is expressed; that is, one is dominant over the other. After the rediscovery and confirmation of Mendel's basic observations on the mode of inheritance of unit factors, some geneticists hypothesized that the dominant factor is the presence of a gene; the recessive factor, its absence. However, this theory rapidly met with difficulties in interpretation when incomplete dominance (intermediate traits) and three or more slightly different alleles for a single gene locus were discovered. Although genes were found to be located at fixed positions on the chromosomes and came to be considered as the material units of inheritance, their apparent complexity was puzzling. Because cellular physiology and the chemical nature of the genetic material were little understood at the time, it is not surprising that interpretations of gene structure and function were limited in scope and understanding.

What is known about how genes act? What does the functional genetic unit mean in biochemical terms? Answers to these questions initially were sought in the relationship between genes and specific biochemical reactions. In the early 1900s, a considerable amount of work was done on the chemistry of the anthocyanin pigments and the genetics of pigmentation in the snapdragon and other flowering plants. Several genes were found to control the onset of various identifiable and specific chemical reactions. These reactions were found to involve modifications in the structure of heterocyclic organic molecules called anthocyanins, and the reactions were found to be catalyzed by enzymes. Also in the early 1900s, Sir Archibald Garrod, a British physician interested in a number of congenital metabolic diseases in man, recognized that certain human biochemical deficiencies were caused by enzymatic abnormalities. But these very important observations, suggesting a relationship between genes and enzymes, had relatively little influence on contemporary genetic or biochemical thought.

In the 1930s, George Beadle, Boris Ephrussi, and Edward Tatum began a series of developmental genetic studies on the fruit fly, *Drosophila melanogaster*. Using a series of eye-color mutants to study the genetics of eye-pigment formation, they were able to show that the synthesis of normal eye pigment proceeded through a series of chemically identifiable intermediates and that each biosynthetic step was under distinct genetic control. From these studies, some of the first principles of biochemical genetics were formulated, some of the technical limitations of the *Drosophila* system were evaluated, and a clear-cut method of attack for studying the problem of gene-enzyme relationships in the fungus *Neurospora crassa* was established. However, until Beadle and Tatum formulated the "one gene–one enzyme" concept in the early 1940s, discussions of primary gene function remained somewhat nebulous and fluid. The theory of Beadle and Tatum states that the gene exerts its influence on the phenotype through its role in the production of an enzyme.

Research in the last two decades has verified and extended this basic conclusion. It has spelled out in more detail the chemical nature of genetic material and important details of the structure of proteins. Figure 2.16 points out that some enzyme activities result from the specific association of different kinds of polypeptide chains, whereas others are due to single polypeptide chains. In addition, a single protein (for example, protein C in Fig. 2.16) may catalyze two different metabolic reactions. Our increasing knowledge of enzymology and of protein structure, along with refined genetic techniques, has allowed the more precise correlation of gene and polypeptide chain rather than gene and enzyme. The gene–polypeptide chain relationship is a simple, far-reaching concept whose validation is one of the triumphs of modern genetics. Both the polynucleotide and the polypeptide are linear structures. In fact, the two molecules are colinear. In the sections below we focus on the approaches and methods that were responsible for establishing this relationship.

Enzymes and Biochemical Pathways

The organic molecules of the cell are metabolized in sequences of chemical reactions. The importance of the multitude of small molecules in the cell stems mainly from their use as sources of energy, as components in the regulation of metabolism, and as building blocks for the different classes of macromolecules (proteins, nucleic acids, polysaccharides, and lipids) that form the foundation of cell structure and function. The pathways of metabolite synthesis (anabolism) and breakdown (catabolism) must necessarily be highly coordinated. Interrelationships between carbohydrate, fatty acid, and amino acid metabolism are many. Converging and diverging metabolic pathways often share common intermediates, as can be seen in Fig. 3.1.

Chorismate is a key intermediate used to make the three amino acids phenylalanine, tyrosine, and tryptophan, as well as the two vitamins p-aminobenzoic acid and p-hydroxybenzoic acid. Enzyme 2 catalyzes the reaction between anthranilic acid, which is made from chorismate, and phosphoribosylpyrophosphate (PRPP) to form an essential intermediate in the biosynthesis of the amino acid tryptophan. PRPP also is used for many other biosynthetic processes in the cell. These are only a few of the hundreds of reactions that comprise the integrated network of intermediary metabolism, which must be maintained in careful balance to assure normal function of the organism.

Elucidation of reaction sequences in many of the pathways of intermediary metabolism has required the application of a wide variety of biochemical technics. Some of these will be discussed in Chapter 5. Of particular value has been the use of microorganisms having specific genetically controlled metabolic defects. Detailed examination of the biochemical basis of such defects in mutant cells has often provided critical information about the nature of metabolic events in the normal cell. Studies of these mutants have also led to many of our current concepts of gene action.

FIG. 3.1. *Pathways of tryptophan biosynthesis.*

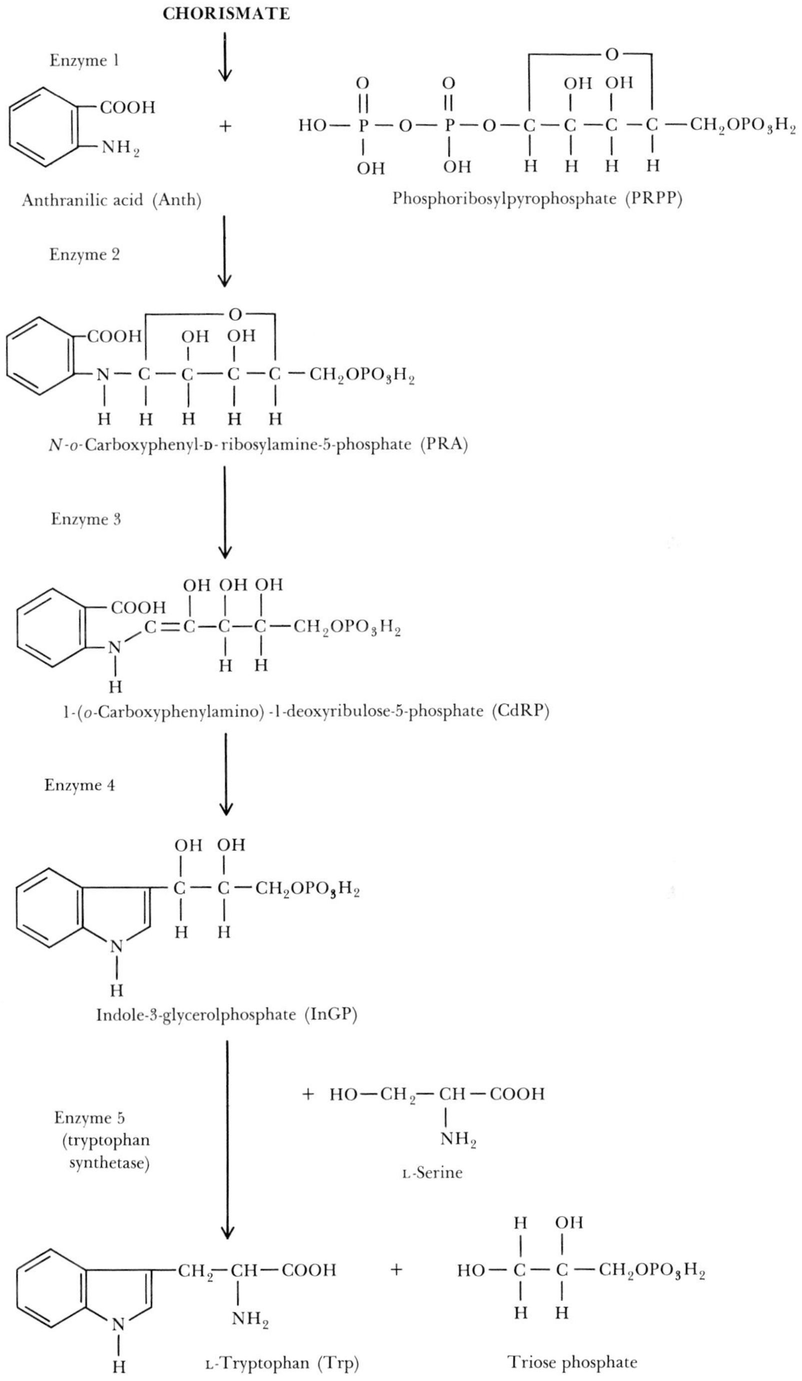

CHORISMATE

Enzyme 1

Anthranilic acid (Anth)

$+$

Phosphoribosylpyrophosphate (PRPP)

Enzyme 2

$N\text{-}o\text{-}$Carboxyphenyl-D-ribosylamine-5-phosphate (PRA)

Enzyme 3

1-(o-Carboxyphenylamino)-1-deoxyribulose-5-phosphate (CdRP)

Enzyme 4

Indole-3-glycerolphosphate (InGP)

$+ \ HO-CH_2-CH-COOH$
$\qquad\qquad\qquad\ \ \ \ NH_2$

Enzyme 5
(tryptophan
synthetase)

L-Serine

L-Tryptophan (Trp)

$+$

Triose phosphate

Gene-Enzyme Relationships

Some of the most valuable mutants isolated to date have been those that cannot synthesize one or another metabolite needed for growth and thus require particular growth factors not required by the wild-type organisms. The reasons for their utility are apparent. Most wild-type enteric bacteria grow in a synthetic medium containing inorganic salts and an organic carbon source. Wild-type *Neurospora crassa* grows on a simple medium supplemented with one of the B vitamins, biotin, and an organic carbon source. From these components in the minimal medium, the organisms can synthesize all of their protoplasmic constituents, including amino acids, purines, pyrimidines, fats, vitamins, etc.

Neurospora mutants defective in the synthesis of metabolites critical for growth are obtained by treating the asexual spores, called conidia, with a mutagen and allowing them to germinate in a minimal medium. Wild-type conidia form long, threadlike structures called hyphae. The hyphae are retained by a cheesecloth filter, but the ungerminated and slowly germinating mutant conidia that cannot grow on a minimal medium pass through with the medium. They are allowed to germinate on a more complex medium, and their specific growth requirements are subsequently determined.

Bacterial mutants that require supplements can be concentrated in a population by using the antibiotic penicillin. Penicillin inhibits the synthesis of bacterial cell walls. When it is added to a minimal medium, the wild-type bacteria grow rapidly but, without cell walls, burst open and are killed. The mutants, unable to grow on a minimal medium, survive. They are transferred to a medium containing added nutrients, and then the specific growth requirement of each mutant is individually tested.

Mutations that affect a particular phenotype (for example, growth requirement for tryptophan) are localized at specific chromosomal sites through genetic tests. Localization of the genetic markers is accomplished by methods analogous to those described in Franklin W. Stahl's *The Mechanics of Inheritance,* in this series, and also discussed by David M. Bonner and Stanley E. Mills in their book, *Heredity,* which is part of the companion Prentice-Hall Foundations of Modern Biology Series.

Biochemical studies of extracts of *Neurospora* have shown that tryptophan, like most other organic molecules of the cell, is synthesized in a sequence of chemical reactions (Fig. 3.1). Mutations in tryptophan-requiring strains map at several genetic locations. Each mutant is defective in one of the steps in the biosynthetic sequence. Those mutations that involve the final reaction, catalyzed by the enzyme tryptophan synthetase (Fig. 3.1), all map in a small section of linkage group 2 called the tryptophan synthetase gene, or *td* gene. Thus the basic gene-enzyme relationship is clear: a mutation in a specific chromosomal region is reflected in the loss of activity of one enzyme. That the *td* gene is a sequence of adjacent DNA nucleotide pairs that dictate the primary structure of the tryptophan synthetase molecule is now assumed. Further evidence, discussed later in this chapter, is necessary to prove that this assumption is correct.

The Genetic Block

The reduction in enzymic activity effected by a mutation is termed a *genetic block*. The block may be complete; that is, it results in complete absence of the enzyme. Or it may be partial (leaky); that is, it results in the formation of altered enzyme that has some limited degree of activity. A particular product, then, is not produced or is produced in insufficient quantity for normal cellular metabolism. Because extreme phenotypic differences usually are easiest to deal with, most biochemical mutants used are those almost totally defective in a particular enzymic activity.

Frequently, precursors that are products of earlier chemical reactions in the biosynthetic sequence (that is, those preceding the blocked reaction) may accumulate in the mutant cells or in the culture filtrate. Identification of some of the precursors accumulated by biochemical mutants has been very helpful in elucidating many pathways of normal intermediary metabolism. Some of the uses and pitfalls in analyses of metabolic pathways in mutants with genetic blocks are described in Chap. 5. At the moment we are concerned with the mutation in the genetic material and its relation to the primary genetic block due to the formation of an altered protein.

Altered Proteins

Genetic crosses between *Neurospora* mutants that cannot form normal tryptophan synthetase demonstrate that many of the mutations are separable by recombination and thus reside at different positions in the polydeoxyribonucleotide chain within the confines of the *td* gene. Some mutants fail to grow at all except in the presence of a tryptophan supplement. In such cases, genetic damage has resulted in the production of an enzyme that is totally unable to catalyze the biosynthesis of tryptophan. Other mutants grow slowly on minimal medium. For example, one mutant, *td24,* forms little or no active tryptophan synthetase at 25°C and has an absolute requirement for tryptophan at this temperature. However, slow growth on minimal medium ensues when the temperature is elevated to 30°C. This type of mutant is known as a temperature-sensitive mutant. The tryptophan synthetase prepared from *td24* is inhibited by a metal constituent in the cell extract. When the enzyme is separated from the inhibitor by fractionation, activity is restored. The mutant protein is much more sensitive to inhibition by zinc ion, and the energy of activation for tryptophan biosynthesis catalyzed by this mutant protein is much higher than the value obtained with the wild-type enzyme. This in vitro temperature effect is in full agreement with the in vivo temperature effect seen when the mutant is grown at 25°C versus 30°C. Only at the elevated temperature, where tryptophan synthetase functions at an appreciable rate, is the mutant able to grow, although slowly.

Mutant enzymes differ from the wild-type protein and from one another in other ways: electrophoretic mobility, sensitivity to heat or acid denaturation, behavior on column chromatography, and so on.

Perhaps the most striking difference so far found between tryptophan synthetase mutants relates to their ability to form a protein that is inactive enzymatically but has immunological properties similar to tryptophan synthetase. This protein is called cross-reacting material (CRM). CRM is detected by the serological methods outlined in Fig. 3.2 and described in the legend to that figure. Those mutants that produce CRM are called *CRM-positive* (CRM+) *mutants*; those that do not are termed *CRM-negative* (CRM−) *mutants*.

Among the CRM+ mutants, immunochemical methods have provided a means of distinguishing several antigenic types of mutationally altered tryptophan synthetase. The formation of these molecules has been related to the genetic locations of mutations within the *td* gene. Furthermore, CRM+ mutants can be classified on the basis of the amount and type of residual enzymatic activity retained by the protein. Wild-type tryptophan synthetase can catalyze at least three biochemical reactions (Fig. 3.3). Some CRM's exhibit no enzymatic activity for any of the reactions. Others retain the capacity to catalyze only one or two of the reactions but lack the ability to catalyze the physiologically important reaction involving the conversion of indoleglycerolphosphate (InGP) and L-serine to L-tryptophan.

How might CRM− mutants be explained? The CRM− phenotype could reflect the formation of unstable molecules, small fragments (free or ribosome-bound), molecules having large regions of the polypeptide chain with an amino acid sequence entirely different from the normal protein, or even polypeptide subunits that have been damaged in certain regions necessary for their association into a specific polymeric form. Indeed, many CRM− mutants do form a molecule that is a grossly abnormal tryptophan synthetase and fails to give the standard immunological test for CRM.

These results tell us that mutations in a particular gene of *Neurospora* exert their effects at the level of a particular enzyme, tryptophan synthetase, and are reflected in specific changes in the structure and properties of the enzyme. Just as the gene can exist in a variety of forms (alleles), so can the protein. The finding of a variety of altered forms of a protein in mutants for a particular gene constitutes strong

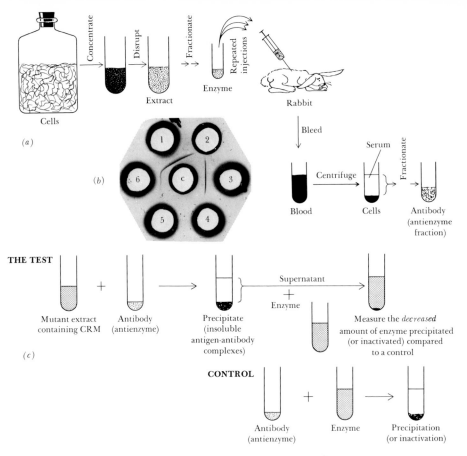

FIG. 3.2. *Preparation of immune serum and detection of CRM. (Above) Some steps in the preparation of immune serum. (Left) Agar diffusion (Ouchterlony technique). Holes are cut into the agar layer in a petri dish. Antienzyme is added to the center well; enzyme is added to well number 1, and extracts of a CRM⁺ mutant are added to wells 3 and 6. After diffusion of the antibody molecules and the enzyme protein (and CRM) molecules, a band of precipitation forms between the extract and antibody wells that coalesces with the band formed between the enzyme and antienzyme wells. Extracts of a CRM⁻ mutant are added to wells 4 and 5, and no band is seen. (Below) Tube titration (blocking power).*

FIG. 3.3. *Reactions catalyzed by tryptophan synthetase. The normal, physiological reaction is pictured in capitals (reaction 1); accessory reactions are shown in lowercase type (reactions 2 and 3). Reaction 3 is separable into two reactions whose interrelationships are not yet clear: a forward reaction (3f) and a reverse reaction (3r) that does not seem to be strictly analogous to a true reversal of reaction 3f.*

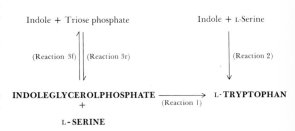

43

evidence that the gene dictates the structure of that particular protein.

The biosynthesis of tryptophan in enteric bacteria proceeds through essentially the same series of reactions as it does in *Neurospora* (Fig. 3.1). The reactions catalyzed by mold and bacterial tryptophan synthetase appear to be similar (Fig. 3.3). However, in contrast to the *Neurospora* enzyme, bacterial tryptophan synthetase is composed of two nonidentical and readily separable protein subunits, termed *components A and B*. Interactions between the A and B components, which are necessary for maximum catalytic activity, are the subject of a section of Chap. 4. Here we shall consider some general observations on bacterial mutants with defective tryptophan synthetase, that is, those CRM+ mutants that cannot carry out the conversion of InGP to tryptophan (Fig. 3.3). Tryptophan synthetase mutants lacking the A component or containing it in an altered form (A-CRM mutants) cannot carry out reactions 1 or 3, but they contain a B component that is normal in all respects and can catalyze reaction 2, the indole-to-tryptophan reaction. Thus A mutants can grow on either indole or

FIG. 3.4. *Genetic map of the gene for E. coli tryptophan synthetase A protein and some amino acid replacements detected in the proteins of particular mutants. The upper portion of the figure shows the genetic map; isolation numbers of some CRM-forming mutants are listed above the line. The numbers in columns indicate that these sites of mutation either are located at identical positions or are extremely closely linked. Some of the properties of the mutant proteins are noted as superscripts to the mutant numbers. They indicate that the respective CRM's are heat labile (●); heat labile, but more stable than A23 (△); heat sensitive to the same degree as the wild-type protein (×); more heat stable than the wild-type protein (○); heat stable, but less stable than A3 or A33 (*); acid precipitable (□). Mutant B51 is located in the adjacent, B, gene.*

Genetic map distances are given as percent recombination immediately below the

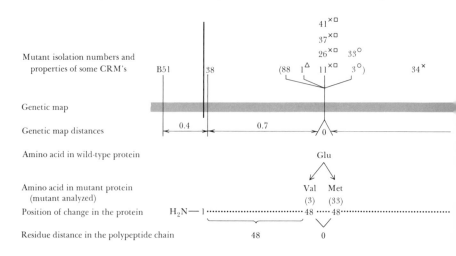

tryptophan. B-CRM mutants contain a defective B component; their A protein is normal, so they can catalyze reaction 3, but they cannot catalyze either reaction 1 or reaction 2. Therefore, they cannot utilize indole for growth, responding only to tryptophan.

In *E. coli,* mutations specifically affecting the A and B proteins are localized in two adjacent sections of the polynucleotide chain known as the *A* and *B* genes, respectively. Recombination tests also show that the *A* and *B* genes are closely linked to three other genes involved in the production of other enzymes in the tryptophan biosynthetic sequence. The clustering of gene loci having related but distinct functions is a subject of Chap. 10.

The top of Fig. 3.4 presents a genetic map of the *A* gene (the lower portion will be referred to in the next section). Numbers listed above the line are stock numbers of independently isolated mutants that form A-CRM. As in *Neurospora,* so in *E. coli* tryptophan synthetase mutants, the CRM's exhibit differences in properties. Their differing responses to heat and acid are included in Fig. 3.4.

line. In cases of clusters of mutations, the mutants used in this analysis are indicated in parentheses lower in the figure. Mutant 34 has not been precisely mapped.

The lower portion of the figure indicates the amino acids found at particular positions in the wild-type protein and the collection of individual amino acid substitutions detected in various mutant proteins, each containing a single amino acid substitution. The sites of mutation within the A gene, located by recombination tests, correspond with the sites of amino acid substitution in the respective polypeptide chains. The genetic map and the polypeptide map are colinear. Compiled from several publications by C. Yanofsky and coworkers, including C. Yanofsky, B. C. Carlton, J. R. Guest, D. R. Helinski, and U. Henning, Proc. Natl. Acad. Sci. U.S., 51 (1964), 266; J. R. Guest and C. Yanofsky, Nature, 210 (1966), 799; C. Yanofsky, G. R. Drapeau, J. R. Guest, and B. C. Carlton, Proc. Natl. Acad. Sci. U.S., 57 (1967), 296.

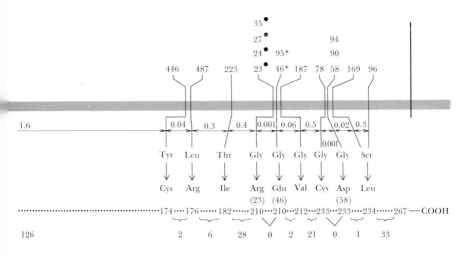

Amino Acid Replacements

In the examples of gene-protein relationships discussed so far, the analyses have shown us only that gene mutations mapping in a restricted portion of a chromosome result in changes in the gross structure and properties of a single species of protein molecule. What evidence is there that these reflect changes in the primary structure of the protein?

This relationship between chromosomal mutation and a discrete, localized change in the primary structure of a protein came first in 1957 from V. M. Ingram's studies of tryptic peptide fingerprints of normal and mutant human hemoglobin. Ingram observed the presence of a single amino acid difference between normal hemoglobin and hemoglobin obtained from individuals suffering with sickle-cell anemia, a congenital abnormality inherited as a single recessive gene. Immediately, other proteins were examined and many mutant forms were found to contain single amino acid substitutions. Among the proteins to receive concerted attention was *E. coli* tryptophan synthetase.

The wild-type A protein component of *E. coli* tryptophan synthetase has been purified and subjected to enzyme digestion and sequence analysis by the techniques described in Chap. 2. The protein has a molecular weight of about 29,000 and contains 267 residues. The protein is hydrolyzed by trypsin into 25 distinct peptides plus a few additional peptide spots that do not separate well on fingerprinting. The number of peptides is greater than the 23 peptides, one might expect from examining Fig. 2.4. Occasionally incomplete hydrolysis may occur at certain points in the polypeptide chain. For example, the lysyl peptide bond at position 200 appears unusually resistant to trypsin, often resulting in a tryptic peptide that includes both peptides XVII and XVIII in addition to the individual peptides XVII and XVIII.

Similar analyses of primary structure have been carried out on a large number of altered A proteins in CRM+ mutants. In all instances, fingerprints of the mutant proteins revealed striking similarities to fingerprints of the wild-type protein. In some cases, differences in one or two peptide spots were seen; in others, no difference was detected by the fingerprint technique. Amino acid analysis and sequence studies of the altered peptides proved that *one* particular amino acid had been replaced by a different amino acid in each of the mutant enzymes. Figure 3.4 diagrams some of the changes found. The figure indicates that the protein of mutant *A3* contains a valine (Val) residue in place of the glutamic (Glu) residue located at position 48 in the wild-type polypeptide chain. The remainder of the *A3* protein does not differ detectably from wild-type protein in amino acid composition. Similar analyses were carried out with each of the other mutant proteins. One of the earliest and most revealing analyses will serve to illustrate the formidable nature of such fine-structure studies.

Fingerprints of tryptic peptides from *A23* CRM showed one wild-type peptide to be missing; this peptide was counterbalanced by the appearance of two new peptides not found on fingerprints of wild-type protein. The mutant protein was assumed to contain an extra trypsin-sensitive residue (arginine or lysine) that is not present in the wild-type protein. An arginine residue is shown in Fig. 3.4, because, upon further analysis, arginine actually proved to be the amino acid that was substituted for glycine at that position in the wild-type protein. Through further carefully controlled enzyme digestions and amino acid analyses, the alteration in the *A46* CRM was shown to involve replacement of this same glycine residue by a glutamic acid residue. As indicated on the genetic map, the *A23* mutant site is very close to, but nevertheless distinct from, the *A46* site. This is strong evidence that more than one nucleotide pair is responsible for determining the specific location of a particular amino acid in a protein.

Finally, a pair of double mutants, *A23, A33* and *A11, A46,* was obtained in recombination experiments. Each of the double mutants had two alterations in the *A* gene. The A-CRMs of each of the double mutants were found to contain both of the peptide alterations noted in the A-CRMs of the original single-site mutants. The results with bacterial tryptophan synthetase indicate most elegantly that individual single-site mutations within the segment of the DNA chain called the tryptophan synthetase genetic region cause single amino acid substitutions in the primary structure of the tryptophan synthetase A protein.

Further confirmation of this relationship between the gene and the primary structure of protein can be seen in studies of the capsid (coat) protein found in tobacco mosaic virus; the TMV subunits are shown in Fig. 2.13. Figure 3.5 shows how mutant forms of the virus were de-

FIG. 3.5. *Lesions produced on a tobacco leaf by wild-type TMV and a mutant strain. A tobacco leaf was inoculated with wild-type TMV on the left half and mutant strain on the right half. The lesions have developed for 10 days. The relative number of lesions is indicative of the virus concentration in the solution used for inoculating the leaves. From H. Fraenkel-Conrat,* **Design and Function at the Threshold of Life: The Viruses,** *New York: Academic Press, Inc., 1962.*

FIG. 3.6.   *Amino acid substitutions found in the proteins of various mutant strains of tobacco mosaic virus. The protein subunits (Fig. 2.13) of the virus rods are repeating polypeptide chains 157 amino acids in length. The composition of the polypeptide chain of one wild-type TMV strain is: Acetyl-Ser(1)-Tyr-Ser-Ile-Thr-Thr-Pro-Ser-Gln-Phe(10)-Val-Phe-Leu-Ser-Ser-Ala-Trp-Ala-Asp-Pro(20)-Ile-Glu-Leu-Ile-Asn-Leu-Cys-Thr-Asn-Ala(30)-Leu-Gly-Asn- Gln-Phe-Gln-Thr-Gln-Gln-Ala(40)-Arg-Thr-Val-Gln-Val-Arg-Gln-Phe-Ser-Gln(50)-Val-Trp-Lys-Pro-Ser-Pro-Gln-Val-Thr-Val(60)-Arg-Phe-Pro-Asp-Ser-Asp-Phe-Lys-Val- Tyr(70)-Asn-Ala-Val-Leu-Asp-Pro-Leu-Val(80)-Thr-Ala-Leu-Leu-Gly-Ala-Phe-Asp-Thr-Arg(90)-Asn-Arg-Ile-Ile-Glu-Val-Glu-Asn-Gln-Ala(100)-Asn-Pro- Thr-Thr-Ala-Glu-Thr-Leu-Asp-Ala(110)-Thr-Arg-Arg-Val Asp-Asp-Ala-Thr-Val-Ala(120)-Ile-Arg-Ser-Ala-Ile-Asn-Asn-Leu-Ile-Val(130)-Glu-Leu-Ile-Arg-Gly-Thr-Gly-Ser-Tyr-Asn(140)-Arg-Ser-Ser-Phe-Glu-Ser-Ser-Ser-Gly-Leu(150)-Val-Trp-Thr-Ser-Gly-Pro-Ala-Thr-COOH.*

Viruses with abnormal growth properties were obtained from lesions appearing on tobacco leaves inoculated with untreated (for spontaneous mutants) or treated (for induced mutants) virus (see Fig. 3.5). Some of the mutations affect other proteins coded for by the virus RNA. However, some of the mutations lead to abnormal virus capsid ("coat protein") subunits, and in over 65 mutants the alterations were due to amino acid substitutions. These encompass substitutions at 33 different residue positions in the protein. A few different substitutions were found at several residue positions, and identical substitutions were found in the proteins of a number of independently isolated mutants. The letter following the residue number indicates whether the mutation was spontaneous (S), or was induced with nitrous acid (N), bromination (B), methylation (M), or by growth in the presence of 5-fluorouracil (F). Compiled from G. Funatsu and H. Fraenkel-Conrat, Biochemistry, 3 *(1964), 1356, and from B. Wittmann-Liebold and H. G. Witmann,* Z. Vererbungslehre, 97 *(1965), 305.*

tected and Fig. 3.6 gives the primary structure of the capsid protein and lists some amino acid replacements found in different TMV mutants. Thus mutations in TMV nucleic acid (which is RNA, not DNA) can lead to the production of coat protein possessing an altered amino acid sequence. All the changes are amino acid replacements. These results reinforce the conclusions reached from our discussion of the work with tryptophan synthetase. However, the tryptophan synthetase system offers one crucial advantage for such studies: *E. coli* undergoes genetic recombination, whereas the small RNA viruses do not. Using the powerful methods of recombination analysis, we can provide unequivocal experimental evidence for the colinear relationship between the genetic map and the amino acid sequence of the protein.

Colinearity of Genetic Map and Amino Acid Sequence

Close inspection of the data presented in Fig. 3.4 allows us to conclude much more than the mere fact that mutations in the DNA lead to amino acid replacements in the primary structure of the protein. Look at the *positions* of the amino acid replacements in the different tryptophan synthetase A protein mutants relative to the sites of the mutations on the genetic map and you will see that they correspond.

Residue number	Amino acid present in wild-type protein	Amino acid present in mutant protein
5 N	Thr	Ile
10 S	Phe	Leu
11 N	Val	Met
15 N	Ser	Leu
19 S	Asp	Ala
20 S	Pro	Thr
20 N, B	Pro	Leu
21 N	Ile	Val
21 N	Ile	Met
21 B	Ile	Thr
24 N	Ile	Val
25 N, B	Asn	Ser
28 N	Thr	Ile
28 F	Thr	Ala
33 S	Asn	Lys
33 B	Asn	Ser
46 M	Arg	Gly
46 N	Arg	Lys
55 N	Ser	Leu
58 F	Val	Ala
59 N	Thr	Ile
63 N	Pro	Ser
65 F, B	Ser	Gly
66 N	Pro	Ser
73 S, N	Asn	Ser
81 M, N	Thr	Ala
95 N	Glu	Asp
97 N	Glu	Gly
107 N	Thr	Met
125 N	Ile	Val
126 B	Asn	Ser
129 S	Ile	Thr
129 N	Ile	Val
136 N	Thr	Ile
138 S, N	Ser	Phe
139 N	Tyr	Cys
140 S	Asn	Lys
148 M, N	Ser	Phe
153 N	Thr	Ile
156 N	Pro	Leu

FIG. 3.6. *Legend on facing page.*

Even the genetic map distances can be related to the number of amino acids along the polypeptide chain; about 0.015 map unit in the *A* gene specifies a single amino acid residue in the A polypeptide chain. Each type of genetic lesion is discrete; it maps as a point mutation and corresponds to the substitution of only one amino acid. In terms of spatial organization, the gene and the polypeptide chain are colinear. We would like to conclude from this that the *A* gene is a linear segment of the deoxyribopolynucleotide chain of the *E. coli* chromosome that determines the corresponding linear sequence of amino acids in the A polypeptide chain.

In only a few other systems do we have information that approaches the refined analysis summarized in Fig. 3.4. In many cases the genetic fine-structure information exists, but analysis of primary structure of the particular polypeptide chain is lacking; in other cases, such as TMV, the unraveling of nucleotide sequence must await the development of chemical rather than genetic methods. It will be several years before sequencing of long genetic messages can be accomplished by chemical techniques.

Genotype versus Phenotype: When Is a Mutant a Mutant?

Genetic analysis always starts with an organism that is the "normal" or "wild type" with respect to as many properties as can be measured. Mutants deviate from the wild type in one or more hereditary characteristics. As you know, *E. coli* ordinarily grows without the addition of tryptophan in the medium, and we can obtain mutants that require tryptophan for growth. Perhaps the genetic block is located in the terminal step of tryptophan biosynthesis and involves the production of a defective tryptophan synthetase (CRM+) with altered properties. Ultimately we may locate an amino acid substitution in the A protein moiety of the enzyme.

Some of these amino acid substitutions are not easy to find. For example, on fingerprint analysis the tryptic and chymotryptic peptides of A-CRM's from *E. coli* tryptophan synthetase mutants *A3, A34,* and *A75* were at first thought to be indistinguishable from the peptides of the wild-type protein. Later, the amino acid substitution in the *A3* mutant was detected (Fig. 3.4) . When one uncharged or neutral amino acid is substituted for another, detection of the replacement requires careful analysis of the amino acid composition of many individual peptides. Obviously, our ability to accurately describe the mutant phenotype at the level of changes in protein primary structure is limited by the precision and extent of our analysis.

When a mutant reverts to the wild-type phenotype, either spontaneously or following mutagenesis, one reasonable assumption is that the original genotype has been restored. Thus, when the tryptophan-requiring mutant *A23* (Arg substituted for Gly at position 210 of the A protein in Fig. 3.4) reverts to growth in the absence of exogenous tryptophan, the genetic code of the *A* gene should be wild type once again and should now specify glycine at position 210 of the A protein. This complete reversion of both genotype and phenotype to wild type has been found. Interestingly, other changes can restore completely or partially the wild-type phenotype, although not the wild-type genotype. Some revertants of mutant *A23* carry Ser at residue 210; some carry Thr. Obviously the genetic code is not specifying glycine at position 210, yet those cells with threonine at position 210 grow slowly in the absence of tryptophan. In fact, those cells with serine at position 210 cannot be distinguished functionally from wild type; A protein with serine at position 210 is catalytically normal. This observation is important, for it proves that some (if not many) mutations in the genetic material may go undetected. If the amino acid replacements occur in a noncritical portion of the molecule or involve the replacement of one amino acid by another possessing similar size and properties, the protein may still retain wild-type activity, although altered in its primary structure.

A similar situation is found among revertants of mutant *A46* (Fig. 3.4). Some revertants are true wild-type (Gly), some mimic wild-type (Val), and others are partially functional in the absence of tryptophan (Ala). In still another class of revertants, called *second-site revertants,* the A protein still retains the original amino acid substitution (Glu in place of Gly); in addition, it contains a second amino acid substitution, a Cys in place of the Tyr normally found at residue 174. *A46* is mutant and so is *A446,* but when the two amino acid substitutions (Gly → Glu, Cys → Tyr) occur together in the same polypeptide chain, they compensate for each other. In some manner the second amino acid substitution modifies the ultimate configuration of the protein, permitting it to function as a catalyst, although at less than normal efficiency. This secondary mutation or second-site reversion is one type of *suppressor mutation,* so called because it suppresses the expression of the original mutant phenotype (tryptophan requirement). The original primary mutation is still present in the *A* gene in unaltered form. This is an example of an *intragenic suppressor mutation,* because the secondary mutation and the primary mutation are located in the same gene.

Second-site reversion of *A46* involves a Tyr-to-Cys change at residue 174 (mutant *A446*), whereas second-site reversion of *A187* involving a Leu-to-Arg substitution occurs at residue 176 (mutant *A487*). These and other second-site reversions all appear to occur within a restricted region of the A polypeptide chain; about 30 amino acid residues separate the two substitutions. This has led Yanofsky and coworkers to speculate that "correction" of the catalytic defect may involve the direct interaction of two critical regions of the protein to form the tertiary structure required for enzymatic activity (Fig. 3.7).

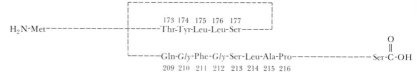

FIG. 3.7. *Possible relationship between different regions of the folded wild-type tryptophan synthetase A protein molecule suggested by second-site (intragenic suppressor) reversion analysis. The amino acids changed in primary mutational events are shown in italic (consult Fig. 3.4) and those changes by second-site reversion are shown in bold type. An amino acid replacement at residue 210 is compensated for by a second replacement in residue 174, and vice versa. Similarly, amino acid substitutions at residues 176 and 212 compensate for each other. The spatial arrangement of compensating changes in the polypeptide chain has led to the speculation that the two segments of the chain interact when the protein achieves its final tertiary structure. After C. Yanofsky, V. Horn, and D. Thorpe,* Science, 146 (*1964*), *1593.*

Gene Mutations and Protein Structure: Some Generalities

The gene is pictured as a sequence of adjacent nucleotides in the polymer deoxyribonucleic acid. The gene is divisible by mutation, because any single nucleotide can be inserted in place of another. The gene is divisible by recombination, for recombinations can take place between pairs of adjacent nucleotides along the polynucleotide chain. The gene is basically a functional unit. Its function lies in the control of the structure of a single class of polypeptide chains.

The amino acid sequence of a polypeptide chain is dictated by the sequence of nucleotides in the corresponding gene. Mutations at different positions within the gene ultimately result in alterations in the structure of the polypeptide chain. A single-site mutation may cause the substitution of one amino acid by another in the polypeptide chain. Thus we can conclude that certain genes control the primary structure of individual and specific protein molecules, and that mutations in a structural gene result in changes in the primary structure of the protein molecule. The gene (DNA) and the polypeptide chain are linear structures, and are colinear with each other.

Amino acid replacements, giving rise to mutant proteins, are qualitative changes. The particular location in which the amino acid substitution occurs within the polypeptide chain is important in determining the ultimate effect of the mutation on the biological activity and other properties of the protein molecule. Also, the type of amino acid substitution is important. Substitution of one amino acid by another containing a very dissimilar side chain generally has a more extreme effect than does replacement with more similar amino acids. In fact, where substitutions involve very similar amino acids, the effect on the configuration and, therefore, on the properties of the protein may be very slight. Such alterations in structure may be detected only by detailed chemical analysis of the purified protein.

Questions

3.1. What is meant by the term *genetic block?* Is a genetic block always complete? Why?

3.2. Look up the original literature and review in about 300 words plus a one-page diagram an additional case of a gene-protein relationship. You may find an appealing example on your own, or you may wish to select your example from among:

(*a*) Lysozyme of T4 bacteriophage.

(*b*) Utilization of a sugar or biosynthesis of a purine, pyrimidine, or amino acid in *Escherichia coli, Salmonella typhimurium, Neurospora crassa,* or *Saccharomyces cerevisiae.*

(*c*) Xanthine dehydrogenase, amylase, or esterases of *Drosophila melanogaster.*

(*d*) Glucose-6-phosphate dehydrogenase in man.

3.3. Normal adult hemoglobin, hemoglobin A, consists of four polypeptide chains, two α chains and two β chains. The primary structures of the two kinds of chains have some similarities but differ at many positions.

(*a*) Is the structure of hemoglobin A dictated by one or by two genes? Justify your answer.

(*b*) A difference in electrophoretic mobility (surface charge) was detected between normal and abnormal hemoglobin by Linus Pauling and coworkers in 1949. What structural alteration in the protein might underlie such a change?

(*c*) Some of the electrophoretically abnormal hemoglobins lead to diseased states (for example, sickle-cell anemia; see Fig. 5.8), but other abnormal hemoglobins are without effect on the phenotype. Explain why such different responses might be predicted.

3.4. What tests does a geneticist apply to determine if two independently isolated mutations affect the same or different genes?

3.5. In tabular form, set out the probable relationships between chemical terms and genetical terms:

	Series of adjacent nucleotide pairs dictating structure of polypeptide chain	Smallest unit of mutation	Smallest unit indivisible by recombination	Smallest unit in which recombination occurs
Chemical term (in relation to structure of DNA)				
Genetical terms that apply				

3.6. Attempt to "explain" the *data* in Fig. 3.4 (that is, genetic map distances and position of amino acid changes) by some device other than an assumption of colinearity.

References

Cairns, J., G. S. Stent, and J. D. Watson, eds., *Phage and the Origins of Molecular Biology.* Cold Spring Harbor, N.Y.: Cold Spring Harbor Laboratory of Quantitative Biology, 1966. Personal and often highly animated recollections by some of those who contributed to formulation of our present concepts of the gene and gene action. Because there is a special emphasis in this book, additional perspective may be gained by consulting the presentation of Carlson (below).

Carlson, E. A., *The Gene: A Critical History.* Philadelphia: W. B. Saunders Company, 1966. The author uses quotations from the original literature in presenting a development of the modern concept of the gene outlined in this chapter.

Cohen, G. N., *Biosynthesis of Small Molecules.* New York: Harper & Row, Publishers, 1967. A good account, in paperback, of some steps in intermediary metabolism concerned with biosynthesis, including chapters on methodology and metabolic regulation.

Cushing, J. E., and D. H. Campbell, *Principles of Immunology.* New York: McGraw-Hill, Inc., 1957. An introductory text to immunology and its applications in biology.

Helinski, D. R., and C. Yanofsky, "Genetic Control of Protein Structure," *The Proteins,* H. Neurath, ed., in Vol. IV, 2nd ed. New York: Academic Press, Inc., 1966, p. 1. A critical review with an emphasis on topics covered in this chapter.

Hogness, D. S., "The Structure and Function of the DNA from bacteriophage λ." *J. Gen. Physiol., 49* (1966), 29: Hogness, D. S., W. Doerfler, J. B. Egan, and L. W. Black, "The Position and Orientation of Genes in λ and λ *dg* DNA." *Cold Spring Harbor Symp. Quant. Biol., 31* (1966), 129. Direct evidence that the linearity of the genetic map resides in the linearity of the DNA molecule.

Ingram, V. M., *The Biosynthesis of Macromolecules.* New York: W. A. Benjamin, Inc., 1966. A paperback book that overlaps the present volume in many respects; the discussion of genetic control of protein structure (Chap. 6) emphasizes studies on hemoglobins and TMV protein.

Sarabhai, A. S., O. W. Stretton, S. Brenner, and A. Bolle, "Colinearity of Gene with the Polypeptide Chain," *Nature, 201* (1964), 14. This paper and the 1964 paper by Yanofsky et al. cited in the legend to Fig. 3.4 constitute the first direct evidence for colinearity.

Yanofsky, C., "'The Tryptophan Synthetase System," *Bact. Rev., 24* (1960), 221. A review of experimental observations on *Escherichia coli* and *Neurospora* tryptophan synthetases.

———, and P. St. Lawrence, "Gene Action," *Ann. Rev. Microbiol., 14* (1960), 311. One of the better reviews of advances in biochemical genetics.

———, "Structural Relationships between Gene and Protein," *Ann. Rev. Genet., 1* (1967), 117. A short review that focuses on several particularly informative microbial systems, including (you guessed it) tryptophan synthetase.

———, "Gene Structure and Protein Structure," *Harvey Lectures, 61* (1967), 145.

Complementation

In Chap. 3 the function of the gene was described in terms of the genetic control of the primary structure of polypeptide chains. The sequence of bases in the polynucleotide chain dictates the positioning of amino acid residues at specific sites in the polypeptide chain. Detailed analyses of this type require that the protein whose structure is controlled by the gene be identified and that the protein be purified. Comparatively few proteins in genetically defined systems have been obtained in the quantities and state of purity required for such analyses. More systems have been described in enzymological terms and still more in general biochemical terms. However, especially in higher organisms, the gross mutant phenotype is at present the only guiding signal. Clearly what we need is an additional, more rapid method to determine whether two different mutations affect the same or separate genic functions.

The average chemical length of a single gene is about 1,000 nucleotide pairs. Recombination tests can tell us if the sites of two mutations are closely linked and could be contained in the relatively short polynucleotide sequence comprising a single gene. If the two mutations lie on different chromosomes, on different arms of the same chromosome, or far apart on a single chromosome arm, they are usually assumed to affect the structures of two different polypeptide chains. There is a second genetic method that can be used to examine further this idea regarding the distinctness of function of the two unlinked or loosely linked genes. The method involves a genetic test of function wherein the phenotype of organisms carrying two separate mutations is examined. The method is in practice not different from descriptions of dominance in diploid organisms.

Dominance and Recessiveness

In diploid organisms, one dose of a functional gene is often sufficient to bring about the wild-type phenotype. That is, the heterozygote cannot be differentiated from the homozygous wild type by gross inspection. The wild-type allele is said to be *dominant,* and the mutant allele is said to be *recessive.* Where such situations are examined at the level of a protein controlled by a wild-type and the mutant gene, we may find in the heterozygote a 50/50 mixture of the active protein (specified by the wild-type gene) and, as pointed out in Chap. 3, an inactive but serologically cross-related protein, a CRM (specified by the mutant gene). Or the wild-type gene may specify a subunit of the active protein, and the polypeptide product of the mutant allele cannot be detected. In these cases the homozygote would have at least a twofold excess of the enzyme needed to bring about the "wild-type" phenotype seen in the heterozygote.

Figure 4.1 illustrates three different dihybrid ratios that arise in genetic crosses. In each case, genetically identical F_1 are crossed to yield the progeny shown in the F_2 squares. The top and left sides of the F_2 squares are labeled with the genotypes of the germ cells produced by the F_1 parents. In all 3 cases the two genes assort independently, and the wild type is dominant. The classic 9/3/3/1 ratio arises from the relative independence of two unlinked genes affecting genetic blocks in different biochemical reaction sequences—coupled with the phenomenon of dominance at the level of gross phenotype (left side of Fig. 4.1). In this example, the products of the two independent pathways are combined to give a final phenotype, such as in the eye colors of insects or the pigmentation of a portion of a plant. In such cases where two quite independent traits are examined collectively, the solid black phenotype is the *combination* of the two differently shaded phenotypes. The other crosses in Fig. 4.1 demonstrate deviations from the classic dihybrid ratio that are explicable by independent genes that control independent, enzymatically catalyzed reactions in the *same* pathway.

In the above examples we can say that the two dominant genes *complement* each other to bring about the wild-type phenotype. We infer that the functions of the two genes are distinct. Their independent assortment during recombination again is evidence of their genetic individuality. Hence, two pieces of information, one obtained

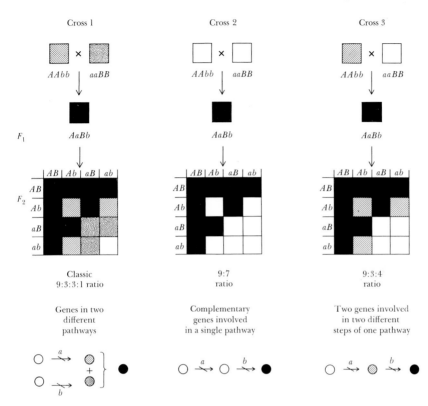

FIG. 4.1. *Clues in genetic data that can assist further study of the mechanism of gene action. Three different crosses between diploid organisms heterozygous for two recessive genes (a and b) in the F₁ generation. The three cases lead to different Mendelian ratios (dihybrid ratios) in the F₂ generation; the genotypes and phenotypes are indicated for the F₂ generation in the Punnett squares. Biochemical interpretation of the data is indicated beneath each cross.*

by recombination and one by complementation analyses, support the same conclusion. However, in the case of mutations involving closely linked genes, one cannot obtain assurance of separate function afforded by the criterion of independent assortment in the above examples. A test for dominance with regard to phenotypic expression, the *cis-trans* (or *complementation*) *test,* is important in initial comparisons of the functions of genes.

Getting Genes Together

The *cis-trans* test is an in vivo method of evaluating the phenotypic effect of two independently occurring mutations. The test (Fig. 4.2) relies on having boh mutations present in two alternative arrangements on the chromosome. The following brief discussion should make clear the difference between the recombination method of analysis and the *cis-trans* test, or *complementation test,* as it is frequently called. For example, let us say that two independently isolated mutations, *a* and *b,* are found to be closely linked and thus could possibly be located within the same gene. They may be brought together on the same chromosome through genetic recombination. The recombinant chromosomes will be wild type (+ +) and the double mutant (*ab*). Along with the two parental types, (*a*+) and (+*b*), we then have four marker arrangements possible among the progeny. If we stipulate that we want the two different mutations in the same cell, there are two ways this may be achieved. The two mutations may be

FIG. 4.2. *General methods for bringing together two mutations (in the* trans *configuration) in single cells.*

   (a) Heterozygous diploids *formed after meiosis and fertilization.*

   (b) Partial diploids in bacteria:

      (1) Following conjugation. *A portion of the chromosome is transferred from the donor cell to the recipient cell. Immediately after gene transfer, the effects of the two elements togther in common cytoplasm may be studied. In special cases the transferred chromosome fragment remains in diploid condition (heterogenote) during subsequent divisions of the recipient bacterium.*

      (2) Following transduction. *When certain bacterial viruses are released from infected cells, they occasionally pick up short chromosome fragments from the killed "donor" bacteria. These chromosome fragments may enter other (recipient) bacteria. In some situations, the fragment multiplies in synchrony with multiplication of the host chromosome (as in the heterogenote shown here). On other occasions, the transduced fragment does not multiply following penetration into the recipient bacterium; it merely is preserved as a single genetic element and is able to function. In this case (called abortive transduction), at each succeeding division of the recipient bacterium, one cell is a genetically altered partial diploid and contains the transduced fragment, whereas the other daughter cell lacks the abortively transduced fragment.*

   (c) Heterocaryon *formed by cell fusion and presence of genetically different haploid nuclei in common cytoplasm. No nuclear fusion (diploidy) occurs.*

   (d) Heterocaryon containing disomic nuclei. *Occasionally, spores are found that carry an extra chromosome (that is,* n + *1). When such a spore germinates, some of the nuclei contain an extra chromosome, but others lose the extra chromosome. If the spore had originated from a genetic cross between strains* a+ *and* +b*, a heterocaryon (pseudo-wild-type) may be formed.*

   (e) Mixed infection by viruses. *This test is made most conveniently under conditions where neither of two genetically different virus particles alone can successfully infect the cell. If the two mutations are in separate genes, the individual virus particles can replicate together in a common cytoplasm. Mutant virus particles, genetically identical with each of the two kinds of the parental infecting particles, are released after the infection has terminated. No genetic recombination is necessary for production of virus progeny through complementation, although the released virus may include a normal proportion of genetic recombinants.*

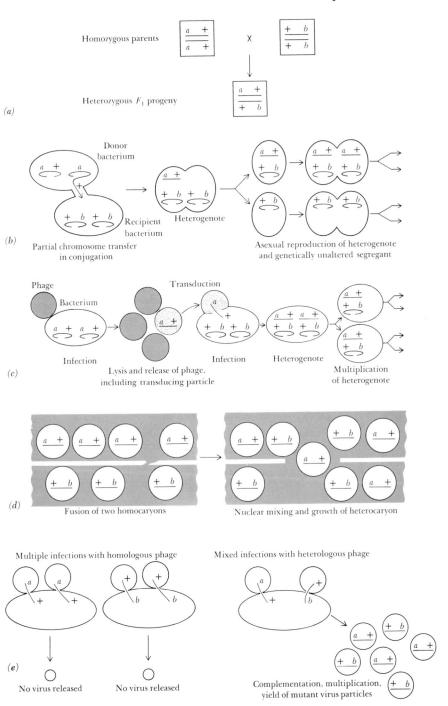

(a) Homozygous parents / Heterozygous F_1 progeny

(b) Partial chromosome transfer in conjugation — Donor bacterium — Recipient bacterium — Heterogenote — Asexual reproduction of heterogenote and genetically unaltered segregant

(c) Phage — Bacterium — Infection — Lysis and release of phage, including transducing particle — Transduction — Infection — Heterogenote — Multiplication of heterogenote

(d) Fusion of two homocaryons — Nuclear mixing and growth of heterocaryon

(e) Multiple infections with homologous phage — No virus released — No virus released — Mixed infections with heterologous phage — Complementation, multiplication, yield of mutant virus particles

carried by one chromosome (the double mutant ab), while the wild-type alleles are on the second chromosome ($++$). This is the *cis configuration*. The alternative arrangement occurs when the two mutations are located on different chromosomes, as denoted by $a+$ and $+b$. This is called the *trans configuration*.

The *cis-trans* test does not depend upon genetic recombination; it depends merely upon genetic function. The main technical problem in the test is the placement of two different chromosomes, or critical portions of chromosomes, together in the same cell. The manner in which this is achieved varies with different organisms, their modes of reproduction, and their normal genetic complement. Figure 4.2 shows some of the primary methods used at the current time to execute the *cis-trans* test. The figure illustrates only the operations involved in obtaining the important *trans* configuration.

Keep in mind the fact that complementation is due to interaction of gene products, not of the genes themselves. This concept is extremely important, for we shall see later in discussions of regulation of protein synthesis that some segments of the genetic material exert their effects directly, rather than through the intermediary of extrachromosomal products which are free to mix and to interact in the cytoplasm.

An Example of the cis-trans Test for Gene Function

The theory underlying the *cis-trans* test is based upon the one gene–one polypeptide chain concept. In thinking about the *cis-trans* test, it may be helpful to consider that genes act as discrete elements that function independently of one another, although some qualification of this general statement will be made in a later chapter. For example, referring to Fig. 4.3, let us assume that mutation a specifically prevents the expression of the normal function of a gene A and the subsequent formation of a normal polypeptide chain$_A$ without affecting the function of another gene B. Now let us say that a second, independent mutational event a' also occurs in gene A but at a different site within the gene A region. The two mutations a and a' are together in the same cell in the *cis* configuration, that is, on the same chromosome, and the other chromosome carries a normal, functional A gene. There will be produced x quantity of a doubly defective polypeptide$_A$, x quantity of wild-type polypeptide$_A$, and $2x$ quantity of wild-type polypeptide$_B$ (upper left in Fig. 4.3). Since both normal polypeptide$_A$ and normal polypeptide$_B$ are present, the phenotype will approach that of wild type and, in fact, may be quite similar to it.

Now examine this situation with regard to the same two genetically separable mutations, a and a', when they are in the *trans* configuration, that is, when they are present on different chromosomes (lower left in Fig. 4.3). Each of the $a+$ and the $+a'$ genotypes causes the formation

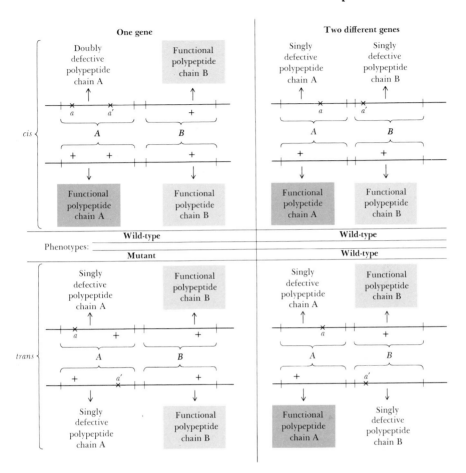

FIG. 4.3. *Theoretical basis of the* cis-trans *test for functional allelism. Two different mutations,* a *and* a', *in one gene and two different genes. The two mutations can be on the same chromosome or chromosome fragment (cis configuration) or on two different choromosomes (trans configuration). The phenotype discerned in the* trans *configuration affords insight to whether two mutations are in the same gene or in two separate genes.*

of a defective polypeptide$_A$. No functional polypeptide$_A$ is produced, and the phenotype of the cell will be mutant even though functional polypeptide$_B$ is formed. Whether the phenotype is wild type or mutant depends upon the relative chromosomal positions of the two mutations *a* and *a'*. This phenomenon sometimes is called the *cis-trans* position effect.

Examination of the right side of Fig. 4.3 will convince you that a single dose of functional polypeptide$_A$ and a single dose of functional polypeptide$_B$ will be produced in both the *cis* and the *trans* configurations if the sites of the mutations *a* and *a'* are in separate genes. Note that it is the *trans* test that critically distinguishes the alternative possibilities. If the two mutations are in the same gene, the *trans* phenotype is mutant; if the two mutations are in different genes, the *trans* phenotype is wild type. In contrast, the phenotype of the *cis* configuration is always wild type. Thus the *cis* test is valuable only as a control. The appearance of the wild-type phenotype in the *cis* test informs us that the mutations are recessive. That is, the wild-type activities continue to be expressed even in the presence of the mutant genes on the opposite genetic element.

One Gene, One Function

The production of a phenotype similar to wild type when two mutations are brought together in the *trans* configuration is called *complementation*. The function of an active gene on one chromosome or chromosome fragment complements the function of a different active gene on a second element. When two mutations fail to complement, the wild-type phenotype is not discerned. Complementation does not occur when the same functional unit is defective on both chromosomes. In this case, neither chromosome can fulfill the functions required to produce a wild-type phenotype. Thus the *cis-trans* (complementation) test can be used as a genetic method for defining the limits of genes.

The following situation is often encountered in complementation tests: (1) every mutation in genetic region (gene) *A* complements every mutation in gene *B,* and (2) no mutations within gene *A* complement each other and no mutations within gene *B* complement each other. In this very restricted case, the genes have been termed *cistrons*. The cistron is defined by purely genetical methods, and represents a functional unit solely defined by the results of unequivocal *cis-trans* tests.

The preceding descriptions assume that mutations affecting one enzyme generally will complement mutations affecting the production of other enzymes. Literally thousands of such tests have been made in a wide variety of organisms. After all, the very concept of recessive mutation depends upon the deficient activity of the mutant gene being compensated for by the presence of the wild-type allele on the other genetic element! In fact, one of the earliest tests of the one gene–one enzyme concept, made by G. W. Beadle and V. L. Conroodt, involved the testing of different biochemical deficiencies by the heterocaryon test (Fig. 4.2c). These workers noted that two tryptophan-deficient mutants, blocked at different steps in the pathway of tryptophan biosynthesis (Fig. 3.1), complemented each other.

There are numerous cases where one functional unit or cistron (defined by the *cis-trans* test) corresponds to one enzymic activity. Mutants defective in this one activity fail to complement one another but do complement mutants defective in any of a wide number of other enzyme activities. In some of the above cases it is known that the enzyme is composed of a single polypeptide chain, accounting for the straightforward correspondence. In other cases the enzyme is known to be composed of identical polypeptide subunits.

Two Cistrons, One Enzyme

Some functional proteins are controlled by two cistrons. Close examination of such systems demonstrates that these functional proteins are composed of two different polypeptide chains. One gene, or cistron, dictates the structure of one of the polypeptide chains, and the other gene dictates the structure of the second polypeptide chain.

Recall, from Chap. 3, the reactions carried out by tryptophan synthetase (Fig. 3.3). Also recall that the bacterial enzyme active in the physiologically significant reaction, InGP to tryptophan, is a composite of two dissimilar proteins, components A and B, each controlled by its own gene. Complementation tests in the *trans* configuration between A and B mutants demonstrate that (1) all A mutants complement all B mutants, and (2) no complementation is found between pairs of A mutants or between pairs of B mutants. The *cis-trans* test thus unequivocally demonstrates the presence of two independent genes, or cistrons, involved in the production of the two protein components of bacterial tryptophan synthetase.

When the B protein is separated from the A protein in vitro, the B protein is found to be a dimer composed of two identical polypeptide chains. The two B polypeptide chains are difficult to separate from each other; but the existence of a dimer was established from the presence of two C-terminal leucine residues per mole of B protein as well as from the fact that the number of tryptic peptides in fingerprints is only half that expected on the basis of the total number of arginine and lysine residues per mole of B protein. In addition, the B protein binds 2 moles of the cofactor, pyridoxal phosphate, per mole of protein. The pure B protein by itself can catalyze the indole-to-tryptophan reaction but at a much lower rate than when it is combined with a wild-type or a mutant A protein component. All mutants defective in gene *A*, responsible for A protein, can grow on indole because each A mutant possesses a B protein. The reaction catalyzed by the B protein becomes physiologically important to bacteria that are mutant in the *A* gene: it allows them to grow on indole as an alternative growth factor to tryptophan. If tryptophan is lacking in the environment, they still can multiply at the expense of any indole that may be present.

The bacterial tryptophan synthetase A mutants are divided into two classes: those containing an altered protein immunologically closely related to active A protein (the CRM$^+$ mutants described in Chap. 3) and those containing no detectable A-CRM (CRM$^-$ mutants). These two classes of mutant can be distinguished from each other on another basis: their rates of growth in the presence of indole. The reason for this difference becomes apparent when the indole-to-tryptophan reaction is studied with purified B protein in vitro. Although purified normal B protein can catalyze this reaction without the presence of A protein, combination of the A and B subunits results in a 30- to 100-fold enhancement of the reaction. Similarly, A protein alone can catalyze the InGP-to-indole reaction in the absence of the B protein, yet in the presence of B protein the reaction rate is greatly increased. Consequently, it would appear that both A and B proteins function at peak efficiency only when physically complexed with each other. This is a specific combination; the proper association is made even in the presence of other proteins.

The physiologically important reaction catalyzed by tryptophan synthetase is the InGP-to-tryptophan reaction (Fig. 3.3). Only the complex of A and B subunits can carry out this reaction. The native synthetase appears to be a tetramer, composed of the two B polypeptide chains (B protein) with two A polypeptide chains attached (see Fig. 2.16). The molecular weight of the complete complex is about 159,000. Free indole is a reactant in the enzymic catalyses carried out by each of the subunits separately, but it is not detected while the intact tetramer functions in the physiological reaction. In this case, indole is thought to be an enzyme-bound intermediate.

The results collectively demonstrate that protein-protein interactions can play important roles in enzyme structure and in physiological regulation of the rates of reactions. Because of the multicomponent structure of many proteins, as demonstrated by bacterial tryptophan synthetase, the original idea of the one gene–one enzyme relationship has been replaced by the concept of the one gene–one polypeptide chain. The *cis-trans* test can give the biochemist some idea of what to anticipate about the structure of a protein. It can provide an initial indication that more than one polypeptide chain may be involved in construction of the enzyme. However, it does not provide insight into the exact nature of the multimer, that is, whether it is a dimer of two dissimilar subunits or a tetramer of two dissimilar subunits.

Geneticists interchangeably use the terms gene and cistron to mean that segment of the genetic material involved in dictating the primary structure of a polypeptide chain. Complementation between mutants in one gene or cistron with those in another is called *intergenic* or *intercistronic complementation*. The word *locus* is used in a more general sense for a particular genetic region associated with a particular phenotype. The reason for this qualification in the use of terms is simple; thorns have been found in the bed of roses!

Intragenic Complementation: The Complexity of Proteins

Very often in biology, exceptional cases are found to seemingly clear-cut rules. When investigated thoroughly, these exceptions frequently furnish important contributions to our basic understanding of the rule itself. The exceptions may even prove to be extensions of the rule, and such is the case with exceptional mutants in the complementation phenomenon.

Complementation has been observed between different mutants whose defects involve the production of nonidentical subunits composing a single enzyme. This was pointed out above for the two genes involved in the production of the A and B components of bacterial tryptophan synthetase. As you recall, pairwise combinations of different A mutants, or pairwise combinations of different B mutants uniformly failed to complement, whereas every A mutant complemented every B mutant. These exceptions, then, help to clarify the relationship of one gene to one enzyme in more precise and correct terms: one gene, one polypeptide chain.

Complementation has also been observed to occur between two mutants, neither of which complements a third mutant. The possibility that the third mutation is an aberration that involves both of the other two sites of mutation can be ruled out by recombination tests. The single gene, therefore, can be further divided into subunits called *complementation units*. Some mutations involve one complementation unit *a*, other mutations involve complementation unit *b*, and still other mutations affect simultaneously both the *a* and *b* complementation units. The best current evidence has led to the working hypothesis that different complementation units within a single gene involve portions of the gene dictating the structure of particular sections of the polypeptide chain. Such sections might, for example, be specific α-helical segments of the protein. These segments of the chain may be the regions involved in protein-protein interactions between identical molecules. In other words, those genes exhibiting intragenic complementation are believed to control the production of enzymes that are multimers composed of one or more types of identical subunits. The single polypeptide chains, the monomers, either are inactive or have very limited enzymic activity. The evidence for these conclusions stems from studies of the general type discussed below.

A simplified complementation map schematizing the complementation behavior of *Neurospora* tryptophan synthetase mutants is shown in Fig. 4.4. Mutants that complement are indicated by nonoverlapping lines, whereas mutants that fail to complement are indicated by overlapping lines. Initially it was thought that CRM⁻ mutants were noncomplementing mutants, but it has recently been found that many of the CRM⁻ mutants do indeed complement with other tryptophan synthetase mutants, although the complementation is often inefficient. Wild-type *Neurospora* tryptophan synthetase, isolated as a pure protein,

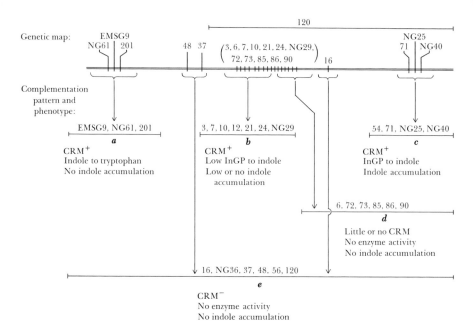

FIG. 4.4. *Genetic and complementation maps of the tryptophan synthetase gene of* Neurospora crassa. *All complementation tests were run in the* trans *configuration in heterocaryons. The heavy bar represents the chromosome; the numbers above the bar are the sites of mutation, mapped by recombination tests, of particular mutants designated by letters and numbers. Included is one mutant (120) that contains a multisite or extended mutation, encompassing a number of individual sites; this mutation is presumed to be a deletion. A number of independent mutations cluster near or at particular spots.*

The complementation pattern and some characteristics of the mutants are listed below the genetic map. The complementation map is read vertically: those mutants whose lines overlap fail to complement; those mutants whose lines do not overlap do complement. Note that there is a good correspondence between behavior in complementation, properties of the protein elaborated by the mutant, and genetic localization on the chromosome. Noncomplementing mutants are scattered through the gene; they are uniformly CRM⁻ mutants and include the multisite mutant, 120. This general pattern is typical of many other gene loci. In some genes the complementation patterns overlap and allow a linear ordering of groups of mutations on the basis of complementation behavior. Based on A. M. Lacy, Biochem. Biophys. Res. Commun., 18 (1965), 812, and previous publications.

has a molecular weight of about 140,000. The quantities of arginine and lysine are approximately equal, the total number of these two basic amino acids being about 130. One would therefore predict that, when *Neurospora* tryptophan synthetase is digested with trypsin (which splits the polypeptide chain at the arginine and lysine residues), about

130 peptide fragments would be detected on a fingerprint profile. However, only 48 to 53 peptides are detected. Two different C-terminal amino acids, leucine and phenylalanine, are detected upon digestion with carboxypeptidase. Finally, when hydrogen bonds are disrupted using an agent such as guanidine hydrochloride, the enzyme dissociates into subunits, each with a molecular weight of about 35,000. From these observations the inference was made that *Neurospora* tryptophan synthetase consists of two pairs of nonidentical subunits, that is, two α and two β polypeptide chains. The analogy to the quaternary structure of the *E. coli* enzyme is striking, but the *Neurospora* enzyme is not readily dissociable into subunits with accessory enzyme activities.

From the above description of *Neurospora* tryptophan synthetase we would predict that complementation tests among *td* mutants would reveal two distinct complementation groups, as in the case of the *E. coli* system. However, one observes a more complicated complementation pattern (Fig. 4.4). Instead of two complementation classes expected, one finds three in the analyses performed to date, and it is quite possible that more will be found as investigations continue. Furthermore, some mutants fail to complement with any other *td* mutant; these noncomplementing mutants are exclusively CRM⁻ mutants, a common observation in other systems.

The results of complementation studies with *Neurospora td* mutants can be interpreted on the basis of knowledge of the tryptophan synthetase in this organism and complementation behavior in other situations. We may speculate that the one group of CRM⁺ mutants with indole-to-tryptophan activity (group *a*) represents mutations in one polypeptide chain analogous to the *E. coli* A protein mutants that still retain active B protein. Similar reasoning suggests that the CRM⁺ mutants that accumulate indole and retain InGP-to-indole activity retain a functional polypeptide chain analogous to the *E. coli* A protein and are defective in B protein activity (groups *b* and *c*). The noncomplementing CRM⁻ mutants of group *e* (bottom of figure) lack one of the proteins A or B; the protein is presumed to be so defective that it also fails to activate the residual activity of the second component. Thus both defects are exhibited. Such noncomplementing CRM⁻ mutants typically are scattered through the gene and ordinarily include extended multisite mutations, as in Fig. 4.4.

So far, our analysis has pointed out similarities with the *E. coli* system in the framework of the one gene–one polypeptide chain concept, but Fig. 4.4 shows some discrepancies from our simplest expectations. Mutants in complementation groups *c* and *d* fail to complement each other. Under similar test conditions they can complement members of group *a*, as expected. Unexpected is their complementation with members of group *b* because all three classes were presumed above to involve mutations in protein "B." Although it is possible that a subunit of B protein is itself composed of two different polypeptide chains, a more likely explanation, in keeping with studies on the structure of the enzyme and with observations on a number of other systems, is that a single class of polypeptide chain is found in B protein. The complementation is intragenic and arises from the manner in which two B polypeptide chains interact to form some critical conformation of the enzyme molecule essential for function. There is a mutual correction of defects in this interaction. The general idea of how effective hybrid molecules might be formed is schematically indicated in Fig. 4.5.

In the case which is presently under discussion, the term "function" may be interpreted in two ways: (1) the ability to give rise to catalytically active B protein, and (2) perhaps concomitantly, the ability of B polypeptide chains to complex with residual A protein. Perhaps the defective proteins of group *b* and group *c* mutants retain only the ability to complex with the A protein. The proteins of each of these mutants can, however, form mixed dimers with other B mutants. Some of these mixed dimers apparently are effective in joining with A protein. This union not only activates the A activity but also restores the enzyme activity characteristic of the normal tetramer, the InGP-to-tryptophan reaction.

Other models involving either chain association or active conformation of the tetramer may also be suggested. The main point is that there is some sort of "correction" mechanism brought about by the interactions of differentially defective chains of multimeric proteins.

Note that the mixed multimer explanation for intragenic complementation specifies that the active product contains defective polypeptide chains whose activity is partially restored when in combination with dissimilar defective chains. In this case we would expect the active enzyme obtained by complementation to differ in some of its properties from normal enzyme. This is the case. Enzymes obtained from extracts of *Neurospora* heterocaryons of complementing alleles differ from wild-type enzyme in their affinities for substrates and cofactors and in their thermostabilities.

Studies on other systems lend plausibility to the interpretations given above. That complementation may occur between mutants defective for a single polypeptide chain is firmly established. The complementation involves different forms or alleles of the same cistron or gene and so is called *interallelic, intracistronic,* or *intragenic complementation.* These all are misnomers because complementation involves the protein products of genes, not the genes themselves. However, these terms are in the genetic literature and can probably be justified by the fact that the *cis-trans* test was, at the outset, a purely genetic one, requiring additional work at the level of protein chemistry for interpretation. The observation of intragenic complementation among mutants defective

FIG. 4.5. *Protein-protein interactions of similar polypeptide chains, giving rise to active enzyme.*

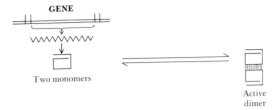

(*a*) Wild type

Two monomers

Active dimer

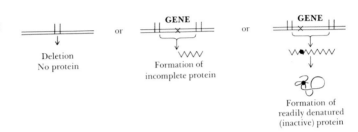

(*b*) Noncomplementing mutants

Deletion
No protein

or

Formation of incomplete protein

or

Formation of readily denatured (inactive) protein

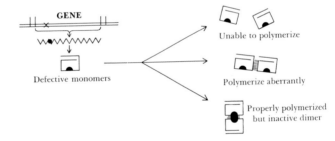

(*c*) Potentially complementing mutants

Defective monomers

Unable to polymerize

Polymerize aberrantly

Properly polymerized but inactive dimer

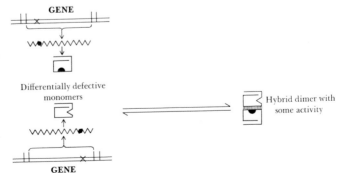

(*d*) Complementation, in the *trans* configuration; between two allelic mutants that complement

Differentially defective monomers

Hybrid dimer with some activity

in a single enzyme activity demonstrates that protein subunits are involved. In some cases the result is clear-cut and the number of different polypeptide chains involved can be specified. In other cases the results are ambiguous. Many of the latter instances may involve mixed multimers of identical and of nonidentical subunits. Further complications in interpretation of *cis-trans* tests could arise from the mode of organization of genes in chromosomes and of their functioning. As we shall discuss in Chap. 10, some genes are arranged in polarized structures known as operons, and mutations in one gene may influence the functioning of certain other nearby genes. Usually, however, this does not interfere with the interpretation of the results of complementation tests.

Genetic Maps and Complementation Maps

In many cases there is correspondence between the positions of mutations on genetic maps and on complementation maps. This accounts for the interchangable usage of the words gene and cistron. Complementation between mutants of two different genes generally is strong and clear-cut.

In instances where there is intragenic complementation, the wild-type phenotype and enzyme level usually are not completely restored. There is generally less enzyme present when the two mutations are present in the *trans* configuration than when they are present in the *cis* configuration. Complementation results in a wide spectrum of activities, from the barely detectable to full restoration. The "cutoff" point varies with the system and is arbitrarily chosen. In vivo tests generally use the criterion of growth as a measure of complementation; however, the time given for a certain amount of growth can be varied and will alter the decision as to whether complementation has or has not occurred.

Variations in cutoff points usually alter the structure of complementation maps quantitatively rather than qualitatively. There is usually a good correlation between positions of mutations on the chromosome and the complementation group to which a mutant belongs. Although the complementation groups in Fig. 4.4 have been arranged arbitrarily so that they correspond to the genetic map, it is apparent that mutations that map closely together by recombination tests often exhibit similar complementation patterns. These correlations are presumed to result from the colinearity of the gene and the polypeptide chain. Certain sections of the polypeptide chain are dictated by certain sections of the polynucleotide chain.

Often one finds that the complementation groups overlap. For example, one might detect during examination of additional *Neurospora td* mutants a class that is unable to complement with groups *b, c,* or *d* but is able to complement with members of group *a*. In other loci this type of situation is quite common and leads to the construction of a complementation map. Occasional mutations do not strictly correlate in position on the two maps. This may be because the final, active protein is a complex, three-dimensional folded structure, not a linear polypeptide chain. Some geneticists believe that complementation behavior of mutants in conjunction with an accurate genetic map can give insight into the tertiary and quaternary structure of proteins. The same type of reasoning is applied here as to the speculations regarding the folding of the bacterial tryptophan synthetase molecule view from back-mutation analyses (Fig. 3.7) . Right now this is merely a prediction that requires the methodology of refined analysis of protein structure for its verification or rejection.

Complementation in Vitro

By measuring the end product of a series of enzyme-catalyzed reactions, in vitro measurements of complex systems can be studied. Using cell-free extracts of mutants with known defects in a metabolic pathway, additions of extracts of unknown mutants in the same pathway can be added to test for complementation, that is, the production of end product from precursors. In this way mutants can be screened rapidly to pinpoint the location of specific enzymic lesions in known multistep metabolic pathways.

In cases where complementing mutants involve defects in the *same* protein, mutant proteins from CRM+ mutants have been mixed in vitro in an effort to detect complementation in intragenic situations. In many cases, even though complementation is detected by genetic in vivo tests, conditions suitable for in vitro complementation have not been found. In a few other instances, however, complementation can be reproduced in vitro. The complementation reactions depend on protein concentration and usually involve placement of the protein in an environment where crucial changes in conformation may occur. For example, agents effective in the reduction of disulfide $(-S-S-)$ bonds are usually added at low concentration. The results indicate that mixtures of inactive multimers (for example, Fig. 4.5c) can rearrange to form hybrid multimers with some activity (for example, Fig. 4.5d) . In the case of *Neurospora* tryptophan synthetase mutants, a small amount of enzyme activity may be obtained in mixing extracts of some CRM+ mutants. Of 15 pairs of mutants that complemented in heterocaryons, 12 gave small but significant amounts of complementation in vitro. Only 3 among the 26 tested combinations that did not show in vivo complementation appeared to give some complementation in vitro. In some instances the enzyme obtained by in vitro complementation was abnormal; its thermostability differed from wild-type enzyme and appeared to resemble more closely that of enzyme formed during in vivo complementation.

Therefore, one can conclude that protein-protein interactions which occur in vitro and lead to reconstitution of enzyme activity through mixed multimer associations also underlie complementation in vivo.

Symmetry in Multimeric Proteins and Mechanism of Intragenic Complementation

We have indicated that intragenic complementation resembling that found in genetic tests can be achieved by mixing different defective mutant proteins in vitro. Protein-protein interactions have been implicated in the reconstitution of enzyme activity. The subunits of the different inactive multimeric proteins exchange to give active hybrid molecules. How are these interactions achieved?

We know little of the three-dimensional structure of multimeric proteins, but what we do know leads us to base our theories of interactions on symmetrical associations of the protein monomers. For example, hemoglobin (Fig. 2.14) has a dual symmetry, and the proteins of tobacco mosaic virus (Fig. 2.13) and the pyruvic dehydrogenase complex (Fig. 2.15) show higher orders of symmetry. The selection of forces leading to axes of symmetry affords a cellular control mechanism; it specifies the state of aggregation that a multimer will possess, be it a dimer, tetramer, or a higher multimer.

The hypothetical dimer shown in Fig. 4.6, with segments of the polypeptide chains designated by capital letters, has a twofold axis of symmetry. Associations of the two chains are shown mainly to occur in homologous regions along the dyad axis (at A, C, H, and F), although some are shown to occur elsewhere (at G–E). One explanation for complementation is that a normal region of a polypeptide chain can "correct" a conformational defect in the segment of the polypeptide chain with which it is paired. Polypeptide chains defective in *different* segments of the chain will mutually correct each other's conformational abnormality, which would result in an active dimer. Polypeptide chains defective in the *same* region of the chain would not be self-correcting in this model. The complementation map will parallel the genetic map in such regions as A through C. Overlaps will occur in the complementation map if, for example, a defective conformation in region B prevents correction through the juxtaposition of chains in regions A and C. An alternative model for intragenic complementation is discussed in the legend of Fig. 4.6.

Although the multimeric nature of a wild-type enzyme may have been established, in some cases no complementation between certain groups of mutants is detected. Perhaps this reflects the presence of self-correcting mechanisms, either in homologous regions (such as A, where the two chains are antipolar) or in nonhomologous, yet paired regions (such as interaction of D with segment I) and a paucity in interactions along the dyad axis of truly homologous parts.

FIG. 4.6. *Model for intragenic complementation based on protein-protein interactions giving rise to a dimer with a twofold (dyad) axis of symmetry. The twofold symmetry axis is shown by a dashed line. Various regions of secondary (α-helical) structure are labeled A through I for the heavily shaded polypeptide chain and A' through I' for the lightly shaded polypeptide chain.*

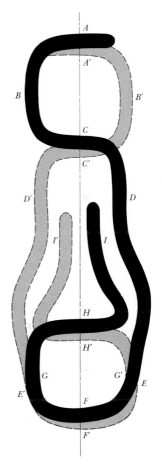

There are two general ideas on how complementation might occur. One model is the "correction" model. It proposes that the C and C' regions, for example, are critical for enzyme activity. A dimer composed of a polypeptide chain with a bad C and a bad C' is inactive. However, the idea is that a bad C can be corrected by pairing with a good C', even though the polypeptide chain carrying the good C' segment may be defective elsewhere. This gives rise to some enzyme activity (complementation). A mutation having its main effect in a region away from the dyad axis, such as at B, might sometimes interfere with corrections at A or at C, thus causing an overlap in the complementation map. It is possible that conformational corrections could also occur between nonhomologous paired segments, as at I and D or at E and G'. In both of the latter cases, mutual correction could occur between two identical polypeptide chains. For example, a mutant protein defective in I could be corrected by the D portion of the same chain; it would not be detected as a mutant phenotype.

The second model can be called a "good parts" model. This model assumes that a region critical to activity is the region, for example, where E pairs with G. There are two such positions in the dimer (E–G' and E'–G). There is no correction; both good E and good G are necessary for normal activity. Therefore, a bad E with a bad E' leads to two inactive catalytic sites. In contrast, a bad E with a good E' will have one active center (E'–G at the lower left in the figure) provided that the chain defective at E is normal at G.

Various combinations and modifications of these possibilities may occur. *Modified after J. R. S. Fincham,* Genetic Complementation, *New York: W. A. Benjamin, Inc., 1966.*

Figure 4.6, a two-dimensional array, is highly speculative and over-simplified. Clearly, the molecular mechanisms underlying intragenic complementation represent an area where the last word is yet to be said. Final resolution of the problem awaits precise description of the three-dimensional structures of several mutant protein systems, as well as analyses of the active multimers produced by complementation.

Why Multimers?

In Chapter 2, the interactions of tobacco mosaic virus (TMV) protein subunits were discussed. The protein monomers aggregate around the RNA in a specific fashion, to form a highly structured particle, the intact virus rod (Fig. 2.13). It is estimated that only a relatively small amount (8 percent) of the total genetic information of TMV is necessary to code for the formation of the monomer. Nevertheless, this amount is sufficient to permit about 2,200 monomeric units to polymerize into the coat that protects the labile RNA core. The advantage of the subunit building-block system is clear; the polymerization process allows the maximum of protection (survival value) for the minimum amount of hereditary baggage.

The multimeric structure of protein molecules also permits the repair of many genetic defects by complementation mechanisms involving protein-protein interactions. In diploid organisms multiple structural forms of many enzymes exist. These "isozymes" can often interchange subunits so that, in the simplest case, three proteins are formed. If two polypeptide chains dictated by two separate genes interact to give active dimers, three forms of the enzyme are possible: A/A, A/B, and B/B. Here, unlike the situation that we ordinarily think of in terms of complementation, all three forms of the enzyme are active. However, each form may be better suited to one particular environment. The polymerization reaction can be influenced by environmental factors, and this allows some environmental control of the rates and direction of intracellular metabolism. For instance, a number of enzymic activities are known to appear suddenly during the birth of a mammal. The enzyme proteins are present before birth but are nonfunctional. The drastic change in the environment that occurs at birth could be conceived as causing the alteration of multimeric forms of certain enzymes and consequently of certain activities. In other words, the monomer-multimer transition systems may provide one type of biological regulation: some of these aspects will be discussed in a later chapter. Ask yourself the question: Why multimers?; you may think of reasons other than these.

Questions

4.1. Based upon Fig. 4.2, set up a *cis* genetic test with a diploid organism. Mention the organism and tell why it was selected for the test.

4.2. Set up a *cis* genetic test for a normally haploid organism. Explain your choice of organism.

4.3. Consult the library and write a short report on the properties of hemoglobin that lead to the view that the functional protein is a tetramer.

4.4. The predominant hemoglobin in adult man is hemoglobin A, a tetramer of two α and two β chains. About 2.5 percent of normal adult hemoglobin (hemoglobin A2) differs from hemoglobin A in that it is composed of two α and two δ chains. The predominant hemoglobin of the human fetus is hemoglobin F, composed of two α and two γ chains. Normal children gradually shift to almost exclusive production of hemoglobins A and A2 within a few months after birth. Individual genes are responsible for each type of polypeptide chain.

(*a*) Hemoglobin A2 has a higher affinity for oxygen than do the other hemoglobins. State how this could be a case of gene evolution.

(*b*) Individuals have been found who produce tetramers composed of four β chains or, in other cases, four α chains. What reasons could you give to explain the failure to find such tetramers in normal individuals? Would you expect the abnormal tetramers to be active? Explain in chemical and in biological terms why you think so. Besides the tetramers comprising four identical chains, what other hemoglobins would you expect to find in these individuals? Why?

(*c*) Certain regions of the hemoglobin polypeptide chains interact to give rise to the functional tetramers. Explain the distribution of mutations you would expect to find: (1) affecting the portion of the molecule involved in the binding of the heme prosthetic group, (2) affecting polymerization, and (3) located in external portions of the polypeptide chain not directly involved with polymerization or with catalytic activity.

4.5. Read the sections of McKusick's *Human Genetics* in this series that deal with the structure of normal and abnormal hemoglobins. Reorganize the material into a one-page synopsis of the critical features of the genetics and protein chemistry of the hemoglobins.

4.6. In the literature find a published complementation map for a gene other than one mentioned in this chapter and interpret its significance relative to the structure of the enzyme concerned.

4.7. Heterozygotes are often found to have a selective advantage over homozygotes. Elaborate on what role you think complementation *between* genes and complementation *within* genes might play in this phenomenon. Give the reasoning behind your arguments.

4.8. Most mutations are recessive mutations. Why? What are some reasons occasional mutations in genes giving rise to multimeric proteins might be dominant or semidominant?

References

Ames, B. N., R. F. Goldberger, P. E., Hartman, R. G. Martin, and J. R. Roth, in *Regulation of Nucleic Acid and Protein Biosynthesis,* V. V. Koningsberger and L. Bosch, eds. Amsterdam: Elsevier Publishing Company, 1967, p. 272; J. C. Loper, M. Grabnar, R. C. Stahl, Z. Hartman, and P. E. Hartman, *Brookhaven Symp. Biol., 17* (1964), 15. Two reviews on the genetics and biochemistry of the histidine biosynthetic enzymes in *Salmonella,* including analyses by complementation.

Brookhaven Symposia in Biology 17 (1964), *Subunit Structure of Proteins: Biochemical and Genetic Aspects.* A symposium that gives a cross section of experiments and views on multimeric proteins, including analyses by complementation.

Carlson, E. A., *Quart. Rev. Biol., 34* (1959), 33. Review of gene loci in *Drosophila,* including discussion of complementation results.

Day, P. R., "Complementation in Dikaryons and Diploids," *Phytopathology, 57* (1967), 808.

Fan, D. P., M. J. Schlesinger, A. Torriani, K. J. Barnett, and C. Levinthal, "Isolation and Characterization of Complementation Products of *E. coli* Alkaline Phosphatase," *J. Mol. Biol., 15* (1966), 32. A recent paper in a series that examines one instance of intragenic complementation in more depth than has obtained in most other systems.

Fincham, J. R. S., *Genetic Complementation.* New York: W. A. Benjamin, Inc., 1966. A thorough treatment that greatly expands upon each of the points made in this chapter and affords increased perspective into methodology and observations in many different systems.

———, "Genetic Complementation," *Sci. Progr., 56* (1968), 165. Simple and concise description of complementation tests and their interpretation.

Gillie, O. J., "Interpretations of Some Large Non-Linear Complementation Maps," *Genetics, 58* (1968), 543.

Klug, A., and D. L. D. Caspar, "The Structure of Small Viruses," *Advan. Virus Res., 7* (1960), 225. A discussion of protein-protein interactions and symmetry in the multimeric proteins of TMV and other small viruses.

Lewis, E. B., "Genes and Gene Complexes," in *Heritage From Mendel,* R. A. Brink, ed. Madison: University of Wisconsin Press, 1967, p. 17. Application of microbial models to higher organisms is not always easy, but progress is being made.

Markert, C. L., "Epigenetic Control of Specific Protein Synthesis in Differentiating Cells," in *Cytodifferentiation and Macromolecular Synthesis,* M. Locke, ed. (21st Symp. Soc. Study of Development and Growth). New York: Academic Press, Inc., 1963, p. 65. A short and cogent discussion of some multiple molecular forms of enzymes (isozymes) and their possible significance in physiology and development. Also consult the articles by C. R. Shaw and N. O. Kaplan in *Brookhaven Symp. Biol., 17.*

Reithel, F. J., "The Dissociation and Association of Protein Structures," *Advan. Protein Chem., 18* (1963), 123. This, and some of the references cited at the end of Chap. 2, pay some attention to relation of enzyme activity to the state of association of subunits in multimeric proteins.

Roberts, C. F., "Complementation Analysis of the Tryptophan Pathway in *Aspergillus nidulans," Genetics, 55* (1967), 233; R. Hutter and J. A. DeMoss, "Enzyme Analysis of the Tryptophan Pathway in *Aspergillus nidulans," Genetics, 55* (1967), 241. Comparison of gene-enzyme relationships in the tryptophan biosynthetic pathway of *Aspergillus* with those in *E. coli, S. cerevisiae* (a yeast), and *Neurospora,* emphasizing genetic control and enzyme aggregates.

Schlesinger, M. J., and C. Levinthal, "Complementation at the Molecular Level of Enzyme Interaction," *Ann. Rev. Microbiol., 19* (1965), 267. A review with 98 references to studies on intracistronic complementation.

Secondary Consequences
of Gene Mutations

The primary effect of a gene mutation is to cause an alteration in the amino acid sequence of a protein molecule. Later chapters will detail the means which the cell utilizes in carrying out primary gene function. For the moment we seek to present some idea of how this seemingly simple primary event, an altered protein, causes a multitude of secondary events that also are part of the mutant phenotype. In fact, descriptions of mutant phenotypes usually concern only the secondary effects. An understanding of the secondary effects of gene mutations is instructive, for they have provided us with much information about normal physiological processes. Because individual biochemical reactions usually are components of more complex anabolic or catabolic sequences in cellular metabolism, relatively few single biochemical reactions in the cell can be disrupted without affecting other metabolic steps.

Localization of Genetic Blocks

The most immediate effect of the alteration of an enzyme is a change in the efficiency of a particular step in a metabolic sequence. If the mutant enzyme is inactive, we say that the reaction sequence is blocked, or that a genetic block is present. We have seen this effect in mutants unable to synthesize the amino acid tryptophan (Fig. 3.1).

If the genetic block in a microorganism shuts off the synthesis of an essential metabolite, thereby creating a nutritional requirement, the metabolite often can be supplied to the organism from the environment. For example, histidineless mutants of microorganisms fail to grow on a minimal medium, but they can grow with a normal growth rate on a medium supplemented with L-histidine.

The growth response of nutritional mutants to known compounds can sometimes provide information about the position of genetic blocks in a reaction sequence and, to a lesser extent, provide clues to the identity of possible biochemical intermediates. For example, histidine-requiring mutants of bacteria are of two types: those that grow on either L-histidine or L-histidinol, and those that respond only to L-histidine (Fig. 5.1). The latter are blocked in reaction 10, the conversion of histidinol to histidine. Mutants that have genetic blocks earlier in the pathway (steps 1 through 9) can grow on histidinol, because they still retain reaction 10. In contrast, no *Neurospora* histidineless mutants can grow on L-histidinol, even though this is an intermediate in histidine biosynthesis; L-histidinol is not normally permeable in *Neurospora,* although the organism can gain the ability to utilize L-histidinol through mutation. Neither *Neurospora* nor *Salmonella* can take up from the medium the phosphorylated intermediates in the pathway: hence they fail to grow on these compounds. Furthermore, these organisms cannot phosphorylate imidazoleglycerol or imidazoleacetol to the active phosphorylated derivatives (Fig. 5.1).

Thus growth on known compounds is sometimes a helpful tool, but its use in biochemical and genetical analyses requires cautious interpretation. Another case in point involves tryptophan biosynthesis (Fig. 5.2). Growth responses to anthranilic acid and indole can differentiate mutants blocked in the various steps of tryptophan biosynthesis. However, the fact that some tryptophan synthetase mutants respond to indole does not necessarily indicate that free indole is an actual intermediate in the biosynthetic pathway. In fact, for a time, the accumulation of indole by bacterial tryptophan synthetase B protein mutants and the growth of bacterial tryptophan synthetase A protein mutants on indole obscured the true nature of the physiological reaction and the relationship between the A and B protein sub-

FIG. 5.1. *Pathway of L-histidine biosynthesis in* Salmonella *and some accessory reactions. The physiologically important pathway of biosynthesis is indicated by solid arrows. Accessory reactions, which are presumed from accumulation and growth data, are indicated by the dashed arrows. Reaction steps are designated by numbers. The circled letter under each enzyme designation is the gene locus involved in dictating the structure of that enzyme. Drawn after B. N. Ames and coworkers, "The Histidine Operon" in* Regulation of Nucleic Acid and Protein Biosynthesis, *V. V. Koningsberger and L. Bosch, eds., Amsterdam: Elsevier Publishing Company, 1967, p. 272.*

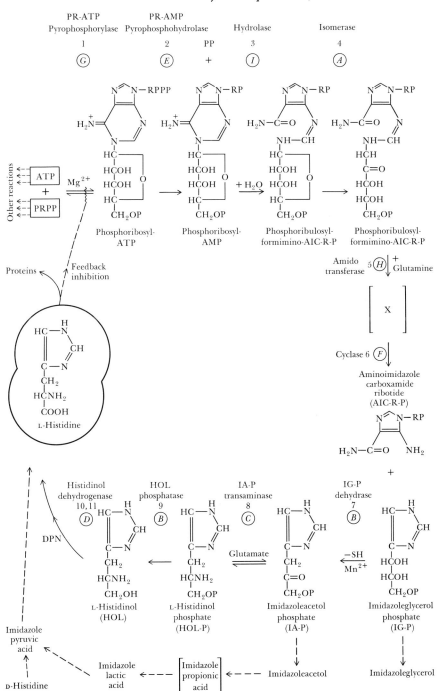

FIG. 5.2. *Growth properties and crossfeeding by tryptophan-requiring mutants of bacteria. A more detailed presentation of the biochemical pathway is shown in Fig. 3.1, and the proteins involved are shown in Fig. 2.16.*

Growth on Known Compounds. *A large number of mutant bacteria (that is 1,000–10,000,000) either are spread directly on the surface of a glucose-salts medium lacking tryptophan or are included in the agar medium when it is poured. Crystals of known compounds are placed with sterile toothpicks at the points indicated. After incubation, the ability to respond to each of the compounds is scored. Photograph a shows a petri dish covered with a lawn of bacteria defective in reaction 5A. There is some inhibition of growth at very high concentrations of indole at the point of application of the crystal. This mutant fails to grow on anthranilic acid but responds to tryptophan and to indole. You can imagine the patterns of growth response obtained with mutants blocked in other reactions. This is an excellent qualitative procedure for screening growth responses and interactions of various compounds.*

Crossfeeding. *The ability of one bacterial strain to feed another can be readily*

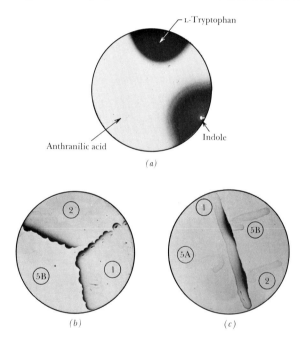

(a)

(b)   (c)

demonstrated by the following methods. In photograph b, cultures of three different tryptophan-requiring strains have been separately streaked on glucose-salts agar lacking tryptophan. The streaking, in a side-by-side boomerang-like pattern, allows compounds excreted by one strain to diffuse to the position of another strain during incubation of the plate. Note that the mutant blocked in reaction 5B is feeding the mutants blocked in reactions 1 and 2. In contrast, the mutant blocked in reaction 5B is not fed by either of these two mutants. The mutant blocked in reaction 2, while being fed by that blocked in reaction 5B, is nevertheless able to feed the mutant blocked in reaction 1. All these interactions can be scored on a single plate. Sometimes, suboptimal enrichment with the end product (in this case, tryptophan) enhances the clarity of the feeding response.

Photograph c shows a modification of the streaking pattern that allows interactions of four different strains to be studied on a single petri dish. Note that mutant 5A does not feed mutant 1; the accumulated intermediates are phosphorylated and cannot be taken up by the mutant 1 bacteria.

---

units that compose tryptophan synthetase. Similarly, growth of bacterial histidineless mutants on D-histidine, imidazole lactic acid, and imidazole propionic acid does not mean that these compounds are involved in the pathway of L-histidine biosynthesis in normal cells (Fig. 5.1).

Incomplete versus Complete Genetic Blocks

The characteristics of the genetic block are largely referable to the unique properties of the altered protein formed by the mutant. The block may be complete, because of the complete absence of active protein, or it may be incomplete (leaky), because of the formation of a protein with altered structure that still possesses slight biological activity.

Leaky mutants are quite common, and they are found whenever the mutant screening method can detect phenotypes that are intermediate between normal and extremely abnormal, as, for example, in eye-pigment mutants of insects and growth factor–requiring mutants of microorganisms. In fact, the vast majority of the mutants observed in higher organisms are of the leaky type; a minority of mutants exhibit extreme phenotypes, sometimes resulting from deletion of the gene (see *Cytogenetics* and *The Mechanics of Inheritance* in this series).

Occasionally genotypes are found in which all mutants are of the leaky type. This is true for mutants of gene *H,* which appear to be blocked in step 5 of histidine biosynthesis (Fig. 5.1). The reason lies in the nature of the reaction. In the presence of enzyme, the reaction proceeds rapidly with very low concentrations of normal substrate (glutamine); in the absence of enzyme, the reaction proceeds slowly and spontaneously when high concentrations of ammonium ion are available. Because relatively high concentrations of ammonium ion are present in all the bacteria, the reaction occurs at a suboptimal rate in the mutants in the absence of the specific enzyme, thereby facilitating slow synthesis of histidine.

Accumulations and Precursors

A single genetic block may be pictured as a specific damming of the flow of metabolites at one spot in a sequence of biochemical reactions. Up to that particular step, the enzymes catalyzing the other steps function normally, so the flow of precursors continues along the pathway until the reaction affected by the genetic block is reached. At this stage, precursors may accumulate because their further conversion is prevented entirely or markedly reduced.

The precursors that accumulate behind a genetic block generally are not inert compounds; they may be substrates for other enzymes. As seen in Fig. 5.1, for L-histidine biosynthesis, a genetic block in reaction 7 leads to the accumulation both of imidazoleglycerol phosphate ester the true intermediate, and of imidazoleglycerol. This is the result of the action of a ubiquitous nonspecific phosphatase that converts the true intermediate to the secondary product, imidazoleglycerol. A block at reaction 8 leads to accumulation of five compounds: imidazoleacetol phosphate ester, imidazoleacetol, imidazoleglycerol phosphate ester, imidazoleglycerol, and imidazole lactic acid (Fig. 5.1). Thus, although accumulations may be indicative of important metabolites in a pathway and provide clues to the reaction sequences, the mere finding of an accumulated compound is insufficient proof of its role as a true intermediate. Other criteria—such as enzyme conversion to end product in cell-free extracts, compound labeling experiments using radioactive or stable isotopes, and so forth—are essential to assure that the reconstructed reaction sequence is physiologically important.

Frequently the intermediate immediately preceding the genetic block is the compound accumulated in highest quantity. However, a word of caution: often one of the side reactions progresses rapidly enough to prevent extensive accumulation of a true intermediate, while causing substantial accumulation of other compounds.

An elegant microbiological method of assigning reaction sequence within a pathway was originally applied to histidine biosynthesis, and its validity was later verified by cell-free enzyme studies. The method consisted of obtaining, by recombination, double mutants that were blocked in two separate reactions in the pathway. The metabolite accumulated by the double mutant was characteristic of the first blocked reaction. The metabolite normally accumulated as a result of the second genetic block was not found, because the supply of its precursor had been shut off at the earlier reaction step.

Accumulations and Feeding

Mutants with genetic blocks that preclude growth on a minimal medium will grow only on intermediates that are located beyond the genetic block or on compounds that can be converted to intermediates. This observation leads one to expect that mutants blocked in later steps in a biochemical reaction sequence would accumulate intermediates that satisfy the growth requirement of mutants blocked in earlier reactions. For example, mutants blocked in reaction 10 of histidine biosynthesis (Fig. 5.1) should accumulate L-histidinol, which can be used by organisms blocked in earlier reactions. Indeed, such crossfeeding phenomena (syntrophism) are found with many mutants. Other examples are shown in Fig. 5.2, where methods for detecting crossfeeding are described.

The crossfeeding technique is useful in ordering the sequence of suspected biochemical reactions as well as in detecting and aiding in identification of biologically significant compounds.

Accumulations and Inhibitions

The accumulation by a mutant of an otherwise normally metabolized intermediate might be expected to have some deleterious effect on the organism. Many examples are known of metabolites that are toxic when they are present at concentrations in excess of their normal levels.

Let us briefly consider the effect in humans of accumulations in front of a genetic block. A more detailed account of inherited metabolic disorders in humans will be found in McKusick's book, *Human Genetics,* in this series. Humans cannot synthesize phenylalanine; they must rely on a dietary intake of this essential amino acid. The excess phenylalanine consumed in the diet is normally converted to tyrosine (reaction 1, in Fig. 5.3), which is metabolized through a series of reactions to acetoacetic acid and fumaric acid. However, some human mutants possess genetic blocks in reaction 1. Such persons retain high blood levels of phenylalanine and excrete phenylpyruvic acid and related compounds into the urine. Intracellular phenylpyruvic acid accumulates in sufficient quantity to inhibit the conversion of tryptophan to serotonin (reaction 3, in Fig. 5.3). Current evidence indicates that serotonin is essential for normal mental processes. Phenylketonuric persons are usually mentally retarded, presumably because of the secondary effects of the genetic block.

Here, then, is an example of a chain of events arising from a single genetic defect. This defect is expressed initially as a metabolic lesion, and eventually it causes a gross phenotypic alteration, mental retardation. Because tyrosine is present in the diet, the intermediates beyond the genetic block are provided. The deleterious effect of the genetic block, then, is caused by the metabolites that accumulate.

End-Product Deficit

Metabolites beyond the genetic block may not be essential to normal growth and development, or they may be supplied by other reactions. For example, persons blocked in reaction 1 (Fig. 5.3) have less tyrosine available than do normal persons and thus are more lightly pigmented (contain less melanin) than are normal individuals. Presumably, the human phenylketonuric, blocked in reaction 1, would show more severe signs of tyrosine deficiency were his diet deficient in this amino acid.

In contrast, the absence of the end product is the most important phenotypic effect elicited by other genetic blocks. The end product may be essential for growth, as with the tryptophan- and histidine-requiring mutants of microorganisms. Hence the effects of the genetic block depend upon the essentiality of the metabolites in the affected pathway, their roles in overall cellular metabolism, and their availability and utilizability from the environment.

FIG. 5.3. *Some aspects of the metabolism of phenylalanine in the human. The numbers signify particular biochemical reactions discussed in the text.*

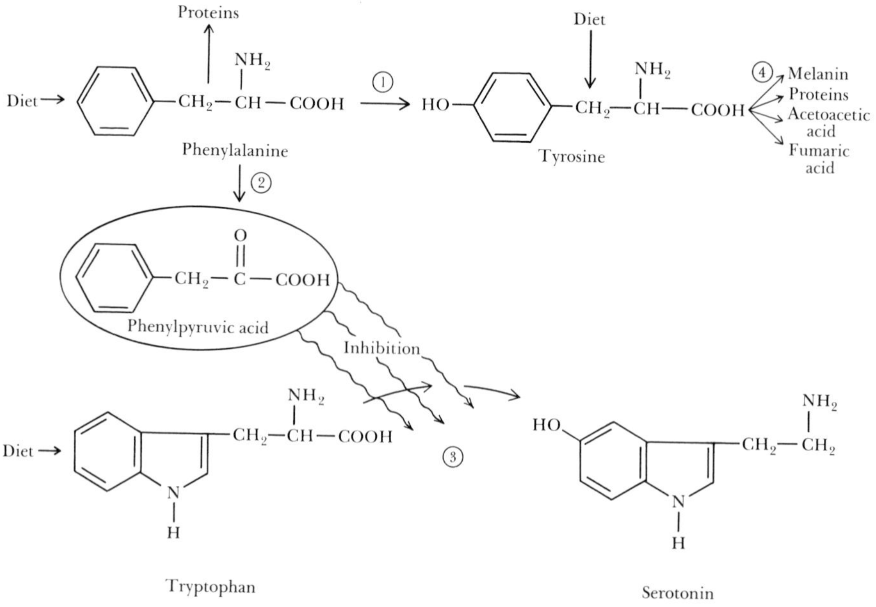

Feedback Inhibition

One of the most striking and important regulatory devices in cellular metabolism is *feedback inhibition*. Since an end product is often involved, some workers use the term "end-product inhibition." Feedback inhibition can be illustrated in histidine biosynthesis in *Salmonella* (Fig. 5.1). The first enzyme (pyrophosphorylase) possesses specific combining sites for L-histidine and for the normal substrates. The inhibition by histidine takes place in two steps. In the first step, histidine is bound to the enzyme molecule. In the second step, the bound histidine elicits a conformational change in the protein that restricts its normal catalytic activity. Since the binding of substrates and histidine occur at different sites on the enzyme molecule, the inhibition is termed *allosteric inhibition*. This is to be contrasted with isosteric inhibition, usually competitive in nature, where inhibitor and substrate bind to the active center of the enzyme.

Systems involving feedback inhibition are generally reversible; the bound histidine gradually dissociates from the enzyme and the protein regains enzymatic activity when the histidine concentration decreases. Feedback inhibition thus acts as a shutoff valve; it allows the cell to tap precursors and energy from the metabolic pool at a rate essential for efficient biosynthesis—and no faster. The concentration of free histidine normally present in *Salmonella* synthesizing its own histidine in a minimal medium is enough to partially inhibit pyrophosphorylase activity. That is, on the average, more total enzyme is present than is functioning to manufacture histidine. The histidine concentration in the pool of an exponentially growing culture is about $1.5 \times 10^{-5} M$, in the same order of magnitude as the K_i value found for in vitro inhibition of the enzyme (K_i is about $5 \times 10^{-5} M$).

Several types of experiments demonstrate that feedback inhibition is important in vivo. One type of experiment uses analogues that mimic the action of true feedback inhibitors without replacing other valuable functions. For example, the synthetic analogue 2-thiazole alanine, which is structurally similar to L-histidine, is a feedback inhibitor, but it cannot replace histidine in proteins. It inhibits bacterial growth because it shuts off production of histidine. Mutants can be readily obtained that are either resistant or are hypersensitive to thiazole alanine. The resistant mutants also resist feedback inhibition by the normal intracellular concentrations of histidine. As a result, in the absence of thiazole alanine, they make excess histidine, which is excreted into the medium (Fig. 5.4). They form altered pyrophosphorylase that retains catalytic activity but is not inhibited by low concentrations of histidine or of 2-thiazole alanine. The feedback hypersensitive mutants are often "leaky" mutants on minimal medium and are stimulated by exogeneous histidine; they make a pyrophosphorylase which is so sensitive to inhibition by L-histidine that not enough histidine is available for protein

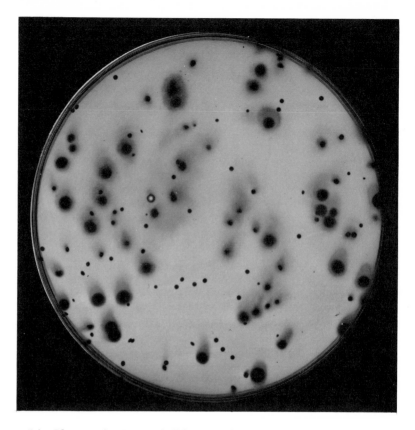

FIG. 5.4. *Photograph of a petri dish of a mineral-salts medium upon which several bacteria have formed colonies. Some of the colonies are formed by wild-type bacteria that excrete no histidine; these colonies have clear edges. Other colonies are composed of mutant bacteria that contain enzyme that is catalytically active but is feedback-resistant; these colonies are surrounded by halos. The halos are due to growth of a large surplus of histidine-requiring mutant bacteria plated as a mixture with the nonexacting strains. The histidine-requiring bacteria use for growth the histidine excreted by the feedback-resistant mutant bacteria. See D. E. Sheppard,* Genetics, 50 *(1964), 611. Photo courtesy of J. H. Wyche.*

biosynthesis. Both types of mutations map in the structural gene for the pyrophosphorylase.

A second type of experiment which also suggests an essential role of feedback inhibition in vivo utilizes labeling with radioisotopes. When bacteria grow in a medium containing radioactive (^{14}C) glucose as sole carbon source, all the carbon-containing compounds of the cell become labeled with ^{14}C at identical specific activities. When ^{12}C (non-radioactive) L-histidine also is present during growth, all carbon compounds still contain high specific activities of ^{14}C, except the histidine that has been incorporated into protein. The exogenous histidine (^{12}C) is thus preferentially utilized, although cell extracts still contain the enzymes involved in histidine biosynthesis. Preferential utilization of an exogenous compound is suggestive of feedback inhibition but must be confirmed by more extensive enzyme studies in cell-free extracts, because control mechanisms other than feedback inhibition could be involved.

The third in vivo method for detecting feedback inhibition is to observe the time course of accumulation of intermediates by nutritional mutants (Fig. 5.5). In histidine-requiring mutants growing in a medium containing a small amount of L-histidine, the potentially competent reactions in the biosynthetic pathway of the cell are arrested until the histidine in the medium is utilized completely. When the histidine supply is depleted, the bacteria stop growing. The previously inhibited reactions in the histidine biosynthetic sequence now proceed, and the intermediates characteristic of the genetic block begin to accumulate.

The process of inhibition can be dissociated from growth and protein synthesis by a refinement of the method shown in Fig. 5.5. This requires suspension of mutant bacteria in an environment that prevents protein synthesis. The bacteria accumulate precursors until the end product is added, at which time further accumulation ceases. In this manner, the ability to accumulate is demonstrated before the feedback inhibitor is added.

The phenomenon of feedback inhibition demonstrates that the concentration of the end product of a metabolic pathway can control the rates of biochemical reactions within the pathway. Therefore, in a mutant deprived of the end product, the reaction that is normally inhibited can be released from inhibition and attain a rapid, uncontrolled rate. The widespread occurrence of feedback inhibition in

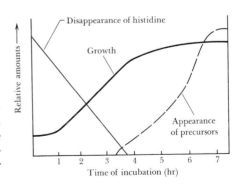

FIG. 5.5. *Idealized curves showing the effects of feedback inhibition on accumulations of intermediates in a histidine-requiring mutant of* Salmonella. *The histidine-requiring bacteria take up histidine from the medium ("Disappearance of histidine") and, after a short lag period, grow exponentially until essentially all of the histidine is exhausted from the external environment, at which time growth ceases ("Growth"). Because of feedback inhibition, the intermediates before the genetic block do not accumulate until the histidine concentration has reached an extremely low level.*

microorganisms as well as in mammals suggests that sensitivities to feedback inhibitions may play important roles in the secondary consequences of many genetic blocks.

Competition for Substrate

The severe consequences of release from feedback inhibition are exemplified in the behavior of histidine-requiring bacteria. Included in Fig. 5.1 is a diagram of the feedback-sensitive reaction in histidine biosynthesis: the conversion of adenosine triphosphate (ATP) and phosphoribosylpyrophosphate (PRPP) to phosphoribosyladenosine triphosphate (PR-ATP). As indicated in the diagram, the two substrates, ATP and PRPP, participate in a number of other reactions; for example, ATP supplies the energy for amino acid activation (Chapter 6). Therefore, the release of feedback inhibition and excessive accumulation of worthless biochemical intermediates behind a genetic block might result in an excessive drain of the energy-rich substrates necessary for other biochemical reactions in the cell. For example, many histidine-requiring bacteria have absolute requirements for L-histidine. However, some leaky mutants grow very slowly on a minimal medium that lacks histidine. They synthesize histidine at a slow rate and use it preferentially for protein synthesis. Thus the endogenous histidine is insufficient to shut down the pathway by feedback inhibition. The result is an abnormally high activity of the pyrophosphorylase enzyme that catalyzes the utilization of ATP and PRPP. This ATP is converted rapidly to PR-ATP and thence to other intermediates, which pile up before the leaky genetic block and are utilized only very slowly. This leads to a severe depletion of the free-ATP supply, vital for other energy-requiring reactions of the cell. The subsequent addition of excess L-histidine to the medium restores normal growth, because it limits the conversion of ATP to PR-ATP and it is also used in protein biosynthesis. The histidine analogue 2-thiazole alanine also supports growth of the leaky mutants. The analogue cannot substitute for histidine in proteins, but it can mimic histidine in the feedback inhibition of the conversion of ATP to PR-ATP, thereby preventing ATP deficiency.

Finally, the addition of adenine stimulates the growth of the leaky mutants. Adenine and its derivatives, adenosine, adenosine monophosphate, and adenosine diphosphate (Fig. 6.1a), probably have two effects. These substances are precursors of ATP. The addition of adenine thus restores the ATP deficit caused by the excessive conversion of ATP to PR-ATP. Also, by competing with ATP for attachment to pyrophosphorylase, the adenine derivatives may reduce the enzyme activity and prevent further loss of free ATP.

As you must have already concluded, the genetic block can seriously disturb the fine balance among several biochemical pathways, and, because many biochemical pathways interconnect, competition for substrate can be an important secondary consequence of a genetic block.

Duplicate Enzymes

Key intermediates in metabolism are often common to several different biochemical pathways. We have just discussed ATP and PRPP, which are used in a variety of reactions. The flow of metabolites through branching pathways often is controlled by allosteric inhibitions of critical enzymes at the branch points. Also, duplicate enzymes have evolved to facilitate control of key reaction steps (see Fig. 5.6).

The reaction sequence at the lower right in Fig. 5.6 should be familiar; it involves the biosynthesis of L-tryptophan from chorismic acid (recall Fig. 2.14). The names of compounds in this reaction sequence and some interrelated pathways are abbreviated in Fig. 5.6. In addition to tryptophan, *E. coli* synthesizes the two amino acids, phenylalanine and tyrosine, as well as several vitamins from chorismic acid. It is at chorismic acid, then, that the biosynthetic pathway has a critical branch point. Tryptophan specifically acts as a feedback inhibitor of enzyme 8, which catalyzes the conversion of chorismic acid to anthranilic acid (ANTH); this interrupts the flow of metabolites when tryptophan is present in excess of that necessary for protein synthesis.

Two duplicate enzymes (enzymes 7, chorismate mutase) convert chorismate to prephenate (Fig. 2.14). One chorismate mutase (enzyme 7a) is specifically inhibited by tyrosine and also has prephenate dehydrogenase activity (enzyme 13). The second chorismate mutase (enzyme 7b) is specifically inhibited by phenylalanine and possesses prephenate dehydratase activity (enzyme 15). Thus, discrete feedback-sensitive enzyme complexes exist that regulate the utilization of chorismic acid for the synthesis of three aromatic amino acids. Now, what about the rate of synthesis of chorismic acid itself?

Duplicate enzymes with unique controlling features also are observed at the first step unique to the aromatic pathway (enzymes 1). There are three separate PKDH synthetases able to convert the precursors, phosphoenolpyruvate (PEP) and erythrose-4-phosphate (ERY-4-P), to 7-phospho-2-keto-3-deoxy-D-arabinoheptonate (PKDH). One PKDH synthetase (enzyme 1c) is feedback-inhibited by phenylalanine, a second (enzyme 1a) by tyrosine, and the *activity* of the third (enzyme 1b) is unaffected by any of the aromatic amino acids alone or in combination. However, the amount of the third enzyme protein is regulated by tryptophan. Mutants blocked in reactions 2, 3, 4, and 6 are readily obtained; for growth they require all three amino acids. Mutants blocked in the first reaction, involving PKDH synthetase, are not found under the same conditions. This is because the two

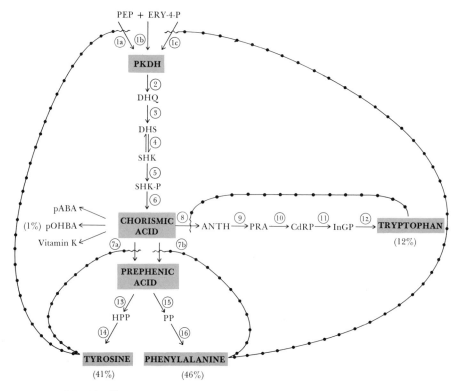

FIG. 5.6. *Duplicate enzymes and metabolic control in biosynthesis of aromatic amino acids and vitamins.*

The names of intermediates in the reaction pathways are abbreviated and enzymes in the pathways numbered. The approximate molar contributions of the various end products in E. coli are given in parentheses (percent).

Duplicate enzymes, under separate genetic control, are present in at least two places in aromatic biosynthesis in E. coli. There are three PKDH synthetases (enzyme 1) that carry out the first step unique to aromatic biosynthesis. There are two chorismate mutases (enzyme 7) that convert chorismate to the prephenate used in tyrosine and phenylalanine biosynthesis. The dotted lines indicate points of feedback inhibition by end products in the E. coli pathways. That is, tyrosine inhibits enzymes 1a and 7a, phenylalanine inhibits enzymes 1c and 7b, and tryptophan inhibits enzyme 8. Activities 7a and 13 are found together on the same enzyme molecule and enzymes 7b and 15 are found together.

In Bacillus subtilis, there is but a single enzyme 1, PKDH synthetase. It is sensitive to feedback inhibition by prephenate and, at higher concentrations, by chorismate. This serves as a main control on the common part of the pathway. The enzyme 1 is in a complex with chorismate mutase (enzyme 7) and with shikimate kinase (enzyme 5). None of these reactions is inhibited by the ultimate end products, tyrosine, phenylalanine, and tryptophan. In B. subtilis, feedback inhibition by tyrosine is exerted on a separate protein, prephenate dehydrogenase (enzyme 13), and feedback inhibition by phenylalanine is exerted on another protein, prephenate dehydratase (enzyme 15). Compiled from B. J. Wallace and J. Pittard, J. Bacteriol., 93 (1967), 237; ibid., 94 (1967), 1297; R. A. Jensen and E. W. Nester, J. Mol. Biol.,

remaining enzymes supply enough of the common intermediate, PKDH, to allow growth when just one of the activities is missing. Mutants lacking each of these enzymes can be obtained under special conditions. For example, in the presence of phenylalanine and tyrosine, which feedback-inhibit their special PKDH synthetases, mutants lacking the tryptophan-specific PKDH synthetase can be obtained. Such mutants grow on minimal medium as do wild-type bacteria, but they are very sensitive to inhibition by tyrosine and phenylalanine.

The presence of two inhibition points in the reaction sequence, and duplications of enzymes, allows *E. coli* to channel its metabolism in a manner necessary for growth. Although the same biochemical sequences are utilized in other organisms, some of these have evolved quite different control mechanisms for this elegant regulation. One example is given in the legend to Fig. 5.6; here not only the end products but also some of the intermediates take part in feedback inhibitions. Examination of other biochemical pathways shows that control mechanisms analogous to those discussed above are applied in some cases, while still another method, concerted feedback inhibition, is used in others. In concerted feedback inhibition, a single enzyme is involved in a critical reaction that ultimately leads to several end products. Each of the end products separately inhibits the activity of the enzyme partially, and these inhibitions are cumulative.

The existence of duplicate enzymes, their association in protein complexes, and their importance in metabolic regulation constitute an additional answer to the question asked in the last section of Chap. 4: Why multimers? Indeed, effects found in in vivo systems indicate that our descriptions above form only a gross outline of intracellular events. Protein-protein interactions allow subtle modes of regulation and intracellular organization about which we still have much to learn. This is an active area of research at the present time and one critical to our understanding of the behavior of cells in tissues and organs.

Channeled Pathways

The pools of intermediates in the bacterial systems described above are interchangeable. For example, mutants defective in one of

12 (1965), 468; K. D. Brown and C. H. Doy, Biochim. Biophys. Acta, 77 (1963), 170; ibid., 104 (1965), 377; ibid., 118 (1966), 157; F. Gibson, Biochem. J., 90 (1964), 256; R. G. H. Cotton and F. Gibson, Biochim. Biophys. Acta, 100 (1965), 76; L. C. Smith, J. M. Ravel, S. R. Lax, and W. Shive, J. Biol. Chem., 237 (1962), 3566; E. W. Nester, J. H. Lorence, and D. S. Nasser, Biochemistry, 6 (1967), 1553; R. A. Jensen and E. W. Nester, J. Biol. Chem., 241 (1966), 3365, 3373; D. Nasser and E. W. Nester, J. Bacteriol., 94 (1967), 1706; E. W. Nester and R. A. Jensen, J. Bacteriol., 91 (1966), 1594; R. L. Somerville, J. Bacteriol., 94 (1967), 1798.

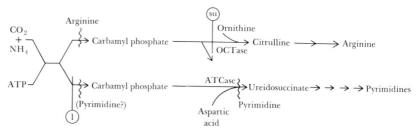

FIG. 5.7. *Interrelations between pathways of arginine and pyrimidine biosynthesis. Arginine and pyrimidines have a common precursor, carbamyl phosphate. Carbamyl phosphate plus ornithine is converted to citrulline by the enzyme ornithine trans-carbamylase (OTCase). Carbamyl phosphate and aspartic acid are converted to ureidosuccinate, a pyrimidine precursor, by the enzyme aspartic transcarbamylase (ATCase). Consult R. H. Davis, in* Organizational Biosynthesis, *H. J. Vogel, J. O. Lampen, and V. Bryson, eds., New York: Academic Press, Inc., 1967, p. 303.*

the enzymes 1 do not regularly appear as requiring several aromatic compounds. Mutants in the enzymes 7 appear, probably due to the associations of enzyme 7a with 13 and 7b with 15. In other bacterial systems, and more prominently in *Neurospora,* biochemical intermediates are not so free to pass from one metabolic sequence to another; they are channeled.

In *Neurospora,* one enzyme catalyzes the synthesis of carbamyl phosphate to be used for arginine biosynthesis, and a presumed second enzyme catalyzes the same biochemical reaction for pyrimidine biosynthesis (Fig. 5.7). The first enzyme is sensitive to feedback inhibition by arginine, and it appears likely that the presumed second enzyme is sensitive to feedback inhibition by pyrimidines.

If the carbamyl phosphates from the two pathways were interchangeable, mutants blocked in carbamyl phosphate synthesis might not be found normally; the one remaining enzyme could supply enough carbamyl phosphate for both reaction sequences. A cell that was mutant for the enzyme in one of the pathways might be revealed only in the presence of the feedback inhibitor appropriate for the other pathway. The two carbamyl phosphate pools ordinarily are not interchangeable, however.

Neurospora mutants that are blocked only in the synthesis of the pyrimidine-specific carbamyl phosphate are pyrimidine-requiring mutants. However, their requirement for pyrimidine is greatly alleviated by a second, independent mutation. Because the original mutant phenotype is suppressed, this second mutation is termed a *suppressor mutation.* It decreases the rate of conversion of carbamyl phosphate and ornithine to citrulline (Fig. 5.7). The suppressed mutant still can synthesize sufficient arginine for normal growth, in spite of possessing only 2 to 3 percent of the normal enzyme activity. In the process, the mutant accumulates excess carbamyl phosphate before the genetic block, and this excess carbamyl phosphate is used to spare the pyrimidine requirement. If exogenous arginine is added, thereby curtailing the synthesis of carbamyl phosphate by feedback inhibition of the arginine-specific enzyme, the suppressed mutant again requires exogenous pyrimidine (which is characteristic of the original primary mutant). In this manner, two ordinarily separate, or channeled, pathways have become linked through mutation. Similarly, arginine-requiring mutants blocked in the synthesis of arginine-specific carbamyl phosphate are relieved of their arginine requirement by a second mutation that imposes an ATC deficiency (Fig. 5.7).

Although the systems described here pertain to biosynthetic sequences, similar observations have been made concerning pathways in catabolism. And instances have been described where one or more reactions in a catabolic pathway are shared with a biosynthetic pathway, each pathway with its unique enzymes. The two pathways are often channeled. The presence of channeled pathways and duplicate enzymes can be seen to create special problems in genetical analysis, resolvable only through close biochemical scrutiny. On the other hand, genetics has supplied a most powerful tool in assisting biologists concerned with the study of these intricacies at the molecular level. Studies on mutants also allow us to assess their significance in vivo.

Consequences Further Removed

We have pointed out a number of metabolic abnormalities that are affected only indirectly by gene mutation. It is easy to visualize that metabolic sequences that are secondarily disturbed by mutation may, in turn, adversely affect other systems in the integrated scheme of normal metabolism.

In higher organisms, the intimate coordination of processes at the cellular, tissue, organ, and organism levels is dependent upon biochemical processes at the intracellular level. Careful analysis is required to uncover the primary source of the multiple effects manifested by various mutant phenotypes. Few mutant phenotypes in higher organisms have been traced back to the primary genetic block. The examples in this chapter may serve as models for further probing of the physiology of the normal organism and its alteration by gene mutation.

One system that has proved very fruitful in the study of higher organisms is the synthesis of the oxygen-transporting blood protein, hemoglobin. Some characteristics of the structure and inheritance of the hemoglobins are summarized in McKusick's *Human Genetics* (in this series). Figure 5.8 shows some of the main abnormalities traceable to a single cause—the replacement of glutamic acid for valine at position 6 in the β-polypeptide chain of hemoglobin. The figure shows

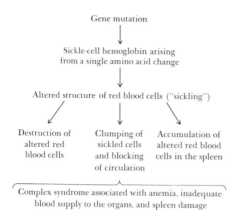

Gene mutation

↓

Sickle-cell hemoglobin arising
from a single amino acid change

↓

Altered structure of red blood cells ("sickling")

| Destruction of altered red blood cells | Clumping of sickled cells and blocking of circulation | Accumulation of altered red blood cells in the spleen |

Complex syndrome associated with anemia, inadequate blood supply to the organs, and spleen damage

FIG. 5.8. *The widespread effects of a gene mutation in humans that alters the primary structure of hemoglobin.*

clearly the many levels of analysis that are required to track down gene mutations in complex organisms. It also points out how a change in a nucleotide pair—effecting a single amino acid replacement—may have multiple (pleiotropic) effects.

Questions

5.1. The normal eye color in *Drosophila,* red-brown, is due to admixture of two main pigments, red and brown, produced by two relatively independent biochemical pathways.

(a) Describe the phenotypes of two independently isolated single mutants, one blocked in the pathway leading to red pigment and one blocked in the pathway leading to brown pigment.

(b) What phenotypes would you expect: (1) When two mutant genes involving two separate reactions in the pathway of brown pigment synthesis are combined *cis,* and when the same two mutations are combined *trans?* Why? (2) When two mutant genes, one blocking a reaction in the pathway of synthesis of red pigment and the other blocking a reaction in the pathway of the synthesis of brown pigment, are combined? Why?

(c) How would you go about analyzing the sequence of pigment synthesis with a series of mutants blocked in different steps in the two biosynthetic pathways?

(d) Recessive mutations at a gene locus, white (w), simultaneously eliminate both red and brown pigments from the eyes of homozygous mutant individuals. Give two plausible theoretical interpretations of this phenomenon.

5.2. Explain pitfalls in the method of localizing genetic blocks solely on the basis of accumulations of metabolites.

5.3. From a biochemistry textbook, locate a series of biochemical reactions leading to an end product. Describe effects caused by a genetic block in the first step of the pathway. Repeat the analysis for a mutant blocked in the last step of the pathway.

5.4. Why do organisms possess some duplicate enzymes with very similar or identical catalytic activities?

5.5. In the library locate a good example of a gene mutation with pleiotropic effects. List the syndrome, attempting to organize the sequence of causes and effects in a manner analogous in general format to the arrangement of the data in Fig. 5.8.

5.6. What properties would you predict for a mutant that is feedback-resistant to tryptophan and, simultaneously, has a genetic block after anthranilic acid? (See Fig. 3.1 for a scheme of tryptophan biosynthesis.)

5.7. Set up several theoretical models of reactions sequences and inhibitions that can account for genes in which both dominant and recessive point mutations occur.

5.8. Can you think of three ways in which a gene mutation can produce an allele that is dominant to the wild-type allele? Outline as a theoretical series of biochemical reactions.

5.9. Some mutations are not expressed in all individuals that carry the mutant gene (incomplete penetrance). Briefly outline some reasons that might offer a biochemical basis for this phenomenon.

5.10. There is a reaction sequence, compound A to compound E, that is controlled by four genes, *1–4*: $A \xrightarrow{1} B \xrightarrow{2} C \xrightarrow{3} D \xrightarrow{4} E$. Compound E is essential for cell growth. Describe what effects mutations in each gene might have with respect to enzyme activity, accumulations, and behavior of the mutants in crossfeeding experiments and in growth tests.

References

Aebi, H. E., "Inborn Errors of Metabolism," *Ann. Rev. Biochem.*, *36*, Pt. I (1967), 271. A brief modern view of a few examples in the biochemical genetics of man.

Atkinson, D. E., "Regulation of Enzyme Activity," *Ann. Rev. Biochem.*, *35*, Pt. I (1966), 85. A review that stresses in vitro studies on modifications in enzyme activity by specific metabolites.

Brew, K., T. C. Vanaman, and R. L. Hill, "The Role of β-Lactalbumin and the A Protein in Lactose Synthetase: A Unique Mechanism for the Control of a Biological Reaction," *Proc. Natl. Acad. Sci. U.S.*, *59* (1968), 491. The substrate specificity of a protein can be different when it is separated as opposed to when it is in union with a second particular protein.

Changeux, J. P., J. C. Gerhart, and H. K. Schachman, in *Regulation of Nucleic Acid and Protein Biosynthesis*, V. V. Koningsberger and C. Bosch, eds. Amsterdam: Elsevier Publishing Company, 1967. Molecular studies on mechanisms of feedback inhibition.

Cohen, G. N., "Regulation of Enzyme Activity in Microorganisms," *Ann. Rev. Microbiol.*, *19* (1965), 105. A review that stresses aspects of feedback inhibition.

Giles, N. H., C. W. H. Partridge, S. I. Ahmed, and M. E. Case, "The Occurrence of Two Dehydroquinases in *Neurospora crassa*, One Constitutive and One Inducible," *Proc. Natl. Acad. Sci. U.S.*, *58* (1967),

1930. *Neurospora* produces two enzymes 3 (Fig. 5.6), a constitutive synthetic enzyme and an inducible enzyme used in 5-dehydroquinic acid (DHQ) degradation.

Ingram, V. M., *The Hemoglobins in Genetics and Evolution.* New York: Columbia University Press, 1963. A thorough treatment that focuses on the molecular basis of some human disorders, the study of which has contributed significantly to many of the concepts outlined in the current text.

Koshland, D. E., and K. E. Neet, "The Catalytic and Regulatory Properties of Enzymes," *Ann. Rev. Biochem.* (1968), 359. Review that ties together material in this chapter with the descriptive presentation in Chapter 2.

Mitchell, H. K., "Biochemical Aspects of *Drosophila*," *Ann. Rev. Genet., 1* (1967), 185. *Drosophila* genetics is still a useful tool in analyses of basic genetic mechanisms.

Monod, J., J. Wyman, and J. P. Changeux, "On the Nature of Allosteric Transitions: A Plausible Model," *J. Mol. Biol., 12* (1966), 88. This article will be of interest with regard to topics discussed in both Chaps. 4 and 5.

Nelson, O. E., Jr., "Biochemical Genetics of Higher Plants," *Ann. Rev. Genet., 1* (1967), 245. Areas in which recent developments lead to promise for future studies of broad interest.

Stadtman, E. R., "Allosteric Regulation of Enzyme Activity," *Advan. Enzymol., 28* (1966), 41. The variety of mechanisms for feedback control of enzymes catalyzing branched biosynthetic pathways are emphasized here.

"Symposium on Multiple Forms of Enzymes and Control Mechanisms," *Bacteriol. Rev., 27* (1963), 155. Three review articles on duplicate enzymes and control mechanisms.

Umbarger, H. E., "Intracellular Regulatory Mechanisms," *Science, 145* (1964), 674. By one of the discoverers of feedback inhibition, this review discusses some microbial systems before examining regulation in multicellular forms.

Wagner, R. P., and H. K. Mitchell, *Genetics and Metabolism,* 2nd ed. New York: John Wiley & Sons, Inc., 1964. Advanced genetics text that introduces a large number of examples of gene-enzyme relationships and secondary consequences of gene mutations.

Protein Biosynthesis:

Components

Our attention in the first five chapters has centered on the structure of proteins, evidence for genetic control of protein structure, and some consequences of changes in protein structure on cellular metabolism. We concluded that the ultimate structure and function of a protein is a direct consequence of the type and order of amino acids in the polypeptide chain. We pointed out that genetic material exerts its control of the phenotypic potential of cells and organisms by dictating the structure of proteins. These two concepts, the importance of proteins and the key role of protein primary structure, are enormously simplifying ones. Armed with them, we can focus attention on how the amino acid sequences are determined by the genetic material and thereby gain insight into a most important phase of gene action.

We are faced, then, with the question of how the correct amino acid gets built into exactly the proper position in the polypeptide chain. Although this question cannot be fully answered, a series of exciting developments during the last 15 years allows us to sketch some of the important steps in the process of protein biosynthesis. Knowledge of these steps allows us partially to resolve the problem of the manner in which the genetic material exercises its control of the phenotype. In other words, we are beginning to understand how genetic information stored in nucleic acid is translated and expressed in the structure and function of specific protein molecules.

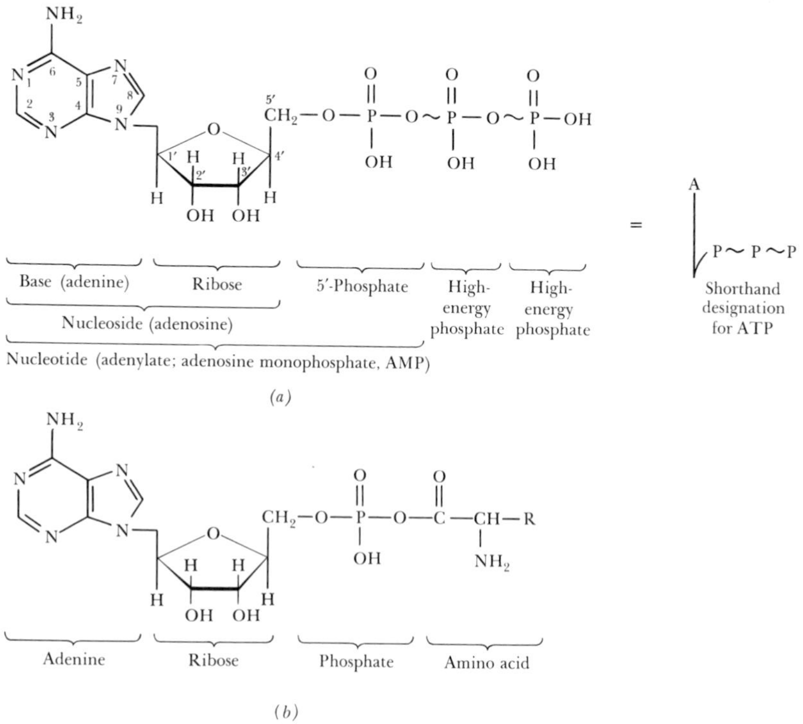

FIG. 6.1. (a) *ATP (adenosine triphosphate), a nucleoside triphosphate, showing structure and the numbering nomenclature for the purine ring and the ribose moiety (the latter are listed as 1', 2', and so on, to differentiate them from the ring carbons of the base).* (b) *Amino acid adenylate. R designates the side chain for any α-amino acid.*

Amino Acid Activation

The first step in protein synthesis is *amino acid activation.* It involves reaction of an amino acid with adenosine triphosphate (ATP); the reaction is catalyzed by a specific "activating enzyme," an *aminoacyl tRNA synthetase.* The first product is an amino acid adenylate in which is conserved the energy required for the second step, the attachment of the amino acid to a specific tRNA molecule. The adenylate remains bound to the enzyme until it is transferred to the tRNA, a transfer that is catalyzed by the same enzyme. The structures of ATP and of an amino acid adenylate are shown in Figure 6.1. Reaction 1 in Fig. 6.2 depicts the activation of amino acid.

The synthetases are highly specific under physiological conditions; that is, each of them usually activates only one kind of amino acid.

Most cells normally contain relatively low levels of free metabolites of small molecular weight, together called a *pool*. However, cells are unable to maintain pool levels precisely enough to prevent an occasional imbalance in concentrations of the different metabolites composing the pool. Theoretically, because the activating enzyme does not have absolute specificity for its substrate, an imbalance in the amino acid pool might occasionally allow it to react with a "wrong" amino acid; such an error could cause chaos in protein synthesis. Fortunately, a crucial control is built into the specificity of an activating enzyme: its affinity for its natural, specific substrate is much higher than for any other. For example, the isoleucine-activating enzyme has a 100-fold higher affinity for isoleucine than it does for valine; even in the presence of abnormally high concentrations of valine, it will preferentially activate any isoleucine present rather than its competitor, valine. The same situation holds for the activation of D- and L-amino acids; the relatively high affinity of the enzymes for the L-isomers allows for their preferential activation, even in the presence of D-amino acids.

There are still further checks on these enzymes. As we shall see in the next section, if the wrong amino acid is activated by an activating enzyme, the enzyme specificity is such that the amino acid adenylate in most cases is unable to take part in the next step of protein synthesis.

We have said that the adenylates remain bound to their activating enzymes (see reaction 1 in Fig. 6.2). And this is fortunate, for they are very reactive when free in solution: they form peptide bonds at random with any amino acid present, or even with amine groups on the side chains of amino acids in proteins. This high reactivity would be

FIG. 6.2. *Amino acid activation and transfer to tRNA. R denotes an amino acid side chain. The shorthand designation for ATP, a 5'-nucleoside triphosphate, is that symbolized in Fig. 6.1a. The configuration of the amino acid–acceptor portion of the tRNA molecule follows the same shorthand convention. The nucleotides adjacent to A in the tRNA are cytidylates, designated as C.*

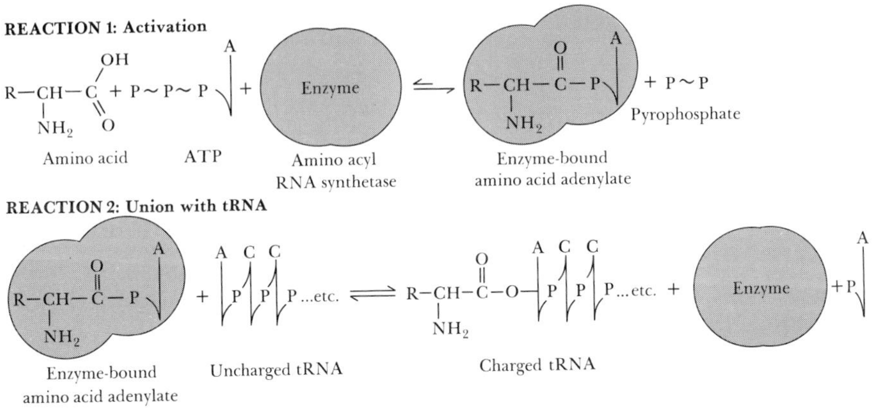

REACTION 1: Activation

REACTION 2: Union with tRNA

detrimental to specific protein synthesis, which requires a particular sequence of amino acids. The bound adenylate is thus protected from reacting nonspecifically. The configuration of the activating enzyme is such that the bound adenylate can react only with the tRNA molecules specific for its particular amino acid (see the next section).

Amino acid activation is a reversible reaction (Fig. 6.2). It is conveniently observed in the reverse direction by adding radioactive pyrophosphate to the aminoacyl adenylate enzyme complex and following the incorporation of radioactive phosphorus into ATP. The ATP can be separated from other components in the reaction mixture, and its radioactivity can be measured.

Genes that specify the structures of the various aminoacyl tRNA synthetases are scattered on the *E. coli* chromosome. Mutants with highly defective synthetases are presumably lethal in these haploid bacteria; however, a number of mutants are known that have temperature-sensitive synthetases or synthetases with altered substrate affinities.

Transfer RNA (tRNA)

Not only does each activating enzyme have a high affinity for ATP and for a specific amino acid, it also exhibits a marked specificity for a particular species of tRNA molecule. In the literature, tRNA molecules have been variously termed tRNA for transfer RNA, sRNA for soluble or supernatant RNA, or adaptor RNA. tRNA molecules are synthesized at particular regions of the genetic material. Each species of tRNA molecule reflects a complementarity in base composition and sequence to its particular gene in the DNA. The complementary bases at certain positions in the tRNA are modified through enzyme action after tRNA synthesis with DNA as template. This leads to the production of rare nucleotides in tRNA; some of these are indicated in the nucleotide sequence of alanine transfer RNA from yeast (Fig. 6.3) and are described in the legend. The presence of these rare nucleotides does not alter the conclusion that tRNA genes and tRNA molecules are very important exceptions to the one gene–one polypeptide chain rule; in this case RNA molecules are the end products of gene action.

The genes specifying tRNA's appear to be scattered on the *E. coli* chromosome but clustered on the chromosome of another bacterium, *Bacillus subtilis*. In bacteria it has been estimated that there are from 40 to 80 genes that can specify tRNA. In *Drosophila*, about 55 genetically distinct semidominant lethal mutations called *minutes* are known; these are thought to be deletions of tRNA cistrons, scattered through the genome.

The nucleotide sequence and schematic representation of the possible conformation of a transfer RNA are depicted in Fig. 6.3. The nucle-

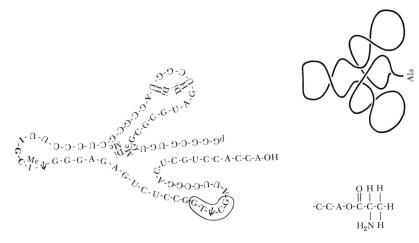

FIG. 6.3. *Cloverleaf model of an alanine tRNA molecule from yeast. Yeast alanine tRNA is the first biologically active nucleic acid molecule to have been isolated in which the nucleotide sequence has been established.* [R. W. Holley, J. Apgar, G. A. Everett, J. T. Madison, M. Marquisee, S. H. Merrill, J. R. Penswick, and A. Zamir, Science, 147 (1965), 1462.]

The three-dimensional structure of tRNA is not known. The cloverleaf model accounts for some of the properties of tRNA, for example, the accessibility of certain nucleotides to hydrolysis by enzymes or to chemical treatments, whereas other regions appear quite resistant. The model allows about half of the 77 nucleotides in the chain to interact through Watson-Crick base pairing involving adenine-uracil and guanine-cytosine base pairs. These paired regions give the molecule appreciable double-helical content. The drawing at the upper right gives a two-dimensional impression of the helical appearance of such cloverleaf molecules.

tRNA's contain unusual nucleosides. In the case of alanine tRNA of yeast these are I, inosine; ψ, pseudouridine; T, ribothymidine; MeI, 1-methylinosine; MeG, 1-methylguanosine; DiMeG, N-2-dimethylguanosine; DiHU, 5,6-dihydrouridine. In the diagram, p represents a terminal 5'-phosphate group and — indicates the phosphodiester linkage of the sugar-phosphate backbone.

The sequence G-T-ψ-C-G, circled in the figure, is a common structural feature of all tRNA's so far examined.

otide sequence was deduced by methods conceptually analogous but chemically quite different from those used in sequencing the structures of polypeptide chains. Purified tRNA was digested with an enzyme, a ribonuclease, that shows a high specificity of nucleolytic activity under certain conditions. The fragments were separated by chromatography on columns and the nucleotide compositions determined. Each fragment was further digested using additional nucleolytic enzymes, and the products separated and characterized with respect to composition and to terminal nucleotides. The various "pieces" were then put together to reconstruct the intact molecule. The content of odd nucleosides greatly facilitated placement of the fragments in proper sequence.

About 15 additional rare nucleotides, whose functions are obscure, have been detected in tRNA's. We shall speculate on the functions of one of them, inosinic acid, in Chapter 8. Others may be involved with prevention of base pairing in the open tRNA loops, or with phenomena of recognition between the tRNA, its aminoacyl tRNA synthetase, or other intracellular structures with which it forms specific associations.

tRNA molecules occur in both active and inactive forms. Inactive molecules lack part or all of the $-C-C-A$ terminal sequence, the terminal adenosine being the site of attachment of the amino acid to the tRNA. This nucleotide sequence may be added to reactivate the inactive tRNA molecule by exposure of the tRNA to an enzyme system that utilizes ATP and cytidine triphosphate (CTP) as substrates to effect the repair.

The enzyme ribonuclease digests tRNA, leaving among the products amino acid–adenylate–dicytidylate. From the known specificity of ribonuclease (which splits RNA at the pyrimidine 3'-phosphate linkages), it is inferred that the amino acid is attached to the terminal A. This attachment has been deduced to be an esterification at the 2'- or 3'-hydroxyl group. When consulting Fig. 6.1, you will see that nucleotides have *cis*-hydroxyl groups at the 2' and 3' positions. Compounds that possess hydroxyl groups in a *cis* configuration are sensitive to periodate oxidation. Internal nucleotides in tRNA are covalently bound to adjacent nucleotides by 3'- and 5'-phosphodiester linkages, and the 3' position of the initial nucleotide is bound in a phosphate ester linkage. These nucleotides are thus resistant to oxidation by periodate. The terminal nucleotide of tRNA is sensitive to periodate oxidation but becomes resistant when the tRNA is charged with an amino acid. Consequently, the amino acid is thought to be attached to the terminal adenosine through either the 2'- or 3'-*cis*-hydroxyl group.

Treatment of tRNA with periodate is used as an indication of the amount of charged versus uncharged tRNA. A mixture of charged and uncharged tRNA is treated with periodate, the amino acids stripped from the RNA by treatment with mild alkali, and the residual acceptor activity measured through incorporation of radioactive amino acids. Periodate is also used to inactivate uncharged species of tRNA after one class has been fully charged with an amino acid in vitro.

tRNA's for different amino acids and among various species are very similar in gross structure: size (molecular weight about 25,000), terminal $-C-C-A$ residues, and content of appreciable double-helical regions. However, as was mentioned earlier, each type of tRNA must have a specific configuration that can be recognized by its own particular aminoacyl RNA synthetase. Attempts to inhibit charging of tRNA's by chemically modified tRNA, fragments of tRNA, and by oligonucleotides of known sequence have so far failed to reveal unequivocally the synthetase recognition site on the tRNA.

Owing to rapid advances in our knowledge concerning the genetic code, specific sites on tRNA's of known sequence have been nominated as candidates for critical roles in the proper placement of amino acids into proteins. This short nucleotide sequence, or *anticodon,* is believed to pair with an antiparallel base sequence in messenger RNA (see below). In the structure for the alanine tRNA shown in Fig. 6.3, the putative anticodon is indicated by bold type at the top of the molecule.

Each cell contains a full complement of tRNA species. There is at least one tRNA for each amino acid, and for a number of amino acids several different tRNA's are present. Some of these multiple tRNA's are present in abundance, whereas others are found only as minor (or trace) components. The reasons for the presence of a high degree of multiplicity of tRNA species are not yet clear, although the presence of some will enter into our discussion in Chap. 8 on the genetic code.

To recapitulate, the amino acid attachment sites of tRNA molecules are the same for most, if not for all, classes of tRNA's. tRNA molecules contain some structural characteristics unique to each class and specific for a given species of aminoacyl RNA synthetase. Finally, tRNA molecules are assumed to contain a unique short sequence of nucleotides that allows them to seek out the proper complementary series of bases on messenger RNA templates during protein synthesis. Later in this chapter we shall review some of the evidence which indicates that the protein-forming system uses the aminoacyl–tRNA complexes as the raw material from which to build polypeptide chains.

Ribosomes

There is a positive correlation between the rate of protein synthesis and the RNA content of various cells. This largely reflects the abundance of ribosomes in actively growing, protein-synthesizing cells. Ribosomes are small particles, about 200 Å in diameter, not resolved in the light microscope. They contain about 60 percent RNA and 40 percent protein. The majority of the RNA and over 5 percent of the total protein of a growing cell is in its ribosomes.

In bacteria, ribosomes are packed throughout the cytoplasm (Fig. 6.4). It is estimated that there are about 1.5×10^4 ribosomes in a growing *E. coli* cell; of these at least one-third are thought to be actively engaged in protein synthesis. Some ribosomes are found free and others are found attached to the cell membrane. Ribosomes purified by centrifugation from a cell extract are shown in Fig. 6.5.

Ribosomes are classified by their sedimentation constants (S), determined by their rates of sedimentation in an ultracentrifuge. Ribosomes and ribosomal subunits from bacteria fall into the general classes de-

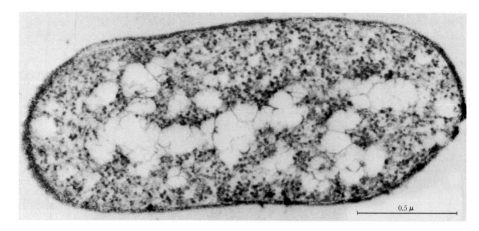

FIG. 6.4. *Electron micrograph of a section through a cell of* E. coli. *A bacterium is surrounded by a cell wall and, interior to this, by a cell membrane. The cytoplasm is packed with ribosomes. The DNA is contained in the lighter (less dense) portions of the cell and is not separated from the cytoplasm by a nuclear membrane. From* S. F. Conti *and* M. E. Gettner, J. Bacteriol., 83 *(1962), 544.*

FIG. 6.5. *Electron micrograph of 70S ribosomes from* E. coli. *The 70S particles, indicated by arrows, show a complex structure, indicative of the union of 30S and 50S components. A few free 30S and 50S particles also are present in the preparation. Magnification 100,000×. From* C. E. Hall *and* H. S. Slayter, J. Mol. Biol., 1 *(1959), 329.*

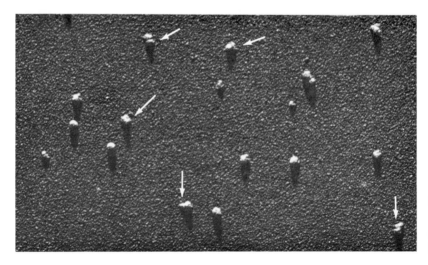

picted in Figs. 6.5 and 6.6. The ribosomal subunits of most organisms dissociate or reassociate into specific complexes depending upon the magnesium ion concentration in the suspending medium; the concentrations shown in Fig. 6.6 apply to ribosomes extracted from cells of the bacterium *E. coli.* The actual sedimentation values depend strongly on the ionic composition of the suspending medium as well as on the source of the ribosomes.

Ribosomes extracted from cellular organelles, for example, from chloroplasts and mitochondria, of higher organisms exhibit the approximate sizes shown in Figs. 6.5 and 6.6. However, the main ribosomal components of higher organisms, as well as of many fungi and yeast, have sedimentation constants in the range of 80S and are composed of proportionately larger subunits (about 60S and 40S). Some of these ribosomes are found free and others are found attached to the surfaces of tubular lipoprotein membranes collectively called *endoplasmic reticulum.* These structures are shown in the frontispiece of this book. When the cell is broken open, portions of the membranes with ribosomes attached are released. The membranes can first be

FIG. 6.6. *Properties of* **E. coli** *ribosomes.*

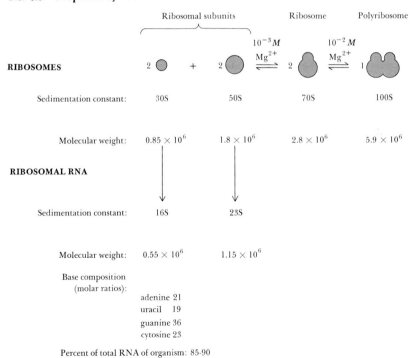

	Ribosomal subunits		Ribosome	Polyribosome
RIBOSOMES	2 ⊙ + 2 ⬤	$\overset{10^{-3}M}{\underset{Mg^{2+}}{\rightleftharpoons}}$ 2	$\overset{10^{-2}M}{\underset{Mg^{2+}}{\rightleftharpoons}}$ 1	
Sedimentation constant:	30S 50S		70S	100S
Molecular weight:	0.85×10^{6} 1.8×10^{6}		2.8×10^{6}	5.9×10^{6}
RIBOSOMAL RNA				
Sedimentation constant:	16S 23S			
Molecular weight:	0.55×10^{6} 1.15×10^{6}			
Base composition (molar ratios):	adenine 21 uracil 19 guanine 36 cytosine 23			

Percent of total RNA of organism: 85-90

sedimented, together with ribosomes, into a pellet called the *microsome fraction* and then the membrane is dissolved with detergents to release the ribosomes.

Ribosomal RNA differs in size and base content from tRNA and from other RNA classes of most cells. Ribosomal RNA from most organisms is relatively rich in guanine and cytosine, and it lacks many of the rare bases found in tRNA, although some methylated bases are present. The base composition of ribosomal RNA given in Fig. 6.6 is for the bacterium *E. coli*. The sedimentation constants for the two types of ribosomal RNA of bacteria are about 16S and 23S; the analogous constants for the two RNA species extracted from ribosomes of higher organisms are about 18S and 28S.

The two classes of bacterial ribosomal RNA's have base sequences that appear complementary by hybridization tests (see Fig. 6.10) to separate regions in the DNA along which they are presumably synthesized. It is estimated that there are between 10 and 200 such ribosomal RNA genes in various bacteria. Whether or not the genes give rise to identical classes of RNA (are duplicate genes) remains to be determined. In higher organisms, the analogous ribosomal RNA components are manufactured along a series of some 200 to 2000 tightly clustered genes. The two types of ribosomal RNA are first made as an elongate unit of high molecular weight (about 45S) which is then severed into discrete sections and methylated in the nucleolus before transmission to the cytoplasm (Fig. 6.7). After their manufacture, the ribosomal RNA's combine with a number of basic proteins, apparently in orderly sequence. Additional proteins attach to the ribosome subunits as they "mature" into the components active in protein biosynthesis. The various proteins are not attached by covalent bonds, so it is difficult to define which proteins associated with ribosomes are truly structural proteins, which perform other functions, and which are insignificant to protein synthesis. This is currently an active field of investigation, holding many clues to the process of protein synthesis outlined in Chap. 7.

At present it appears that the ribosomal RNA's are final gene products whose sole function is of a structural nature. This point is not firmly established, for some workers point to evidence indicating that the ribosomal RNA's might have a second function in serving as template for the synthesis of at least some of the ribosomal proteins. In either event, the ribosomal RNA's and the genes specifying them are exceptions to the one gene–one polypeptide chain rule. Like the genes dictating the structures of tRNA's, the ribosomal RNA genes have unique functions in the cell. Besides the larger RNA components, each ribosome contain a small, 5S, RNA (Fig. 6.7) whose origin and function is unclear.

Although the reasons for the complex structure and the RNA content of ribosomes are not yet clear, their importance in protein synthesis is well established. We shall see in Chap. 7 that free 30S and 50S subunits form specific associations with mRNA molecules in the presence of other factors. The 70S ribosome produced by this association is the component active in protein synthesis. The union of

FIG. 6.7. *Outline of some major events in the generation of ribosomal subunits in cells of higher organisms. Each of a series of contiguous ribosomal RNA genes at the nucleolar organizer region of the chromosome (DNA) is transcribed into 45S RNA. The 45S RNA is methylated (+CH₃), complexed with protein, and cleaved via a series of steps into 18S and 32S pieces. The 18S RNA associated with protein forms the small ribosomal subunit which is released into the cytoplasm. The 32S component undergoes a further change to 28S RNA which when associated with protein forms the large ribosomal subunit. About one-third of the 45S molecule, coded for by the DNA regions, X, is lost during this conversion process. One molecule of 5S RNA, transcribed from genes located outside the nucleolar organizer, becomes associated with each large ribosomal subunit. The function of 5S RNA is unknown. All of these events take place in the nucleolus.*

Upon entry into the cytoplasm the subunits attach to messenger RNA (mRNA). Polyribosome formation ensues. Certain (accessory) proteins, which are part of the newly emerging subunits, are shed during polyribosome formation. The structural proteins and RNA of the ribosome are relatively stable, and the ribosomes are utilized a number of times. However, some breakdown occurs. Adapted after R. P. Perry, "The Nucleolus and the Synthesis of Ribosomes," Progr. in Nucleic Acid Res. Mol. Biol., 6 (1967), 219. Also see D. G. Comb and co-workers, J. Mol. Biol., 23 (1967), 441; 25 (1967), 317; E. F. Zimmerman and B. W. Holler, J. Mol. Biol., 23 (1967), 149; E. Knight, Jr., and J. E. Darnell, J. Mol. Biol., 28 (1967), 491.

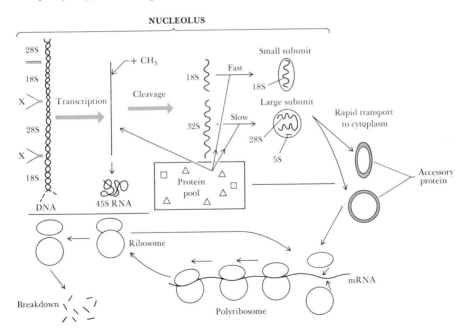

ribosomes with mRNA generally leads to aggregates of 70S ribosomes, *polyribosomes,* held together by the mRNA.

The Messenger: mRNA

Ribosomes are relatively nonspecific workbenches to and from which tRNA molecules shuttle, carrying amino acids for the synthesis of polypeptide chains. The specific order in which these charged tRNA molecules are utilized depends upon the code contained in mRNA molecules, bound to the ribosomes. These far-reaching ideas stem from in vivo experiments that demonstrate the utilization by virus mRNA of ribosomes made before virus infection. Also, as we shall see in the ensuing chapters, ribosomes can be programmed by addition of various specific mRNA's in vitro. In each case the polypeptide products predominantly reflect the source of messenger rather than the source of ribosomes.

mRNA in bacteria is rapidly synthesized. But, since it is also rapidly degraded, having a half-life of only a few minutes, it does not accumulate in the cell. Only a few percent of the total RNA of a bacterium is mRNA. mRNA of other cells, for example, the reticulocytes that manufacture the blood protein hemoglobin, is much more stable. The stability of mRNA appears to depend upon the cell type in which it is present as well as on other factors little understood at present. Also, the processes and the mechanisms leading to the destruction of mRNA remain ambiguous in spite of intensive efforts to obtain answers to these exceedingly important questions.

RNA with the properties of mRNA has been synthesized in vitro by an enzyme called RNA polymerase. RNA-polymerase action requires the presence of a DNA polymer as primer. This suggests that the enzyme preferentially synthesizes RNA complementary to the DNA rather than joining nucleotides in a random fashion. Supporting this idea is the requirement of the presence of all four ribonucleoside triphosphates—ATP, guanosine triphosphate (GTP), cytidine triphosphate (CTP), and uridine triphosphate (UTP)—for maximal RNA synthesis in the presence of DNA primer. All four ribonucleotides are incorporated in the RNA product. If the primer is deoxy-A–T copolymer, however, only UTP and ATP are used for synthesis of the U-A ribonucleotide polymer, and if it is deoxy-T homopolymer, only ATP is used for synthesis of the A ribonucleotide polymer.

Although some nucleic acids isolated from different organisms are alike in gross base content, they usually differ in the average frequencies with which particular bases are found in juxtaposition along the chain. These frequencies are called nearest-neighbor frequencies, and the method for their determination in RNA is shown in Fig. 6.8. Data from experiments using this technique have shown that the RNA prod-

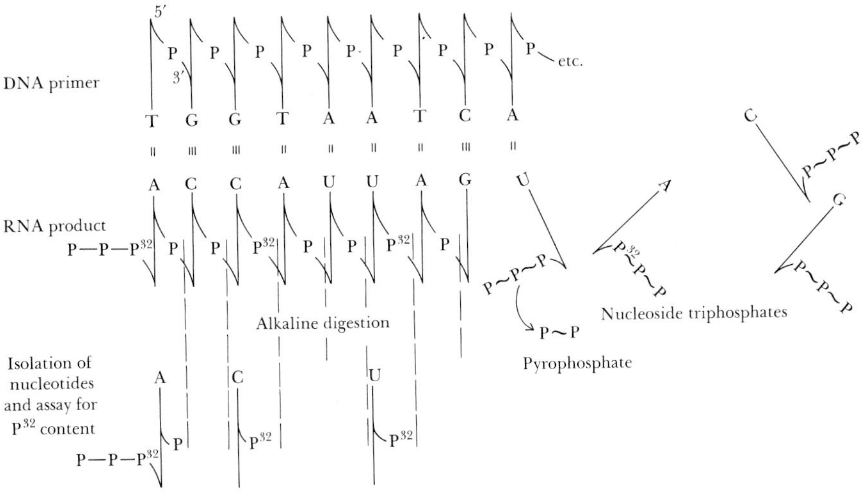

FIG. 6.8. *Determination of nearest neighbors in RNA synthesized along a DNA template. A portion of the base sequence of the effective DNA (template) strand is shown on the top row. All four nucleoside triphosphates (ATP, UTP, GTP, and CTP) are required for RNA synthesis. Only the ATP in the phosphate adjacent to the sugar (α-phosphate) is labeled with radioactive phosphorus (*32P). Recall that the free nucleoside triphosphates are 5'-phosphate esters (see Fig. 6.1a).*

In the presence of RNA-polymerase, RNA is synthesized by addition of the 5'-nucleotides and release of the two terminal phosphates as pyrophosphate (center row). As you can see, the standard base-pairing rules apply. The RNA product is isolated and subjected to alkaline hydrolysis. Alkali splits all the internucleotide 5'-phosphate diester linkages in the RNA. The nucleotides are separated, and the presence of radioactivity is determined. The 5' radioactive phosphate, originally esterified to the adenine-ribose moiety, is now isolated as the 3' ester of the nucleoside to the "left" of adenosine. The amount of radioactive phosphorus in each nucleotide gives an accurate estimate of the frequency with which that base occurs next to adenine in the newly synthesized RNA. The experiment can be repeated with the radioactive phosphorus in each of the other nucleoside triphosphates. Note also that the number of mRNA chains can be estimated by the number of free nucleosides (from the end of the chain) and nucleoside tetraphosphates (from the beginning of the chain) released by alkaline hydrolysis.

uct has a structure complementary to the DNA primer (Fig. 6.9). Furthermore, in vitro, some of the product of RNA polymerase action is a hybrid of complementary RNA and DNA chains. The chains are wound about each other and thus are relatively resistant to digestion either by deoxyribonuclease (which digests free DNA) or by ribonuclease (which digests free RNA) (Fig. 6.10a).

When radioactive phosphorus is presented to cells, sampling at short intervals of time shows that much of it enters their mRNA. The radioactive label is found first in the nucleus and later in the

Labeled triphosphate	Isolated 2',3'-nucleoside monophosphates			
ATP³² (dATP³²)	UpA (TpA) 0.010 (0.011)	ApA 0.016 (0.019)	CpA 0.058 (0.052)	GpA 0.063 (0.065)
UTP³² (dTTP³²)	UpU (TpT) 0.016 (0.017)	ApU (ApT) 0.023 (0.022)	CpU (CpT) 0.054 (0.050)	GpU (GpT) 0.052 (0.056)
GTP³² (dGTP³²)	UpG (TpG) 0.053 (0.054)	ApG 0.045 (0.049)	CpG 0.143 (0.139)	GpG 0.112 (0.112)
CTP³² (dCTP³²)	UpC (TpC) 0.065 (0.063)	ApC 0.054 (0.054)	CpC 0.110 (0.113)	GpC 0.125 (0.121)

FIG. 6.9. *Comparison of nearest-neighbor frequencies of RNA synthesized in vitro from a DNA template by RNA polymerase.*

DNA from Micrococcus lysodeikticus, rich in G and C, was used as template for RNA polymerase. In each experiment, one of the nucleoside triphosphates was labeled with radioactive ³²P while the other three triphosphates were unlabeled. After the enzymatic reaction, the RNA product was hydrolyzed with alkali. The proportion of radioactivity in each of the four nucleotides was determined. Consult Fig. 6.8 and its legend for a view of the expected alkaline digestion products and the theory underlying nearest neighbor determinations.

Nearest-neighbor frequencies in the DNA, determined by a similar type of experiment where DNA template was copied with DNA polymerase, are shown in parentheses for comparison. When the same RNA polymerase was used with other DNA templates having quite different base ratios, the RNA product mimicked the DNA in composition and in nearest-neighbor frequencies.

The tight similarities in nearest neighbors observed with RNA polymerase products reflect the fact that with some DNA's the two strands are very similar in base composition and in nearest-neighbor frequencies. Also, strand selection for mRNA synthesis is often imprecise in vitro. The nearest neighbors in some RNA products deviate from those found in DNA since the sequence in only one DNA strand serves as template.

Data on RNA polymerase product from nearest neighbors are from S. B. Weiss and T. Nakamoto, Proc. Natl. Acad. Sci. U.S., 47 (1961), 1400; data on nearest neighbors in the DNA primer are cited by Weiss and Nakamoto from J. Josse, A. D. Kaiser, and A. Kornberg, J. Biol. Chem., 236 (1961), 864.

cytoplasm, bound to the ribosomes. Since the mRNA is not tightly bound to ribosomes, as is the bulk of the RNA (ribosomal RNA), it can be separated from the ribosomes and tRNA by dissociation and differential centrifugation. The mRNA fraction is composed of nucleotides that mimic the DNA in base composition, or, in cases where the base compositions of the two strands of DNA can be differentiated, it is found that the mRNA made in vivo has a base composition precisely complementary to only one of the two strands of DNA.

mRNA has an affinity for hybrid formation only with DNA from the same or from genetically very closely related organisms. The formation, in vitro, of such specific RNA-DNA hybrids first requires that the DNA be denatured by heating, so that the hydrogen bonds between the Watson-Crick base pairs are disrupted. If the DNA is then quickly cooled, few of the hydrogen bonds reform, leaving a collapsed, tangled molecule whose bases are free to pair, by hydrogen bonding, with added mRNA (Fig. 6.10*b*). No specific, ribonuclease-resistant complexing

FIG. 6.10 (a) *A portion of a DNA molecule along which mRNA has been synthesized in vivo. This hybrid segment is insusceptible to digestion with nucleases specific for DNA or for RNA.* (b) *Formation of RNA-DNA complexes between specific mRNA and single-stranded DNA extracted from the same organism. No specific complexes form between mRNA and double-stranded DNA, or between mRNA of one organism and DNA from another, nonhomologous, organism.*

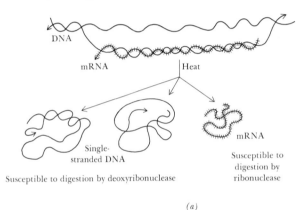

is observed between mRNA and DNA of genetically dissimilar organisms, even if they have very similar overall base compositions.

Even greater selectivity in DNA-RNA hybrid formation has been demonstrated. mRNA that has been synthesized along a particular segment of DNA will complex only with DNA from the wild-type organism. It will not complex with the DNA of a mutant whose homologous DNA segment has been deleted. This striking finding indicates that the process of DNA-RNA hybrid formation is not only organism-specific but also gene-specific.

Certainly, what is implied here is the need for identical or very similar base sequences. Hybridization studies have been used to study the genetic relatedness of species (Chap. 11), to identify cistrons for tRNA, ribosomal RNA, and mRNA, and to determine which strand of the DNA is functional. It represents a most important technique in modern genetical analysis.

mRNA with biological activity has been synthesized in vitro with appropriate DNA templates and RNA polymerase. The demonstration of an active RNA product depended on the specific source of the template DNA and on an amplification system for detection of active RNA. In one case, the system used for the biological assay was a vitamin-deficient bacterial mutant, competent to take up the RNA product as an RNA–DNA complex and requiring only traces of ultimate product (vitamin) for growth. In another case, the RNA product was detected by its ability to be translated into a protein product with some of the functional properties of normal enzyme.

Not all mRNA is copied along DNA templates. Certain viruses—for example, tobacco mosaic virus—contain RNA instead of DNA as the genetic material. This RNA can serve directly as mRNA. It also can be replicated in the host cell during virus growth through the mediation of an enzyme complex, RNA replicase, that first synthesizes a complementary RNA chain using as template the infecting single-stranded RNA chain. This complementary strand in the duplex molecule then serves as template for the synthesis of numerous RNA chains of identical base sequence to the original infecting RNA found in mature virus particles and active as "virus-specific message." Insofar as is now known, this mechanism for formation of new RNA applies only to replication of viruses. The RNA species found in normal cells all appear to depend upon one or more DNA-primed RNA polymerases for their formation.

Direction of mRNA Synthesis—from 5' to 3'

The experiments illustrated in Figs. 6.8 and 6.9 were used to determine the nearest neighbors in RNA. Only one of the ribonucleoside triphosphates used in the synthesis was labeled in any single experiment. It was labeled with ^{32}P in the α position. In the synthesis of mRNA in vitro with DNA-primed RNA polymerase, one can equally well utilize a ribonucleoside triphosphate labeled with ^{32}P in the γ phosphate group. In this case, with label entering the reaction solely from the terminal phosphate of the nucleoside triphosphates, only small amounts of label are detected in the reaction products. After alkaline digestion, these counts are found in a nucleoside tetraphosphate, readily separated from the nucleoside monophosphates by electrophoresis. The nucleoside tetraphosphate is shown in the lower left corner in Fig. 6.8.

The ease of separation of the nucleoside tetraphosphate from the other alkaline digestion products applies equally at the other end of the molecule, where, after alkaline digestion, a nucleoside is formed (G, guanosine, in Fig. 6.8). Thus one can separate and identify the bases in the internal portion of the RNA product as opposed to those at each of the ends. This methodology is applicable both to messenger made in vivo and in vitro; such experiments indicate that mRNA's (a mixture in each case) contain A and less frequently G as the predominant base at the 5' end of the molecule.

It is from the results of in vitro kinetic experiments that the direction of mRNA synthesis has been established. First, ^{3}H-labeled ATP is added to an RNA-synthesizing system at time zero. Incorporation is allowed to proceed for 8 min. The RNA product is separated from unincorporated ^{3}H-ATP and subjected to alkaline hydrolysis. The hydrolysis products are resolved by paper electrophoresis. Next, cold ATP is added to an identical in vitro system during the first 8 min, and ^{3}H-labeled ATP is only introduced for an additional 2 min. Figure 6.11 shows the two possible mechanisms for the direction of mRNA chain growth and the predicted alkaline hydrolysis products. Figure 6.12 shows the data for the two experiments. In the second experiment only about one-fourth as much ^{3}H incorporation occurred in the major, or Ap, peak, because the reaction proceeded only 2 min instead of 8 min. The pppA peak is the same in the two experiments, as expected if it were due to unincorporated ^{3}H-ATP substrate incompletely separated from the products of RNA hydrolysis. The activity in the first peak on the left, A, for the 2-min incorporation is about half that found when ^{3}H-ATP is present for the full 8 min of incubation. Presumably, about half of the RNA molecules have stopped growing by the end of 8 min, the time when the tritium label was introduced in the late labeling experiment. In contrast to these results, we see that the activity in the peak on the far right, pppAp, is less than one-tenth that of the 8-min labeled sample. This indicates that mRNA chain synthesis *started* with *nonlabeled* ATP during the first 8 min of the reaction and *failed to incorporate label into the starting end during the last 2 min*. The significant labeling of the adenosine (A) peak in the short-labeling experiment indicates that *adenosine represents the growing end of the*

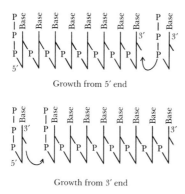

Growth from 5' end

Growth from 3' end

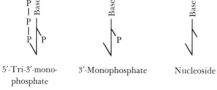

5'-Tri-3'-mono-
phosphate

3'-Monophosphate

Nucleoside

Products generated by alkaline hydrolysis

Fig. 6.11. *Possibilities for the direction of chain growth in RNA synthesis and the expected three products of alkaline hydrolysis of the ribopolynucleotide product. From G. S. Stent, Proc. Roy. Soc. (London), B164 (1966), 181.*

RNA molecule. Finally, the presence of three to four times as much label in the pppAp peak as the adenosine peak in the long-labeling experiment indicates that chains are *initiated* predominantly by adenosine nucleotides.

The average molecular weight of the product and some idea of the molecular-weight distribution can be estimated directly by its sedimentation properties. The average molecular weight (RNA chain length) also can be determined by the ratio of the number of chains initiated (nucleoside tetraphosphates) to the total incorporation. In this estimate, the preference for initiation with A and G and the overall nucleotide composition of the product have to be taken into account.

The above calculations apply to purified in vitro systems using DNA as primer for RNA polymerase. In vivo there are enzymes present that can cleave the terminal phosphates from RNA. Although the importance of these enzymes in cellular metabolism is unknown, clearly they limit the applicability of the above in vitro experiments to in vivo situations. However, some studies of in vivo message formation have been made in spite of the possible uncertainties introduced by other metabolic reactions. Such studies show that the radioactivity of 3'-terminal nucleosides released by alkaline digestion become constant early after addition of a labeled nucleoside to cells, whereas total radioactivity continues to increase. These kinetic experiments were performed with

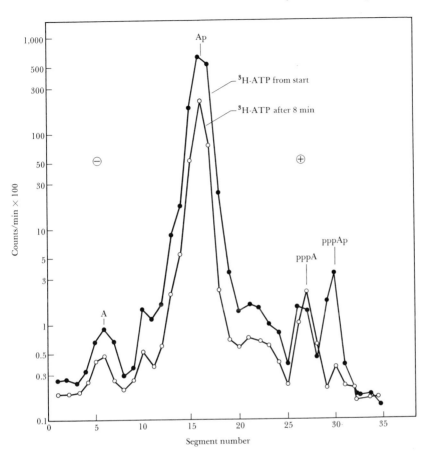

FIG. 6.12. *Paper electrophoresis of the products of alkaline hydrolysis of two RNA-polymerase reaction mixtures contain T4 phage DNA as template. One mixture contained ^{3}H-labeled ATP among the substrates from the beginning and was incubated for 8 min. To the other mixture, which initially contained unlabeled ATP, ^{3}H-labeled ATP was added after the eighth minute of reaction, and the re-action was then allowed to progress for 2 more minutes. The positions of the radioactivity corresponding to adenosine, Ap, and pppA were identified by ultraviolet absorption of the corresponding unlabeled carrier compounds added to the hydrolysates prior to electrophoresis. The identification of the rightmost peak as pppAp is inferential. Measurements for radioactivity were made upon successive segments of electrophoresis papers upon which samples of the reaction mixtures had been applied and electrophoresed. The major peak that contains most of the total radioactivity (pA) represents incorporation into the body of the polymer while the pppAp and A peaks represent incorporations at the termini (see Fig. 6.11). From H. Bremer, M. W. Konrad, K. Gaines, and G. S. Stent, J. Mol. Biol., 13 (1965), 540, and G. S. Stent, Proc. Roy. Soc. (London), B164 (1966), 181.*

E. coli at 0°C, where *initiation* of new chains does not appear to proceed as readily as the elongation of existing chains.

The in vitro data and scanty in vivo results certainly indicate that the direction of mRNA synthesis is from 5′ to 3′. In Chap. 7 we shall see that this also is the direction in which the genetic code, contained in the messenger, is read by the tRNA molecules with the aid of the ribosomal workbenches.

The Protein-Synthesizing System

The importance to the cell of the protein-synthesizing system is indicated by an examination of the components found in growing *E. coli* cells. The genetic material, the DNA, comprises only about 4 percent of the total dry mass of the cell. The outer layers of the cell, the cell wall and cell membrane, constitute perhaps 20 percent of the dry mass. On the other hand, the ribosomal RNA and proteins make up about 25 percent of the dry mass and the transfer RNA another 4 percent. One must also add in the mRNA molecules and enzymes involved in protein biosynthesis. Thus, over 30 percent of the dry mass of the cell is taken up by components of the protein-synthesizing system. This investment is made by the cell to synthesize an approximately equal mass of soluble proteins, the enzymes and proteins responsible for giving the cell its ultimate unique phenotype.

Numerous observations implicate mRNA and rule out tRNA and ribosomal RNA as the template in the synthesis of these soluble proteins. For example, *E. coli* tRNA and activating enzymes can transfer amino acids to rabbit reticulocyte ribosomes containing rabbit mRNA and synthesizing the rabbit protein, hemoglobin, in vitro. Also, when f2 phage RNA is used as mRNA with *E. coli* tRNA, ribosomes, and the necessary enzymes from *E. coli,* phage protein is synthesized. In vivo experiments show that ribosomes made before phage infection are programmed by phage mRNA made after infection and produce phage-specific proteins. These experiments, and many reviewed in Chap. 8, tell us that the ribosomes are "workbenches" which, in conjunction with charged tRNA's and the necessary enzymes, interpret the messages transcribed from DNA and contained on mRNA molecules.

Questions

6.1. In tabular form, list the distinguishing characteristics of the three classes of RNA molecules: ribosomal, soluble, and messenger.

6.2. Describe one experiment which indicates that ribosomes are workbenches that must be programmed by other molecules in order to dictate protein structure.

6.3. Outline a DNA-RNA hybridization experiment that presents evidence for the specificity of the process.

6.4. Which of the two processes carried out by aminoacyl tRNA synthetases is the most specific: amino acid activation or the transfer reaction? Outline an experiment that might give you an answer to this question.

6.5. Trace the curve from Fig. 6.12 for ^{3}H-ATP from the start. Now draw in a second, hypothetical curve for the results that you would expect from addition of ^{3}H-ATP after 8 min if mRNA chain elongation progressed from 3′ to 5′ instead of the way it actually occurs (5′ to 3′).

6.6. Describe what a metabolic pool is and tell what factors you would expect to influence its size.

6.7. Draw out a sequence of 20 nucleotides at random (using A, G, U, and C). Now see if you can get any short sequences on the molecule paired (Watson-Crick base pairing) in an antiparallel fashion. What *proportion* of the bases can be matched up in this way? Would you expect these bases to be paired if they were on an RNA molecule in solution?

6.8. Just based on what you know about protein synthesis now (without looking at later chapters), how many amino acid–activating enzymes would you expect to have? How many different classes of tRNA molecules? How many different classes of ribosomal RNA molecules? mRNA molecules?

References

Bautz, E. K. F., "RNA Synthesis—Mechanisms of Genetic Transcription," in *Molecular Genetics*, Pt. II, J. H. Taylor, ed. New York: Academic Press, Inc., 1967, p. 213.

Borek, E., and P. R. Srinivasan, "The Methylation of Nucleic Acids," *Ann. Rev. Biochem., 35*, Pt. I (1966), 275; *Progr. Nucleic Acid Res. Mol. Biol., 5* (1966), 157. Two reviews on methylation of nucleic acids, including tRNA. The first review stresses biochemistry and the second evidence for methylation at the macromolecular level.

Brenner, S., F. Jacob, and M. Meselson, "An Unstable Intermediate Carrying Information from Genes to Ribosomes for Protein Synthesis," *Nature, 190* (1961), 576. Ribosome workbenches are programmed by mRNA in vivo.

Brown, G. L., S. Lee, and D. Metz, "Active Sites of RNA's," in *Genetic Elements: Properties and Function*, D. Shugar, ed. New York: Academic Press, Inc., 1967, p. 57. Structure of RNA's in relation to their function.

Chantrenne, H., *The Biosynthesis of Proteins*. New York: Oxford University Press, 1961. A detailed summary of the subject with a useful guide to the original literature and presentation of the development of ideas leading to our current concepts.

Clowes, R. C., ed., "Recent Research in Molecular Biology," *Brit. Med. Bull., 21*, No. 3 (1965), pp. 183–273. Some good summary articles on subjects ranging from complementation to discussions on components involved in protein biosynthesis.

DeVries, J. K., and G. Zubay, "DNA-directed Peptide Synthesis. II. The Synthesis of the α-Fragment of the Enzyme β-Galactosidase." *Proc. Natl.*

Acad. Sci. U.S., 57 (1967), 1010. Indications that RNA polymerase transcribes with fidelity in vitro.

Forget, B. G., and S. M. Weissman, "Nucleotide Sequence of KB Cell 5s RNA," *Science, 158* (1967), 1695.

Georgiev, G. P., "The Nature and Biosynthesis of Nuclear Ribonucleic Acids," *Progr. Nucleic Acid Res. Mol. Biol., 6* (1967), 259. Discussion of the main classes of cellular RNA and their biosynthesis with an accent on studies with higher organisms.

Goldstein, L., ed., "The Control of Nuclear Activity," Englewood Cliffs, N.J.: Prentice-Hall, Inc., 1967. Articles include studies on the various RNA components of higher cells, sites of their syntheses, and sites of their function.

Hadjiolov, A. A., "Ribonucleic Acids and Information Transfer in Animal Cells," *Progr. Nucleic Acid Res. Mol. Biol., 7* (1967), 196.

Hurwitz, J., A. Evans, C. Babinet, and A. Skalka, "On the Copying of DNA in the RNA Polymerase Reaction," *Cold Spring Harbor Symp. Quant. Biol., 28* (1963), 59. The first evidence, often overlooked, that RNA synthesized in vitro carries biological activity.

Jacob, F., and J. Monod, "Genetic Regulatory Mechanisms in the Synthesis of Proteins," *J. Mol. Biol., 3* (1961), 318. Reviews the early evidence for the existence of messenger RNA.

Kelley, W. S., and M. Schaechter, "The 'Life Cycle' of Bacterial Ribosomes," *Advances in Microbial Physiol., 2* (1968), 89.

Kirby, K. S., "Isolation of Ribonucleic Acids for Studies in Protein Biosynthesis," in *Techniques in Protein Biosynthesis,* Vol. I. New York: Academic Press, Inc., 1967, p. 265.

Leoning, U. E., "RNA Structure and Metabolism," *Ann. Rev. Plant Physiol., 19* (1968), 37.

Lipmann, F., "Messenger Ribonucleic Acid," *Progr. Nucleic Acid Res. Mol. Biol., 1* (1963), 135. A view of messenger RNA; its measurement, synthesis, and function.

Maaløe, O., and N. O. Kjeldgaard, *Control of Macromolecular Synthesis.* New York: W. A. Benjamin, Inc., 1966. Quantitative aspects of DNA, RNA, and protein synthesis in bacteria.

Madison, J. T., "Primary Structure of RNA," *Ann. Rev. Biochem., 37* (1968), 131.

Muira, K.-I., "Specificity in the Structure of Transfer RNA," *Progr. Nucleic Acid Res. Mol. Biol., 6* (1967), 39. Discussion of tRNA structure and functional sites on tRNA.

Osawa, S., "Ribosome Formation and Structure," *Ann. Rev. Biochem., 37* (1968), 109.

Penman, S., "Ribonucleic Acid Metabolism in Mammalian Cells," *New Engl. J. Med., 276* (1967), 502.

Petermann, M. L., *The Physical and Chemical Properties of Ribosomes.* Amsterdam: Elsevier Publishing Company, 1964. A thorough account.

Prescott, D. M., "Cellular Sites of RNA Synthesis," *Progr. Nucleic Acid Res. Mol. Biol., 3* (1964), 33. A review that stresses autoradiographic and kinetic experiments.

Roberts, R. B., R. J. Britten, and B. J. McCarthy, "Kinetic Studies of the Synthesis of RNA and Ribosomes," in *Molecular Genetics,* Pt. I, J. H. Taylor, ed. New York: Academic Press, Inc., 1963, p. 292. Review of kinetic studies on formation of ribosomal precursors and ribosomes in *E. coli.* The sequence of events described in this article may be compared with that outlined in Fig. 6.7 and the reference cited therein for ribosomes of higher organisms.

Singer, M. F., and P. Leder, "Messenger RNA: An Evaluation," *Ann. Rev. Biochem., 35,* Pt. I (1966), 195. An excellent review that critically examines the properties of mRNA and means of its detection.

Spirin, A. S., *Macromolecular Structure of Ribonucleic Acids,* J. A. Stékol, transl. New York: Reinhold Publishing Corporation, 1964. A good review of RNA structure and its role in ribosome structure.

Vincent, W. S., and O. L. Miller, Jr., eds., "International Symposium on the Nucleolus, Its Structure and Function," *Natl. Cancer Inst. Monogr., 23* (1967). Original work on the fine structure, biochemistry, and genetic control of nucleoli are presented together where one may compare methodology and form an integrated picture of our present knowledge and its limitations.

Zachau, H. G., and H. Feldmann, "Amino Acid Esters of RNA, Nucleosides, and Related Compounds," *Progr. Nucleic Acid Res. Mol. Biol., 4* (1965), 217. Review of chemical studies on aminoacyl tRNA and other amino acid esters.

Lengyel, P., and D. Söll, "Mechanism of Protein Biosynthesis," *Bacteriol. Reviews 33* (1969), 264-301.

Seven

Protein Biosynthesis:
The Process

The main components of the protein-synthesizing machinery are described in Chapter 6. Each of these plays a key role in the process and is of particular significance from the standpoint of genetics. In addition to these components, protein biosynthesis requires the concerted and sequential efforts of a number of enzymes as well as the input of energy. The detailed steps in protein synthesis are being studied intensively at the present time. Our main emphasis here will be on the general framework of the process and its relationship to genetic control.

Amino Acid Incorporation

The incorporation of radioactive amino acids into protein is conveniently followed by precipitating the proteins and larger polypeptides with acid. The amino acids and small peptides remain soluble. The amount of radioactive amino acid that becomes *acid-insoluble* during incubation is an initial measure of the extent of protein synthesis.

Several criteria can be applied to assure that amino acid incorporation indeed represents the formation of protein—that is, the building of amino acids into polypeptide chains. Labeled amino acid incorporation should be irreversible; that is, no radioactivity should be released from the polypeptide product on subsequent addition of excess nonradioactive amino acid. Labeled amino acid which has been incorporated into protein can be converted into acid-soluble form by hydrolysis of the protein. Chromatographic analysis and identification of the labeled amino acid released from the protein is accepted as evidence of incorporation and protein synthesis. Also employed as a criterion is the observation that amino acid incorporation is prevented by compounds that specifically inhibit protein synthesis, such as chloramphenicol and puromycin.

The general methodology and criteria for studying protein synthesis apply to amino acid incorporation both in vivo and in vitro. In vitro studies allow further resolution and examination of the components of the protein synthesis system. In vitro amino acid incorporation into protein requires ribosomes, mRNA, and a complete set of charged tRNA's. If free amino acids are used in place of the charged tRNA's, then ATP, tRNA's, and aminoacyl tRNA synthetases also are required. These additions usually are sufficient if crude ribosomal preparations and crude synthetase preparations are used in the analyses. However, when the ribosomes are thoroughly washed to eliminate contaminating soluble proteins, and partially purified synthetase preparations are used, it is found that a number of additional protein components are necessary to mediate the assembly of charged tRNA–mRNA–ribosome complexes and the catalysis of peptide-bond formation between amino acids in the growing polypeptide chain. The addition of guanosine triphosphate (GTP) is necessary also.

Polyribosomes as Active Structures

Free 70S ribosomes are not the units most highly active in protein synthesis in normal cells. The most active units are aggregates containing a mRNA molecule to which a number of 70S ribosomes are attached. The ribosomes appear to be spaced along the mRNA molecule as if translating different portions of it. Evidence for the activity of polyribosomes in protein synthesis stems mainly from the incorporation of amino acids into proteins in cell-free and in in-vivo systems. Techniques as illustrated in Fig. 7.1 are often used. Centrifugation through a sucrose gradient separates materials found in cell extracts. The large particulate elements of the cell sediment most rapidly while smaller macromolecules are distributed toward the top of the centrifuge tube.

In the experiment of Fig. 7.1, bacteria were labeled with radioactive uracil. About 1 min later, the cells were disrupted and centrifuged. Centrifugation was done in the cold to reduce loss of the active components by enzymic degradation, and magnesium ion was present to lessen dissociation of ribosomes. The different species of ribosomes were located by examining each centrifuged fraction for its ultraviolet absorption at

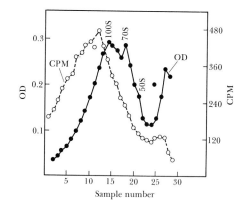

FIG. 7.1. *Sedimentation of radioactivity associated with pulse-labeled RNA. Bacteria infected with bacteriophages were allowed to incorporate radioactive (¹⁴C) uracil for a very brief (pulse) period. They were then broken open, and the unbroken cells and debris of high molecular weight were sedimented from the extract. The clarified extract was then layered on top of a sucrose gradient in a centrifuge tube. The tube was centrifuged for several hours at high speed, the bottom of the tube was punctured with a hypodermic needle, and 10-drop samples were collected for analysis. The optical density (OD) of each sample was measured at 2,600 Å as an indication of its nucleic acid content. Each fraction was precipitated with trichloracetic acid, and its content of radioactive uracil was measured in counts per minute (CPM). The acid-precipitable radioactivity (contained in RNA) was found to be associated predominantly with a rapidly sedimenting fraction greater than 100S in size.*

If a similar extract is prepared from nonradioactive bacteria, allowed to incorporate radioactive amino acids in vitro, and then centrifuged, curves are obtained for OD and CPM that are qualitatively similar to those shown here. This indicates that the fractions containing pulse RNA are the ones competent in protein biosynthesis. Redrawn from R. W. Risebrough, A. Tissieres, and J. D. Watson, Proc. Natl. Acad. Sci. U.S., 48 *(1962), 430.*

a wavelength where nucleic acids strongly absorb. The small amount of newly synthesized material was traced by assaying the various samples for their radioactivity.

The rapidly synthesized RNA of the virus-infected bacteria used to obtain the data in Fig. 7.1 is mRNA. It enters material that sediments faster than the 70S ribosomes. Similar experiments using labeled amino acids show that these also rapidly enter and become fixed for a short time in the same polyribosome fractions. Upon treatment with ribonuclease, radioactivity in the heavy components shifts into the 70S peak. Exposure for several minutes to nonradioactive precursors also displaces much of the label from the heavy fractions to the 70S peak.

Similar types of observations have been made on a wide variety of cells. For example, rabbit reticulocytes that predominantly synthesize the blood protein hemoglobin contain clusters of polyribosomes whose mean size is a pentamer and appear to be the active sites of hemoglobin synthesis (Fig. 7.2).

These experiments demonstrate that attached mRNA allows ribosomes to cluster into polyribosomes and that protein synthesis is associated mainly, if not exclusively, with such polyribosomes. The 70S ribosomes that have completed synthesis may leave the polyribosome cluster with a completed polypeptide chain still attached. The 70S ribosomes are unable to participate in protein synthesis again until they have become reattached to mRNA, after first dissociating to 30S and 50S subunits.

FIG. 7.2. *Polyribosome clusters (sometimes called polysomes) of 80S ribosomes obtained from reticulocytes synthesizing the protein hemoglobin. The most common polyribosome size class contains five 80S ribosomes, although some larger and smaller size classes are also detected. The polyribosomes are held together by mRNA molecules about 1,500 Å long. Magnification: 100,000×. From J. R. Warner, A. Rich, and C. E. Hall,* Science, 138 (1962), 1399. *The mRNA has been dissociated from such polyribosomes and determined to have a sedimentation constant of about 9S, indicating a molecular weight of about 150,000. This is a length sufficient to code for one polypeptide chain, about 145 amino acids long, of a hemoglobin tetramer (see Fig. 2.14). Reviewed in H. Chantrenne,* Arch. Biol., 76 (1965), 307, *and H. Chantrenne, A. Burny, and G. Marbaix,* Progr. Nucleic Acid Res. Mol. Biol., 7 (1967), 173.

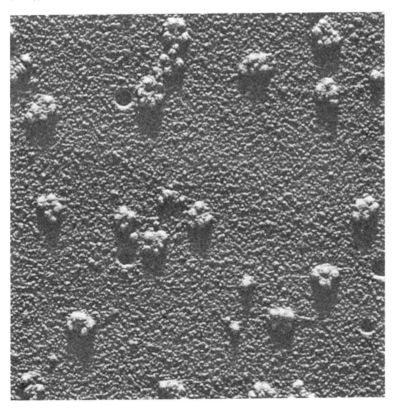

Association of mRNA and Ribosomes

The singular primary structure of a species of polypeptide chains dictates that all chains begin at identical and end at identical positions. How are the chains so precisely initiated and terminated?

Proper binding between mRNA and ribosomes is an essential step in translation of the message into the amino acid sequence of a polypeptide chain. It ensures polypeptide chain initiation at the proper positions on the messenger. Early in vitro studies on the interaction of mRNA and ribosomes or their subunits relied on the position of radioactivity in sucrose density-gradient experiments akin to that shown in Fig. 7.1. mRNA is added to ribosomes and the complexes are centrifuged. The complexes can be followed by using radioactive mRNA or by allowing incorporation of radioactive amino acids prior to centrifugation. These early studies suggested that mRNA binding could occur to the 30S component of 70S ribosomes and to the isolated 30S subunits but not to free 50S subunits. Binding occurs with various synthetic mRNA's containing, for example, only uracil (poly-U) or only adenine (poly-A). The sole requirement is for a fairly high concentration of a cation, usually magnesium; binding of mRNA to 70S ribosomes occurs at low temperature and requires no energy, GTP, or aminoacyl tRNA.

More recent experiments suggest that the earlier observed mRNA-ribosome binding is, in part, an in vitro artifact. Although able to lead to amino acid incorporation in vitro, the binding is less specific than operates in vivo. More specific attachment of ribosomes to mRNA can be achieved in vitro by lowering the magnesium-ion concentration to a more physiological level (about 0.005 M). Furthermore, more carefully prepared cell extracts contain few free 70S ribosomes, but free 30S and 50S ribosome subunits are present. It appears that the free 30S ribosomal component, a protein factor, and a special "initiating" charged tRNA molecule first form a complex with mRNA under normal in vivo conditions. This complex next unites with a 50S ribosomal component to give rise to the 70S ribosome active in peptide-bond formation. When this active 70S ribosome moves along the message, attachment of another 30S subunit takes place at the initiating site on the mRNA and the process is repeated, leading to polyribosome formation (Fig. 7.3). We will return to this subject later in this chapter and again in Chap. 9.

The mRNA–tRNA–Ribosome Complex

The attachment of tRNA to ribosomes can be studied in sucrose density gradients or by pouring the tRNA-ribosome mixture through a cellulose nitrate filter. In the latter instance, free tRNA

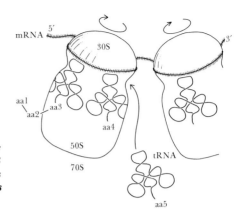

FIG. 7.3. *One portion of a polyribosome active in protein synthesis. Each 70S ribosome component is pictured as rotating as the code in the mRNA is successively read.*

passes through whereas that bound to ribosomes is trapped on the filter. Studies of this type indicate that there are two high-affinity attachment sites for tRNA on the 50S component of the ribosome. This attachment does not require that the tRNA be charged with an amino acid. It does require the presence of the −C−C−A end (see Fig. 6.3) and high concentrations of magnesium ion. There are some 20 to 50 additional sites to which tRNA can bind with lower affinity.

The binding of tRNA as well as that of mRNA is greatly costimulated. The two RNA species act synergistically, and the associations are specific. For example, poly-U binding to ribosomes is enhanced in the presence of tRNA for phenylalanine, a tRNA species that "recognizes" the UUU sequence; also, the presence of poly-U, which contains the UUU coding sequence for phenylalanine, stimulates phenylalanine tRNA binding. Even more strikingly, short synthetic polynucleotide mRNA's behave similarly; the cooperative binding is only strong when the tiny synthetic mRNA's are trinucleotides or longer. This is one indication that the genetic code is read in series of three-letter sequences. By use of various short and long polymers of known sequence, such binding studies have facilitated the elucidation of the genetic code (see Chap. 8).

In contrast to the binding in the absence of mRNA, the binding of tRNA in the presence of mRNA occurs on the 30S ribosomal component. Again, a high magnesium concentration is necessary to achieve binding. Although a useful instrument for in vitro studies and relatively specific in nature, the binding is not truly physiological. At lower magnesium-ion concentrations, and in the presence of mRNA, only a special "initiator" tRNA is bound to the 30S ribosomal subunit. Other tRNA's are not bound to the complex until 50S components are added. In the formation of the resultant complex—30S component–mRNA–tRNA–50S component—a second high-affinity binding site is created on the 50S subunit. This is the prelude to peptide bond formation and growth of the polypeptide chain.

The aminoacyl tRNA molecules are the immediate precursors of the amino acids in protein. The amino acids do not again become free before incorporation. When tRNA, charged with radioactive amino acid, is added to the mRNA-containing ribosomes, the radioactive amino acid rapidly becomes incorporated into polypeptide chains that are first found associated with the polyribosomes and are later released as soluble proteins. If a great excess of nonradioactive free amino acid is added to such a system, the incorporation of the tRNA-bound radioactive amino acid into protein is not decreased.

The polypeptide chains that are bound to the ribosomes contain single tRNA molecules attached to the C-terminal end of each polypeptide chain (Fig. 7.3). The tRNA molecules are not altered by their binding to the ribosome and the subsequent transfer of the amino acid to the growing polypeptide chain. The tRNA molecules are free to pick up another charge of specific amino acid for transport to the sites of protein synthesis. The fact that amino acids attached to tRNA are incorporated directly into protein without the addition of activating enzymes shows that incorporation into polypeptide chains is not mediated by the aminoacyl tRNA synthetases. Indeed, other enzymes have been found which participate in the linear growth of the polypeptide chain.

Growth of the Polypeptide Chain—from N- to C-Terminal

That a tRNA molecule is attached to the C-terminal end of a polypeptide chain extracted from ribosomes suggests that the chain grows linearly, starting at the N-terminal end and progressing toward the C-terminal end. Better evidence for this linear growth is derived from the following experiment (Fig. 7.4).

Rabbit reticulocytes (cells that synthesize predominantly hemoglobin) contain ribosomes with incomplete hemoglobin polypeptide chains of various length (time t_1 in Fig. 7.4). After various times of exposure to radioactive amino acids (time t_2, time t_3, time t_4), the soluble hemoglobin is separated from the ribosomes. The incomplete polypeptide chains are dissociated from the ribosomes and subjected to tryptic digestion, and the soluble hemoglobin also is treated with trypsin (the vertical lines in the figure indicate places where trypsin fragments the molecules). The various peptide fragments, whose sequence in the hemoglobin molecules is known, are then characterized and analyzed for the presence or absence of radioactivity.

The experimental results matched those depicted in the figure. At short times of exposure to radioactive amino acid, label was found near the C-terminal (finish) end in soluble hemoglobin. With increasing time, the label penetrated deeper into the molecule, with a gradient of label through the array of peptides that decreased with increasing time.

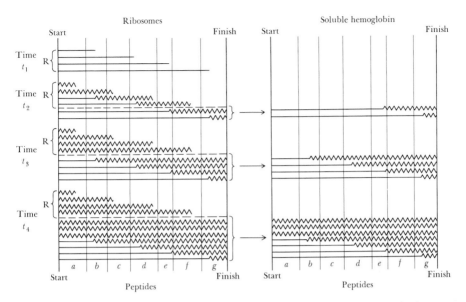

FIG. 7.4. *Model of sequential chain growth from the N-terminal to the C-terminal end. The experiment is described in the text. The straight lines represent unlabeled polypeptide chains. The zigzag lines represent radioactive polypeptide chains formed after the addition of a radioactive amino acid at time t_1. The groups of peptides designated R are unfinished and remain attached to the ribosomes. The rest of the chains, having been completed, are assumed to be present in the soluble hemoglobin. In the ribosomes at time t_2, the top two lines represent peptide chains formed completely from amino acids during the time interval between t_1 and t_2. The middle two lines represent chains that have grown during the time interval but have not reached the finish line and are, therefore, still attached to the ribosomes. The bottom two chains represent those that have crossed the finish line, left the ribosomes, and are to be found mixed with other molecules of soluble hemoglobin. Redrawn from H. M. Dintzis and P. M. Knopf, in* Informational Macromolecules, **H. J. Vogel** *et al., eds., New York: Academic Press, Inc., 1963, p. 376.*

The incomplete peptide fragments on the ribosomes were approximately uniformly labeled at early time (time t_1) and as time went on developed a gradient that was the reverse of the gradient in the soluble hemoglobin.

In addition to demonstrating that growth of the polypeptide chain progresses from N-terminal to C-terminal ends, this experiment is one of the best demonstrations that chain growth actually occurs on the ribosomes.

Figure 7.5 indicates schematically one highly simplified idea of how elongation of the polypeptide chain may proceed. There are two highly effective sites on the ribosome (shaded) where tRNA molecules are tightly bound; the presence of a tRNA molecule in one site (the *donor*

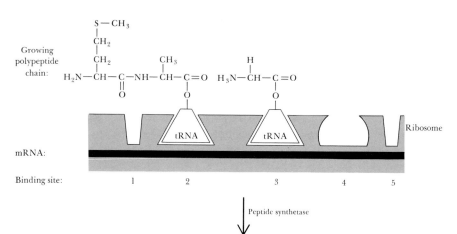

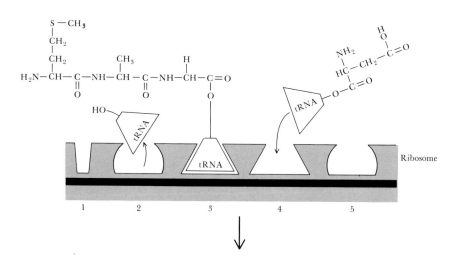

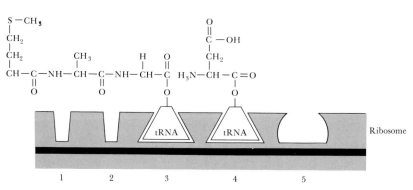

site) activates the adjacent (*acceptor*) *site* for this binding. These two tRNA molecules are shown in sites 2 and 3 at the top of Fig. 7.5. The precise tRNA to be bound is selected by the base sequence in the mRNA. The growing polypeptide chain is attached to the first of these two tRNA molecules in the "donor" site. Shortly after the second tRNA enters with its amino acid, an enzyme, peptidyl transferase (peptide polymerase or peptide synthetase), transfers the growing peptide from the donor tRNA to the newly arrived aminoacyl tRNA in the acceptor site. The conformation of site 2 is changed, squeezing out the deacylated tRNA molecule that formerly held the growing polypeptide chain, and site 4 is in a high-affinity conformation ready for the next tRNA molecule specific for the subsequent sequence on the mRNA. The transformation of sites may be achieved by an enzyme (s), a "translocase." At the bottom of Fig. 7.5, the new tRNA molecule is shown bound to site 4, ready for the action of peptidyl transferase. The process is repeated stepwise until the peptide chain is completed. A tRNA that starts the polypeptide chain can be pictured as having the conformation to bind to any one of the sites, each site being structured partially by the 30S ribosomal component and partially by the 50S ribosomal component. The peptidyl transferase and translocase contributed by the 50S ribosomal component may activate the neighboring site and initiate the sequence of events leading to sequential building of the polypeptide chain.

Of various inhibitors of these reactions, puromycin appears to release peptide attached to tRNA at the donor site, chlortetracyline may inhibit tRNA binding to the acceptor site, chloramphenicol the peptidyl transferase, and erythromycin the translocation enzyme.

FIG. 7.5. *Some steps in growth of the polypeptide chain.*

Binding sites on the ribosome allow orientation of charged tRNA molecules and messenger RNA. Although there are a large number of binding sites for tRNA, only two are active at one time on each ribosome. One of the tRNA molecules is responsible for maintaining the nascent polypeptide chain bound to the ribosome. The second tRNA enters a site adjacent to the one containing the polypeptide chain (top). Peptide synthetase catalyzes the formation of a peptide bond between the incoming amino acid and the polypeptide chain. The products of this reaction are deacylated tRNA, which then leaves the ribosome, and a polypeptide chain, which has increased by one amino acid in length. A new, charged tRNA, specific for the messenger RNA, at site 4, enters this activated site (center) ready for a repetition of the sequence of events (bottom). A series of sites that undergo conformational changes are shown, alternating between inactive and active states. It is also possible that a ribosome merely contains only one active donor and one active acceptor site. For discussions of observations underlying this model, consult R. Schweet and R. Heintz, Ann. Rev. Biochem., 35, Pt. 2 (1966), 723; H. Noll, in Developmental and Metabolic Control Mechanisms and Neoplasia (University of Texas M. D. Anderson Hospital and Tumor Institute Nineteenth Annual Symposium on Fundamental Cancer Research), Austin: University of Texas Press, 1966; G. Attardi, Ann. Rev. Microbiol., 21 (1967), 383; H. P. Ghosh and H. G. Khorana, Proc. Natl. Acad. Sci. U.S., 58 (1967), 2455.

Termination of the polypeptide chain, pictured as the end of a particular part of the message, may be due either to entry of a special tRNA with no amino acid attached or to absence of any tRNA (either charged or uncharged) for the particular sequence on the mRNA. One of several enzymes (release factors) is involved in the hydrolysis of the polypeptide chain from the final tRNA to which it is attached. The polypeptide chain is then released.

These events in protein synthesis, speculative to be sure, are being questioned in many research laboratories; the current literature will provide you with developments we are unable even to outline now.

Translation of mRNA—from 5′ to 3′

The polypeptide chain grows in a linear fashion from the N- to the C-terminal. Its sequential synthesis is mediated by adaptor tRNA molecules and is based upon the chemical information in the mRNA template. We have seen that RNA molecules also have a polarized direction; this is due to the orientation of the 3′- and 5′-phosphodiester linkages (Figs. 6.8 and 7.6). mRNA molecules are linear molecules synthesized by the addition of the nucleoside triphosphates to the 3′-hydroxyl group of the preceding nucleotide in the chain (review Chap. 6). Hence growth of the chain during mRNA synthesis (transcription) is said to occur in the direction 5′ to 3′. Although some conjectural reports earlier appeared in the literature, it is now clear that mRNA is read (translation) in the same direction that it is synthesized—from 5′ to 3′.

Two lines of evidence support this contention. Both lines of evidence are based on our current knowledge of the genetic code. Although the genetic code will come in for more intensive scrutiny in Chap. 8, experiments pertinent to the direction of messenger translation will be described here for additional background.

FIG. 7.6. *The direction of synthesis of mRNA (transcription) is oriented identically with the order in which it is used as a template for protein synthesis (translation).*

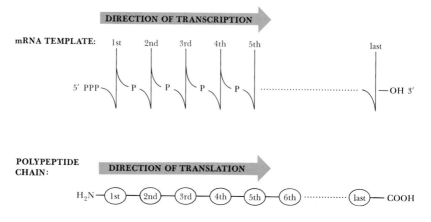

The first type of experiment utilizes synthetic ribopolynucleotides of known composition and/or sequence which can be made in several ways. The earliest method used for preparing these polynucleotides was enzymic synthesis with polynucleotide phosphorylase extracted from microbial cells. This enzyme differs from DNA- or RNA-primed RNA polymerase in several ways. Polynucleotide phosphorylase uses nucleoside diphosphates as substrates instead of the triphosphates. The equilibrium of the reaction is strongly in the direction of ribopolynucleotide breakdown rather than synthesis, although enough synthesis occurs to use the reaction for the preparation of polynucleotides in vitro. Most important, the composition and sequence of the polymer depends heavily upon the relative concentrations of the dinucleotide substrates in the incubation mixture rather than on the base sequence of a primer DNA or RNA molecule. Consequently, polynucleotide phosphorylase proved to be inappropriate as the catalyst in a replicative or copying scheme for mRNA. Its function in vivo remains uncertain, but it is thought to be related to some aspect of RNA breakdown. Nevertheless, the enzyme proved exceedingly useful for the in vitro synthesis of various types of copolymers where base composition could be chemically determined and triplet frequencies calculated statistically knowing the number and concentration of nucleoside diphosphates employed in the reaction mixture.

Since polynucleotide phosphorylase also catalyzes the addition of nucleotides to preexistant polynucleotide chains, one can construct "block polymers" with very short sequences known. For example, incubation of ApU and polynucleotide phosphorylase in the presence of GDP gives rise to polymers of the type ApUpGpGpGp...G, containing various numbers of guanine nucleotides (mixed chain lengths). The products can be separated chromatographically (for example, ApUpG from ApUpGpG from ApUpGpGpG, and so on) and these products used in a second reaction mixture with the enzyme and, let us say, UDP. In this case, addition of ApUpG to initiate the reaction will lead to synthesis of the polymer ApUpGpUpUp . . . U. Addition of ApUpGpG will give rise to ApUpGpGpUpUp...U, and so on. Other more complicated initiating sequences of known order can be obtained by more intricate treatments and fractionations. Furthermore, the specificity of two different ribonucleases assist the preparation of pure types of polymers. Pancreatic ribonuclease attacks natural and synthetic polynucleotides at pyrimidine residues. This allows the construction, for example, of a chain of A's terminating in a U or C from chains having variable numbers of U's or C's at the end. Another ribonuclease, T1 RNase, preferentially hydrolyzes adjacent to guanine residues.

The most elegant method of preparation of large polyribonucleotides of known sequence utilizes chemically synthesized short deoxyribonucleotides of known repeating sequences as primer for DNA polymerase. The DNA polymerase repeatedly copies the short primer DNA into long redundant sequences. This product, then, is used as primer for

DNA-dependent RNA polymerase and the enzymatic manufacture of synthetic messenger RNA's of known sequence results. Remarkable as it may seem, numerous studies, including nearest-neighbor analyses, demonstrate the fidelity of copying by the DNA and RNA polymerases.

The various synthetic polymers have proved extremely useful in establishing the genetic code. They have also established the orientation of reading of mRNA. Two of the more simple polymers will illustrate this latter use. Work with larger and more complicated polymers confirms these observations.

One polymer was isolated having the sequence ApApApUpUpU (we shall use the designation A_3U_3 as shorthand for this polymer). When placed in an amino acid–incorporating system, this polymer stimulated the synthesis of the product lysylphenylalanine; no phenylalanyllysine was made (Fig. 7.7). Since poly-A alone stimulates lysine incorporation and poly-U stimulates phenylalanine incorporation, one concludes that the 5'-ApApA end of the block polymer led to N-terminal incorporation of lysine, whereas the UpUpU-3' end of the block polymer led to C-terminal incorporation of phenylalanine. The product, lysylphenylalanine, was shown to contain both lysine and phenylalanine, and it behaved chromatographically as expected and differently from synthetic phenylalanyllysine. Finally, the synthesized product, lysylphenylalanine, was split by carboxypeptidase A; this enzyme splits at the N-ter-

FIG. 7.7. *Outline of experiments demonstrating the synthesis of lysylphenylalanine from the block polymer ApApApUpUpU (termed A_3U_3 below). After R. E. Thach, M. A. Cecere, T. A. Sundararajan, and P. Doty, Proc. Natl. Acad. Sci. U.S., 54 (1965), 1167.*

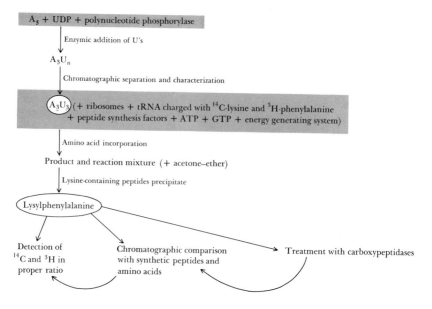

minal side of aromatic amino acid residues. Carboxypeptidase B, which preferentially acts at the C-terminal side of aromatic residues, failed to act on the product.

A similar experiment was carried out with a longer polymer having an Ap repeating sequence terminating in C. When placed in an amino acid–incorporating system, this polymer led to the synthesis of a polypeptide chain of lysine residues containing a C-terminal asparagine.

The results of amino acid incorporation using polymers of known sequence as mRNA demonstrate that the message is read from 5' to 3' in vitro. In vivo studies confirm this observation. The in vivo studies involve the use of mutants in which bases have become added or deleted from the DNA. Analysis of the amino acid sequences of proteins isolated from wild-type and appropriate mutants, and inspection of the known codon assignments for the affected amino acids, allows a perfect correspondence if reading in vivo also occurs 5' to 3'. Attempts to construct alternative mRNA coding sequences which would allow 3' to 5' reading have been unsuccessful. The concordance of 5' to 3' reading with the established genetic code, in every instance so far examined, constitutes strong evidence that the in vitro results with synthetic polymers reflects intracellular events: mRNA is read 5' to 3', the same direction in which it is synthesized.

The Overall Scheme

In Chapter 3 we discussed evidence for the colinearity between the genetic map and the amino acid sequence of the protein. We have now seen the importance of another linear polymer, mRNA, as an intermediate between the master template, DNA, and the polypeptide chain. The information for the linear sequence of amino acids in the polypeptide chain is contained in the sequence of bases in the mRNA, and this template is read from its 5' to its 3' termini. The amino acid residues of the polypeptide chain are added consecutively from the N- to the C-terminal end. We are forced to conclude that all three molecules are colinear. As you progress through the remainder of this book, you will find other experiments mentioned that substantiate this conclusion.

The rate of formation of these cellular products is amazingly rapid in the bacterium *E. coli*. A conservative estimate would specify 5 min, one-twelfth of a generation time, for the synthesis of an mRNA molecule 3,000 nucleotides long, or 10 nucleotide pairs per second. To account for the production of new hemoglobin in reticulocytes, it has been estimated that these cells must, on the average, make one polypeptide chain of hemoglobin per ribosome every $1\frac{1}{2}$ min. Since there are about 150 amino acids per hemoglobin chain, these estimates indicate that the polypeptide chains grow at a rate of about 2 amino acids per second.

In spite of their speed, the processes of RNA and of protein synthesis are highly coordinated. Figure 7.8 reviews some critical steps in protein biosynthesis as we picture them at the current time. Amino acids are selected from the intracellular amino acid pool by specific aminoacyl RNA synthetases. The activated amino acids remain attached to the enzymes until they are transferred to specific tRNA molecules. The amino acid–tRNA molecules become bound to ribosomes actively engaged in protein synthesis (polyribosomes) and are specifically oriented in the proper positions on the template mRNA. The mRNA, synthesized along one strand of the duplex DNA molecule, is bound to the ribosome in a manner that makes it accessible to the amino acid–tRNA molecules. The polypeptide chain is initiated at the N-terminal end. Amino acids are added to the growing C-terminal end of the polypeptide chain one at a time in a reaction catalyzed by an enzyme system composed of peptidyl transferase and translocase. The specific organization and alignment of amino acids in the chain is dictated by the base sequence of the mRNA, which selects the correct complementary base sequence from the pool of charged tRNA molecules. The polypeptide chain appears to fold into the final biologically active configuration while still attached to the ribosome. In release from the ribosome, the completed polypeptide chain is enzymatically hydrolyzed from the last tRNA molecule to which it was attached.

What Next?

What are the unique structural features of active ribosomes that allow adsorption and release of mRNA and that allow such rapid and specific attachment and transfer of amino acids by the sRNA molecules? What determines the N- and C-terminal ends of a protein? What are the mechanisms underlying the linking of amino acids into a polypeptide chain? What determines that the polypeptide chain will be released from the template once its sequence is complete? What is the fate of mRNA? Do different mRNA molecules function different numbers of times? What is the basis for the dual specificity of the tRNA molecule (for both a specific amino acid and a particular site on the mRNA-ribosome template)? Are all cellular proteins synthesized through the intermediary of charged tRNA molecules?

Many important questions remain to be answered, and even the fundamental hypotheses behind our model are continually being subjected to more critical experimental tests in the laboratory. Remember that the scheme in Fig. 7.8 is a diagrammatic, simplified picture of our notions and not analogous to an actual photograph of an existing

FIG. 7.8. *A model for the genetic control of protein biosynthesis. The organization of genes into operons and the synthesis of more than one protein from a single mRNA molecule are topics discussed in Chaps. 9 and 10.*

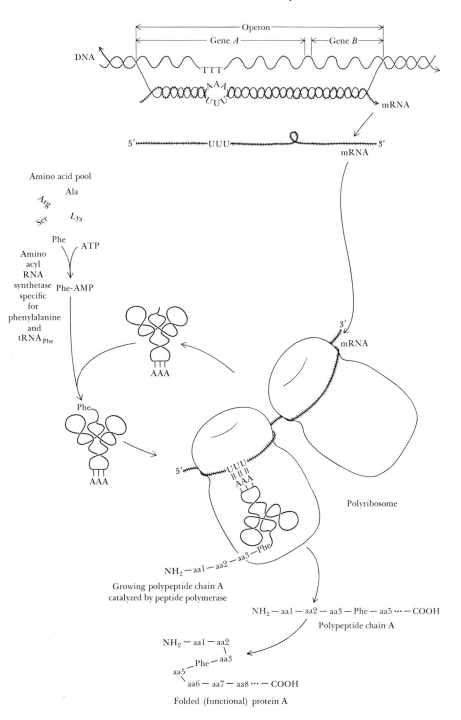

Growing polypeptide chain A
catalyzed by peptide polymerase

NH_2 — aa1 — aa2 — aa3 — Phe — aa5 ··· — COOH
Polypeptide chain A

Folded (functional) protein A

assembly line in a real factory! At the risk of preaching, may we suggest that in all intellectual ventures and especially in science, a receptive mind, unprejudiced by immutable models, is a true asset. Nevertheless, there are advantages to conceptual models consistent with the best data currently available. With such models in mind, further experiments can most readily be designed to explore, verify, extend, modify, or even eliminate hypotheses.

So for its utility, let us retain this model; and as you read further in this book, you will find that the principles fundamental to it will be helpful in understanding a number of genetic phenomena.

Questions

7.1. What components are required in an in vitro amino acid–incorporating system?

7.2. In tabular form, list the function of each component in an amino acid–incorporating system.

7.3. What features of protein biosynthesis pointed out schematically in Fig. 7.8 require more substantiation than is given in this chapter? Describe what you consider to be three important voids in our knowledge.

7.4. How does tRNA recognize the proper activating enzyme? How does tRNA recognize the proper position on the template mRNA?

7.5. Write a brief summary of the purpose and results of a paper reporting on original research published within the last 12 months and pertaining to the subject of this chapter.

7.6. What forces hold the 30S and 50S components of ribosomes together? What forces hold the mRNA to the ribosome? The tRNA to the ribosome?

7.7. Of what importance is the fact that the direction of transcription *and* translation is $5' \rightarrow 3'$?

7.8. What is the function of peptidyl transferase? Of translocase?

7.9. What properties of polynucleotide phosphorylase lead to the view that it is not involved in mRNA synthesis in vivo?

7.10. You know that tRNA's bind to specific trinucleotides in the presence of ribosomes, and you can obtain triplets of known composition and sequence. Can you describe a series of experiments that will assist in analysis of the genetic code?

7.11. In what way is tRNA binding to ribosomes and ribosomal subunits influenced by the level of magnesium ion? Set out your information in tabular form for 70S, 30S, and 50S components in the categories of high and low magnesium-ion concentration.

7.12. What results would you expect from the Dintzis experiment (Fig. 7.4) if you had taken the newly synthesized free hemoglobin and exposed it to carboxypeptidase? To aminopeptidase?

7.13. What "practical" applications can you think of that could be developed from a firm knowledge of the biochemistry of protein synthesis in various organisms?

References

Attardi, G., "The Mechanism of Protein Synthesis," *Ann. Rev. Microbiol., 21* (1967) , 383. One of the better modern reviews.

Campbell, P. N., "The Biosynthesis of Proteins," *Progr. Biophys. Mol. Biol., 15* (1965) , 1.

Cold Spring Harbor Symp. Quant. Biol., 28 (1963) ; *31* (1966) . Two excellent symposium volumes containing many original papers on topics described in this chapter.

Koningsberger, V. V., and L. Bosch, eds., *Regulation of Nucleic Acid and Protein Biosynthesis,* Biochimica Biophysica Acta Library, Vol. 10. Amsterdam: Elsevier Publishing Company, 1967. Thirty-four papers presented at a 1966 symposium and partially overlapping, partially complementing topics in the 1966 Cold Spring Harbor Symposium held in the same month and published under a 1966 dateline.

Lipmann, F., Y. Nishizuka, J. Gordon, J. Lucas-Lenard, and M. Gottesman, "Bacterial Amino Acid Polymerization," in *Organizational Biosynthesis,* H. J. Vogel, J. O. Lampen, and V. Bryson, eds. New York: Academic Press, Inc., 1967, p. 131.

Mans, R. J., "Protein Synthesis in Higher Plants," *Ann. Rev. Plant Physiol., 18* (1967) , 127.

Monro, R. E., B. E. H. Maden, and R. R. Traut, "The Mechanism of Peptide Bond Formation in Protein Synthesis," in *Genetic Elements: Properties and Function,* D. Shugar, ed. New York: Academic Press, Inc., 1967, p. 179.

Neidhardt, F. C., "Roles of Amino Acid Activating Enzymes in Cellular Physiology," *Bact. Rev., 30* (1966) , 701. A clearly written discussion of work on mutant aminoacyl tRNA synthetases and information it has provided relating to cellular control mechanisms.

Novelli, G. D., "Amino Acid Activation for Protein Synthesis," *Ann. Rev. Biochem., 36* (1967) , 449.

Rich, A., "Polyribosomes." *Sci. Am., 209* (Dec. 1963) , 44. A nicely illustrated description of the discovery of polyribosomes.

Schweet, R., and J. Bishop, "Protein Synthesis in Relation to Gene Action," in *Molecular Genetics,* Part I, J. H. Taylor, ed. New York: Academic Press, Inc., 1963, Chap. VIII. A good, relatively concise and up-to-date review of the steps in protein biosynthesis with references to the original literature.

———, and R. Heintz, "Protein Synthesis," *Ann. Rev. Biochem., 35,* Pt. II (1966) , 723. A recent compilation of observations and references to the literature, stressing biochemical aspects.

Volkin, E., "Biosynthesis of RNA in Relation to Genetic Coding Problems," in *Molecular Genetics,* Part I, J. H. Taylor, ed. New York: Academic Press, Inc., 1963, p. 271. A particularly good account of observations leading to the implication of mRNA as the key carrier of genetic information from the DNA to the production of proteins.

Zamecnik, P. C., "Historical and Current Aspects of the Problem of Protein Synthesis," *Harvey Lectures, 54* (1960) , 256.

———, "Unsettled Questions in the Field of Protein Synthesis," *Biochem. J., 85* (1962) , 257.

The Genetic Code

This chapter will bring together experimental evidence that outlines many general, and some specific, features of the genetic code.

The generalization will be made that primary gene action consists of the transcription of the coded genetic information in DNA into the ribopolynucleotide sequence of mRNA and the subsequent translation of this information, contained in the four-letter alphabet, A, U, G, and C, of mRNA, into specific amino acid sequences. We will find that the four-letter alphabet is arranged into adjacent, nonoverlapping, three-letter words or coding units (*codons*). Each codon in the mRNA molecule dictates the positioning of a specific amino acid in a polypeptide chain.

General Types of Codes

Figure 8.1 shows some theoretical types of codes. In Fig. 8.1*a*, discontinuous groups of nucleotides code for two amino acids, aa1 and aa2, that are adjacent to each other in the polypeptide chain. In Figs. 8.1*b–d*, the codons are short, continuous sections of the polynucleotide chain; but in Fig. 8.1*b* the codons overlap, whereas in Figs. 8.1*c* and 8.1*d* they do not. Overlapping means that a particular nucleotide serves in more than one codon. Finally, Figs.

(*a*) Discontinuous:

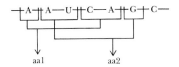

(*b*) Continuous, overlapping:

(*1*) Double-letter overlap

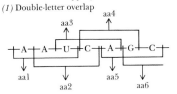

(*2*) Single-letter overlap

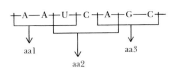

(*c*) Continuous, nonoverlapping, with commas:

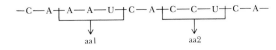

(*d*) Continuous, nonoverlapping, commaless:

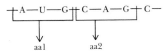

FIG. 8.1. *General theoretical coding possibilities of mRNA containing the four bases A, U, G, and C.*

8.1*c* and 8.1*d* differ in that Fig. 8.1*c* contains spacers (commas) between the codons.

The information presented in this chapter will rule out general models shown in Figs. 8.1*a–c*, while remaining compatible with the model shown in Fig. 8.1*d*. The codons appear to be short, continuous, adjacent sections of the polynucleotide chain.

Deciphering the Code

Four main types of experimental approaches have yielded most of the current information on the general nature of the genetic code and on the nucleotide compositions and nucleotide sequences of the codons themselves.

The first method is analysis of the primary structures of wild-type and mutant proteins (Chapter 3). In each of the mutant proteins so far analyzed, a mutant amino acid replaces a particular wild-type amino acid. The accumulation of data on such amino acid replacement sets restrictions on the genetic code, as will be indicated in later sections of this chapter.

The second method is the use of synthetic ribopolynucleotides to stimulate amino acid incorporation in cell-free systems. The third method depends upon the mutual enhancement of *binding* to ribosomes of specific tRNA's and of synthetic mRNA's of various chain size and base sequence.

The final means of delineating the genetic code involves inference from the results of purely genetical experiments. The experiments are of a variety of types. Some consider the activities of certain mutagens in reversing particular kinds of mutations; others involve placing two or

FIG. 8.2. *The genetic code. The table shows the code words, or codons, using the designations based on mRNA nucleotides. Each word is composed of three nucleotides, a triplet. Beginning at the 5′ end, the letters are read from the left column, the top, and the right column, respectively. Thus AUG is the codon for Met, methionine. The abbreviations for amino acids are the same as those presented in Fig. 2.2. The triplets shown as "ochre," "amber," and "nonsense" are described in the text. The codons depicted here pertain to E. coli because to date most critical research on the code has been performed using this organism. Studies on other organisms are sufficient to support the statement that the code is universal; that is, the code is very similar, if not identical, in all forms of life.*

1st letter	2nd letter				3rd letter
	U	C	A	G	
U	Phe	Ser	Tyr	Cys	U
	Phe	Ser	Tyr	Cys	C
	Leu	Ser	Ochre	Nonsense	A
	Leu	Ser	Amber	Trp	G
C	Leu	Pro	His	Arg	U
	Leu	Pro	His	Arg	C
	Leu	Pro	Gln	Arg	A
	Leu	Pro	Gln	Arg	G
A	Ile	Thr	Asn	Ser	U
	Ile	Thr	Asn	Ser	C
	Ile	Thr	Lys	Arg	A
	Met	Thr	Lys	Arg	G
G	Val	Ala	Asp	Gly	U
	Val	Ala	Asp	Gly	C
	Val	Ala	Glu	Gly	A
	Val	Ala	Glu	Gly	G

more mutations on the same DNA strand and observing the resultant phenotype. Each kind of genetical experiment is described in the section most pertinent to the information it has provided.

It is the observations on mutant proteins and genetic experiments that give us confidence in the genetic code as deduced from in vitro experiments. Furthermore, extraction of various tRNA's from cells and studies of the nucleotide sequences found in certain regions of these isolated tRNA's—all converge to give a single, consistent picture of the code. This is shown in Fig. 8.2 and represents a great achievement of modern genetics. Let us examine some of the evidence for the codon assignments shown in Fig. 8.2.

The Coding Ratio

Recall that there are only four letters available in mRNA: A, U, G, and C. If the coding units for amino acids were composed of just two letters, there would be only 4^2, or 16, possible sequences to code 20 amino acids. Furthermore, there is strong evidence that more than one codon can code for a single amino acid (degeneracy). The shortage of codons in a two-letter code would be circumvented if some other material, for example, the ribosomal RNA, were to assist in the coding. But, as has been shown (Chaps. 3 and 6), such major assistance has been ruled out. Three-letter codons offer 4^3, or 64, possibilities. Codons larger than three letters would seem wasteful but might still be worthy of consideration, except that accumulated evidence already has suggested that such larger units are unlikely.

The coding ratio is equal to the number of nucleotides in the mRNA (or nucleotide pairs in double-stranded DNA) divided by the number of amino acids in the polypeptide chain product; thus it expresses the average number of nucleotides per codon. In each of several genes, the number of nucleotide pairs has been estimated by genetic techniques and compared with the number of amino acid residues of the protein coded by the gene. All the estimates give coding ratios close to three; that is, three nucleotides compose a codon. Such a code is called a *triplet code*. A wide variety of genetic experiments is consistent with a triplet code, but measurement techniques are not precise enough generally to distinguish a ratio of exactly three from a ratio close to three (for example, two, four, or even five or six), except in the case of bacteriophage T4. We mentioned earlier that the mRNA bound to reticulocyte polyribosomes approximates the length of a polynucleotide chain which, assuming a triplet code, would be expected for one of the hemoglobin chains. Although each of these measurements is crude in comparison to the criteria discussed below, they support the concept that the codons in the master template, DNA, and its copy, RNA, are indeed triplets of nucleotides.

Mutations and the Code—Some Jargon

As each branch of science develops, it adopts its own means of communication. The tests of time, usage, chance, and developments in the area determine which bits of jargon become the permanent language of that science. A few terms of recent vintage seem most descriptive and are widely used in molecular genetics today. Figure 8.3 illustrates some of these.

The genetic code presented in Fig. 8.2 is *degenerate*. This means that there is more than one coding unit for a single amino acid, as indicated by the top arrow in Fig. 8.3. Note that degeneracies occur frequently in the *third* letter of the codon; we shall return to this point later. If a codon, for example, AAA, is changed to another codon, for example, AAG, which codes for the *same* amino acid, obviously no amino acid substitution will occur in the protein. Under these conditions, the mutation giving rise to an altered mRNA is expected to remain unobserved in the final phenotype. About the only way we have of detecting such changes at the moment is by mutational analyses. By reference to Fig. 8.2 you can see that Lys codon AAA can mutate by a single-base change to the AUA codon of Ile but not to the AUG codon of Met, and vice versa; the Lys codon AAG can mutate by a single-base change to AUG but not to any of the Ile codons. One assumes that degeneracies in the genetic code would be selected for in evolution, for they would provide a "buffer" against possible deleterious effects of mutation. The proportion of these "silent" mutations is higher among transition mutations involving a substitution of a purine for a purine (A to G or G to A) or a pyrimidine for a pyrimidine.

Besides mutation to a degenerate codon, the coding unit may be changed so that it now represents a codon for a different amino acid (*missense*). Two possibilities are shown in Fig. 8.3. The amino acid substitution caused by a missense mutation may lead to a grossly altered protein if, for example, the acidic amino acid, glutamic acid, replaces the basic amino acid, lysine. This is due to the dependence of the activity of a protein on its tertiary structure and, in turn, the primary structure. The mutant phenotype is readily detected and, in a fingerprint of the protein, the charge difference on the peptide containing the amino acid replacement usually leads to altered migration and subsequent detection. Conversely, the mutation may not be detected as a change in phenotype if the incorrect amino acid that has been inserted in the polypeptide chain does not appreciably change the conformation and subsequent function of the protein product. The missense mutation might be recognized only by examination of the primary structure of the protein, not by examination of other properties of the protein. Some cases of this type were mentioned in Chap. 3. Note from Fig. 8.2 that similar amino acids have similar codons, differing by only one letter. For example, look at the codons for the acidic amino acids,

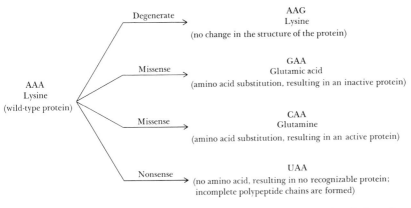

FIG. 8.3. *Some possible phenotypes resulting from one-letter mutational alterations of a hypothetical coding unit.*

Asp and Glu, or for the codons for the basic amino acids, Glu, Asn, Lys, and Arg. In this way selection during evolution may have minimized the effects of mutations on the phenotype.

Finally, in Fig. 8.3, we see that the codon may be changed from sense (lysine) to *nonsense*. There are three nonsense codons: UAA (ochre), UAG (amber), and UGA. They represent triplets that fail to code for an amino acid under normal conditions. Because no amino acid is specified at that position, premature termination of the polypeptide chain results at the position of the *adjacent proximal residue*. We shall return to discuss these three chain-terminating, nonsense codons in Chap. 9. Right now we want to stress evidence for the code itself; in some of these experiments, the nonsense codons serve as "controls."

Adjacent Nucleotides

Most of the basis for establishing code-word assignments has come from in vitro studies of the enhancement of tRNA binding to ribosomes by synthetic ribonucleotide polymers and trinucleotides and from amino acid incorporation work such as that cited in Chap. 7 and later in this chapter. Genetic methods have also offered strong evidence that the individual nucleotides of each coding unit are adjacent to each other in the DNA and mRNA.

In Fig. 3.4 the relationship between the genetic map and amino acid replacements in the *E. coli* tryptophan synthetase A protein was illustrated. The more distantly linked mutations affected amino acid replacements in more distantly related positions in the polypeptide chain. In addition, several mutants having different amino acid replacements at the same residue in the polypeptide chain have been obtained. At

FIG. 8.4. *Amino acid pedigree at position 210 in the tryptophan synthetase A protein of* E. coli. *Many tryptophan-requiring mutants were isolated from wild-type bacteria. Among these mutants, 23 were found to contain CRM's with amino acid replacements at residue 210. Glycine is the amino acid normally present in wild type (Fig. 2.4). Fifteen mutants, including A23, contained arginine at residue 210, one contained valine, and seven mutants, including A46, contained glutamic acid. The genetic sites of the two mutations, A23 and A46, are very close to each other but, nevertheless, are separable by recombination tests (Fig. 3.4). Crosses between them give rise only to the wild type containing Gly at position 210. The proteins of 81 revertants and partial revertants also were analyzed, and the amino acid replacements at residue 210 are listed in the figure. Reference to the genetic code (Fig. 8.2), based mainly on in vitro experiments, allows assignment of codons for each type of mutant. Each mutational event is limited to a single base-pair change. The glutamic acid codon GAA was selected because both the A46 glutamic acid codon and the A23 arginine codon AGA must be related to a common glycine codon; AGA was selected for the A23 arginine codon because only this arginine codon could give rise to the codons corresponding to the amino acids that replace arginine at the A23 position. Here, M indicates that a mutator gene in E. coli greatly increases the frequency of that revertant class; in all cases examined, the codon change is from A to C. Similarly, the base analogue, 2-aminopurine (AP at the arrows in Fig. 8.4) enhances the frequency of certain mutant classes. The "mutator" mutation is one of a class of mutations called "transversions" since it involves a purine-pyrimidine change; the 2-aminopurine–induced mutation is an example of a "transition"-type mutation which involves the substitution of a purine for a purine or a pyrimidine for a pyrimidine. The results of mutation experiments of this kind, correlating supposed base substitutions with amino acid replacements and codon assignments, provide us with the best approach toward understanding the molecular basis of mutagenesis. For further information on chemical mutagenesis, see the reference list (and Stahl, in this series).*

Note in the figure that not all possible single base-pair mutation classes are detected among the revertants. Some classes are lacking, probably due to degeneracy of the code; mutation of the arginine AGA codon to AGG, for example, would still result in the presence of arginine at residue 210 and result in a mutant protein. Other mutation classes also are undetected, presumably because the protein remains inactive when certain other amino acid substitutions occur. For example, mutants in which the AGA arginine codon has mutated to AAA would still contain a basic amino acid, now lysine, at residue 210. Adapted after C. Yanofsky, J. Ito, and V. Horn, **Cold Spring Harbor Symp. Quant. Biol., 31** *(1966), 151. Also see* C. Yanofsky, **Sci. Am., 216** *(May 1967), 80.*

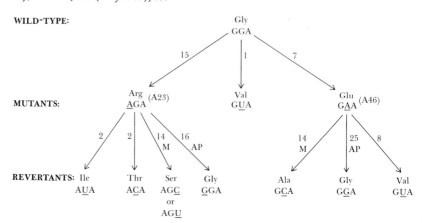

144

residue 233, in place of the glycine normally present in wild type (Fig. 2.4), mutant *A58* contains aspartic acid and mutant *A78* cysteine. These two mutations recombine at very low frequency to yield wild-type bacteria containing glycine at position 233. Similarly, the glycine residue at position 210 has been replaced by an arginine in mutant *A23* and by glumatic acid in mutant *A46* (Fig. 3.4). Crosses of *A23* with *A46* yield wild-type bacteria with very low frequency; the A protein of these bacteria contains glycine at position 210.

Mutational analyses in conjunction with protein chemistry provide additional information on genetic coding in vivo (Fig. 8.4). These experiments show that the codon for an amino acid in the DNA is composed of more than one nucleotide pair. The member nucleotides of a coding unit are contiguous in all cases tested.

Triplet Code

Some critical information on the nature of the coding unit evolved from studies of the mutagenic effects of acridines. A brief digression on the mode of action of an acridine, proflavin, is warranted here, for interpretation of the genetic data depends upon some understanding of the interaction of proflavin with polynucleotide chains.

Proflavin is a powerful mutagen for some bacterial viruses when it is present during DNA replication. Figure 8.5 shows a model, based on physicochemical data, of the interaction of proflavin with native double-stranded DNA. The flat, planar proflavin molecules become intercalated between the stacked nucleotides of the double-stranded DNA, thereby stretching and stiffening the backbone structure of the DNA. Thus proflavin is believed to exert its mutagenic effect by distorting the DNA molecule during replication or during recombination. Intercalation of a proflavin molecule between two nucleotides of one strand of the DNA almost exactly doubles the distance between them. This might allow the insertion of an extra nucleotide in the strand during replication or might shift the paired nucleotides by a single base during the events leading to recombination (that is, lead to unequal crossing over). Through one or both of these mechanisms,

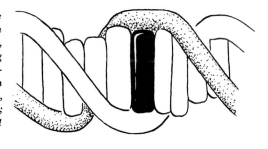

FIG. 8.5. *Acridines (black disk in the figure) are believed to intercalate between the base pairs of the DNA double helix, stretching the backbone and causing mutations through the deletion or addition of one or more base pairs. Based on* L. S. Lerman, Proc. Natl. Acad. Sci. U.S., 49 (1963), 98; J. Mol. Biol., 10 (1964), 367; J. Cellular Comp. Physiol., 64, Suppl. 1 (1964), 1.

Part	Genotype	Phenotype	Description
I	− or +	} Mutant	Individual single-site mutations
II	− − or + +	} Mutant	Double mutants of the same kind
III	− − − − or − − − − −	} Mutant	Quadruple and pentuple mutants of the same kind
IV	− +	} Wild-type	Double mutants of the opposite kind
V	− − − or − − − − − − or + + +	} Wild-type	Triple mutants of the same kind or multiple of triple mutants of the same kind

FIG. 8.6. *Changes in the reading frame. The plus and minus signs denote independently isolated mutants of two classes; the two classes are isolated by selection for their ability to suppress the mutant phenotype of a particular mutant, arbitrarily labeled* − (*in which case the suppressor is denoted* +) *or to suppress one of the* + *mutations* (*in which case the designation is* −). *This wild-type phenotype is indicated in part IV of the table. Each of the mutations individually determines a mutant phenotype (part I), as do any two* + *or any two, four, or five* − *combinations (parts II and III). However, either three or six* − *mutations give rise to the wild-type phenotype, and any three* + *mutations, together on the same chromosome, give a wild-type phenotype (part V). Based on F. H. C. Crick, L. Barnett, S. Brenner, and R. J. Watts-Tobin,* Nature, 191 (*1961*), 1227; *also see* F. H. C. Crick, Sci. Am., 207 (*1962*), 66.

proflavin is believed to lead to the deletion or duplication of one nucleotide pair or several adjacent pairs. What genetic evidence supports such a model of proflavin-induced mutation?

Proflavin-induced mutants revert to the wild-type phenotype spontaneously, and they can be induced to revert at high frequency with additional proflavin treatment. They do not revert to the wild-type phenotype after treatment with mutagens that cause replacements, rather than deletions or additions, of bases in the DNA molecule. (See the discussion of base-pair substitutions presented in the legend of Fig. 8.4.) Conversely, proflavin does not cause analogue-induced mutants to revert. The basic assumption, then, is that proflavin causes a base pair or base pairs to be deleted or duplicated.

In experiments with bacteriophage T4, spontaneous revertants were isolated from a proflavin-induced mutant of the *rIIB* gene. The reversions were not true back mutants to the original nucleotide sequence present in the wild-type DNA. By recombination tests with wild type, these revertants were proved to have a second mutation in the same short section (about a fifth) of the *B* cistron containing the original mutation. Individually, each of the two mutations elicits a mutant phenotype, but together they produce a wild-type phenotype. Because the secondary mutant sites are separable by recombination from the original site of mutation, but are located in the same gene, they are termed intragenic suppressor mutations. These are arbitrarily designated as + mutations in Fig. 8.6, and the original mutation, *a*, is arbitrarily termed a − mutation.

Several of these secondary (+) mutations were separated from the original mutation by recombination with wild type. Further reversions to the wild-type phenotype were isolated from the secondary (+) single-site mutants. Once more, these revertants did not represent true back mutations at the original site but proved instead to be double mutants. The individual single-site mutants from this third class of double mutants also were obtained by recombination with wild type (bottom line of Fig. 8.7).

FIG. 8.7. *Reading-frame interpretation. In this diagram it is assumed that the nucleotide sequence is read from left to right during protein synthesis and that the amino acids at positions 1, 2, and 3 are not critical to the function of the protein but that amino acids beyond position 3 are critical. The − and + mutations are assumed to move the reading frame so that coding triplets are missense or nonsense. The reading frame can be readjusted on center either by a second mutation compensating for the first mutation, as shown here, or by two additional mutations of the same kind as the original single-site mutation. Based on F. H. C. Crick, L. Barnett, S. Brenner, and R. J. Watts-Tobin,* Nature, **191** *(1961), 1227; also see F. H. C. Crick,* Sci. Am., **207** *(1962), 66.*

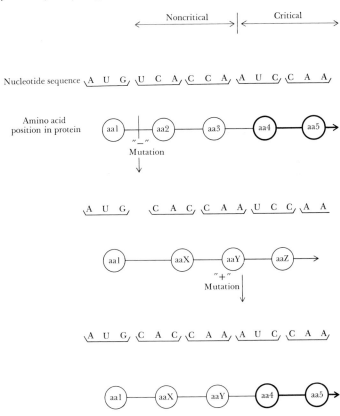

Hence three classes of mutants were recognized: the original single-site *rIIB* mutant (−), suppressors of this original mutant (+), and suppressors of the suppressors (−).

By genetic crosses, recombinants can be obtained having one, two, three, or more of the various − or + mutations in the same gene (*cis* configuration). The various combinations and their phenotypes are shown in Fig. 8.6. Two − mutations or two + mutations are still mutant, whereas most pairs of − and + mutations can form the wild-type phenotype. Furthermore, almost any three − mutations, or any three + mutations also form the wild-type phenotype. Six − mutations also form the wild-type phenotype.

The interpretation of these results is that the mutation shifts the reading frame of a triplet code (see Fig. 8.7). If the code is thrown off by deletion of one letter, the subsequent triplets mainly form missense. This means that the triplet still codes for an amino acid, but

FIG. 8.8. *Effect of frameshift mutations on the amino acid sequence of tryptophan synthetase A protein of* E. coli.

The amino acid sequence of a portion of the wild-type protein is shown in the center of the figure (see Fig. 2.4 for the complete sequence). Single frameshift mutants generally contain no detactable A protein (for example, mutant 9813). From these, partial revertants with detectable A protein can be obtained; the partial revertants of frameshift mutants are double frameshift mutants. The amino acid sequences found in analogous portions of two proteins, one from the double mutant 9813 **PR11** *(top) and the other from another double mutant 9813* **PR8**

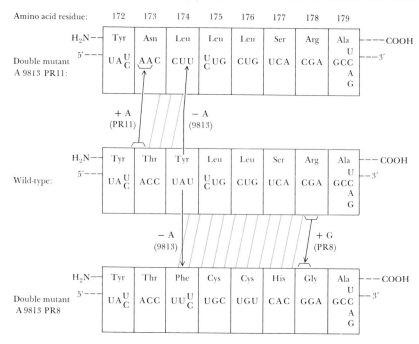

it is the wrong amino acid for that particular position in the polypeptide chain. If the triplet reading frame is shifted one letter to the right, all subsequent triplets are read incorrectly until a second (suppressor) mutation occurs that can offset the first error by shifting the reading frame back one letter to the correct position. Therefore, as long as this second mutation occurs in the same cistron and near the original mutation, the small jumbled segment of the code located between the two mutant sites may cause damage insufficient to prevent formation of a functional gene product.

The suppressor mutations occur in a restricted portion of the *rIIB* gene. It is assumed that the amino acid sequence dictated by this portion of the *B* gene is not essential for *B* activity. In fact, a mutant is known that has functional *B* activity, yet this portion of the *B* gene has been deleted. Thus it is important only that the reading frame be thrown back into correct position *before* the code for some *critical* portion of the amino acid sequence is copied.

Although polypeptide products of the *rIIB* gene have been detected

---

(bottom), are cases in point. Triplets compatible with the three sequences of amino acids can be selected from the codons in Fig. 8.2 only if the triplets are oriented 5′ to 3′ as shown and the N- and C-terminal orientation of the polypeptide chain is known (Fig. 2.4). The first position of the Leu codon at position 176 is assigned as C rather than U because the residue has been shown to be replaced by Arg in mutant A487 (see Fig. 3.4); the selection of G as the last letter of the triplet stems from the amino acid replacements found in the 9813 PR8 double-mutant protein. The loss of the A in mutant 9813 is inferred from the replacements found in 9813 PR8, in addition, mutant 9813 fails to recombine to give wild type with mutant 446, which contains substitution of Cys for Tyr at residue 174 (see Fig. 3.4). The assignment of the triplet ACC [rather than ACU, ACA, or ACG (see Fig. 8.2)] to Thr coding for residue 173 depends upon its conversion to an Asn codon in PR8. In the same manner, the degenerate codon used in the wild type for Arg at position 178 is deduced to be CGA by amino acid sequence data obtained on another double mutant, 9813 ICR-13, not shown here. Thus the frameshift mutations allow specification of which codon in a degenerate set of codons is used at a given place.

The addition or deletion of a single base is most common, although occasionally more than one base is involved. Note that the addition mutations involve the addition of a base identical to an adjacent base (that is, A next to A and G next to G). This is a most common occurrence; it indicates that additions or deletions of one or few bases in frameshift mutagenesis occur through "slippage" during DNA replication or synthesis, or during events associated with genetic recombination (for example, "unequal crossing over" at the molecular level). A sequence of codons that do not match the wild type (for example, the codons for Phe-Cys-Cys-His-Gly in double mutant A9813 PR8) is sometimes called "gibberish." Note that the protein-synthesizing apparatus cannot discern the proper (wild-type) phase once polypeptide synthesis has begun; the protein-synthesizing apparatus merely reads what is written in the mRNA. After W. J. Brammar, H. Berger, and C. Yanofsky, Proc. Natl. Acad. Sci. U.S., 58 (1967), 1499. Also see H. Berger, W. J. Brammar, and C. Yanofsky, J. Mol. Biol., 34 (1968), 219, and J. Bacteriol., 96 (1968), 1672. Some properties of frameshift mutants in bacteria are reviewed by B. N. Ames and H. J. Whitfield, Jr., Cold Spring Harbor Symp. Quant. Biol., 31 (1966), 221, and R. G. Martin, J. Mol. Biol., 26 (1967), 311.

recently, they remain to be purified and further characterized before relationships between gene mutations and amino acid sequences can be definitively established. In the meantime, studies on other systems confirm the expectations based on the *rII* system. In these studies, frameshift mutants have been first obtained and then crossed with one another to obtain a double mutant that is only partly defective in its gross phenotype. Or, partial revertants have been obtained from frameshift mutants. Organisms containing two frameshift mutations in a restricted portion of a gene have been obtained by both means. It has been possible to study the amino acid sequence in the proteins of such double mutants in cases where the stability of the protein lends itself to purification. Two examples are given in Fig. 8.8. The center of Fig. 8.8 shows a short portion of the amino acid sequence of the tryptophan synthetase A protein. This is compared with amino acid sequences for two double frameshift mutants, each carrying one + and one − mutation. In fact, the altered amino acid sequences in the mutant proteins allow us to specify which mutation is a + (addition) and which is a − (deletion). The code-word directory (Fig. 8.2) was used to select codons for each of the amino acids in the wild-type and mutant proteins. A perfect fit was obtained, as shown, if codons were arranged so that reading of mRNA takes place from the 5′ to the 3′ direction, and if the base additions and deletions occurred as shown.

Let us emphasize several important conclusions from our discussion. First, the experiments demonstrate that combinations of three similar mutations, that is +++ or −−− generally allow effective protein to be made. Single mutations and combinations of 2, 4, or 5 similar mutations do not allow effective protein to be made. This is strong evidence that the codon is a triplet. Second, the studies on amino acid substitutions in proteins elicited by +− frameshift mutants show that the nucleotide members of the triplet are contiguous. Third, the gene is a polarized structure, owing to its property of serving as template for a polarized molecule, mRNA, synthesized from 5′ to 3′ (Chap. 6). The mRNA is translated in the same direction, from 5′ to 3′, into the polypeptide sequence. The amino acid substitution data (Fig. 8.8) show that this translation must progress from the N- to the C-terminal, as concluded also from other experiments presented in Chap. 7; there is a perfect matching between the codons, whose orientations are known, and the amino acid substitutions in the polypeptide chains. The results of studies of frameshift mutations also indicate, as will be discussed below, that the code does not contain commas or nucleotide punctuations between codons for a single polypeptide chain. The genetic code is nonoverlapping.

Nonoverlapping and Continuous Code

Sequences of amino acids are now known for a large number of different polypeptide chains. The sequences appear to be almost completely at random. This could not be so if two coding units over-lapped. For example, if overlap occurred, in two letters, the amino acid would always have the same four nearest neighbors (Fig. 8.1*b*). Even allowing for degeneracy of the code (Fig. 8.2), this constancy in nearest neighbors would be observed at measurable frequency. Actually, in the case of amino acids coded for by only one or two codons, many more than four amino acids are found in adjacent positions.

One can also see in Fig. 8.1*b* that a single mutation involving over-lapping codons would affect the positioning of two or more adjacent amino acids in the polypeptide chain; yet only single amino acid changes have been found to arise from single-site mutations (see Figs. 3.4 and 3.6 for a few of many known examples). We can believe that the codons dictating the structures of single polypeptide chains do not overlap.

The simplest hypothesis that accounts for all relevant experimental data is that no nucleotides, or "commas," exist between codons for an individual polypeptide chain (Fig. 8.1*d*). The data shown in Fig. 8.8 lead to this view. The studies cited below further consolidate this conclusion.

Triplet Composition

In the preceding discussions, interpretations have been based on the genetic code illustrated in Fig. 8.2. We have yet to describe in detail the two series of in vitro experiments that led to elucidation of the code. The first method was developed by M. W. Nirenberg and J. H. Matthaei in 1961. It involved the use of synthetic polyribonucle-otides in amino acid–incorporation studies. A cell-free extract was prepared containing the constituents necessary for incorporation of amino acids into polypeptide linkage (Chap. 7): amino acids, tRNA, energy source, ribosomes, and so on. To this was added a radioactive amino acid and a synthetic polyribonucleotide prepared as described on page 131. The amount of radioactivity incorporated into acid-insoluble material (that is, polypeptide) was determined. Figure 8.9 shows data from an experiment that measured amino acid incorpora-tion using ribopolynucleotides containing only A and C (poly-AC) in varying amounts. From this experiment, the authors concluded that two triplets, one containing C and the other A and C, coded for proline. One of the triplets was CCC and the other triplet was either ACC, CAC, or CCA.

Incorporation experiments with randomly ordered synthetic ribo-polynucleotides provided information on the *composition* of coding triplets. A polymer that coded for several amino acids was considered to contain the codons for these amino acids and to lack the codons for others. Amino acid replacement data in mutant proteins of the type shown in Fig. 3.6 substantiated these assignments.

There are many pitfalls in methodology with the above synthetic systems. Incorporation of nucleotides into synthetic ribopolynucle-

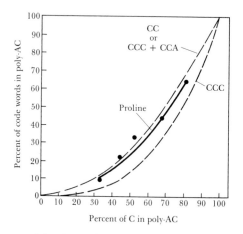

FIG. 8.9. *Determination of the composition of coding triplets through amino acid incorporation efficiencies with various polymers. The activities of a series of poly-AC preparations with different proportions of bases were tested in an amino acid–incorporating system. The theoretical proportions of the four doublet (CC, AC, and so on) and eight triplet (CCC, CCA, CAC, and so on) permutations were calculated for each of the polymers. The dashed lines show theoretical frequencies of some of the RNA code words. The observed relative abilities in amino acid incorporation are shown, for proline, by the solid line. It is concluded that the doublet CC, or the two triplets CCC and CCA, code for proline.*

The four doublet permutations do not contain enough specific information to code for the six amino acids incorporated in experiments similar to that shown here with the poly-AC templates, whereas the informational content of the eight triplet words is adequate. The percent incorporation of lysine, asparagine, glutamine, and histidine agrees well with triplet code-word frequencies but not with doublet frequencies. Redrawn from M. W. Nirenberg, O. W. Jones, P. Leder, B. F. C. Clark, **and S. Pestka, Cold Spring Harbor Symp. Quant. Biol., 28 (1963), 549.**

otide polymers is not always strictly random, and one must directly ascertain the base content and the average distribution of bases in the polymers to have a reliable estimate of the frequency of occurrence of particular triplets. Second, aberrant incorporation may occur. For example, the stimulation both of phenylalanine and of leucine incorporation by poly-U embarrassingly indicated that both amino acids might be coded by the same triplet. However, because appreciable leucine incorporation occurs only in the absence of phenylalanine and the presence of abnormally high concentrations of magnesium ion, it is assumed that UUU codes for phenylalanine and that the leucine incorporation is an artifact. Other artifacts may arise from impurity of radioactive amino acids, metabolism of the amino acids in the impure extracts used for incorporation (for example, conversion of glutamine to glutamic acid), and alterations in the polymers by polynucleotide phosphorylase or other enzymes present in the extracts.

The more recent use of messengers of known sequence has extended the earlier studies on triplet composition and confirmed many of our notions as to the sequence of the nucleotides within triplets. Studies of amino acid substitutions in mutant proteins have supplied the essence of reassurance, the in vivo test.

Base Sequence within Triplets

In 1965, M. W. Nirenberg and P. Leder introduced a method that led to assignment of base sequences within codons. The method, referred to in Chap. 7, makes use of the ability of tRNA's and mRNA's to mutually stimulate the binding of each other to ribosomes. It was observed, for example, that stimulation of tRNA binding was achieved with poly-U and, to a lesser but still signficant extent, with short-chain ribonucleotides containing U (Fig. 8.10). Two highly significant observations were made when a number of short-chain messengers were tested. First, a chain length of three was necessary and sufficient for enhancement of tRNA binding; dinucleotides stimulated little or no binding (Figs. 8.10 and 8.11). Second, there was differential specificity in binding stimulated by triplets of constant composition but differing in sequence (Fig. 8.11). This provided the basis, in most cases, for unequivocal assignment of base sequences. Once the method was developed, the main problem lay in the synthesis of the 64 combinations of trinucleotide sequences inherent in a triplet code using four bases.

Some binding of tRNA's other than the major one is sometimes observed in the in vitro assay. A number of these anomalies are not found when amino acid incorporation, rather than binding per se, is used as a measure of triplet composition and arrangement. Some of these are the polymers, described on page 133, containing repeat base sequences of one type followed by a few different bases of known se-

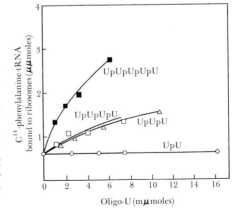

FIG. 8.10. *Stimulation of specific binding of phenylalanine tRNA to ribosomes using synthetic polymers of various sizes.*

Poly-U of chain lengths 2, 3, 4, and 5 at increasing concentrations were added to ribosomes in the presence of tRNA which had been charged with radioactive phenylalanine. The triplet UUU stimulated binding whereas the doublet UU did not. The methodology is described in the legend to Fig. 8.11. From M. Nirenberg and P. Leder, Science, *145 (1964), 1399.*

Experiment	Addition (Base residues), μμmoles	C14-amino-acyl-tRNA bound to ribosomes, μμmoles		
		C14-*Val*-tRNA	C14-*Phe*-tRNA	C14-*Leu*-tRNA
1	None	0.38	0.22	0.37
	4.7 Poly U	0.23	**4.73**	0.22
	4.7 Poly UG	**2.65**	1.93	0.24
2	None	0.40	0.22	0.62
	4.7 GpUpU	**1.11**	0.27	0.56
	4.7 UpGpU	0.40	0.25	0.55
	4.7 UpUpG	0.37	0.25	0.44
3	None	0.18	0.22	0.69
	4.7 GpU	0.20	0.22	0.69
	4.7 UpG	0.19	0.21	0.71
	4.7 UpU	0.18	0.20	0.67

FIG. 8.11. *GUU as a codon for valine and elimination of UGU and UUG: the alternative possibilities.*

Ribopolynucleotides, dinucleotides, or trinucleotides were added as messenger to ribosomes in the presence of tRNA's charged with radioactive valine, phenylalanine, or leucine. Only one labeled charged tRNA was added to each aliquot. The mixture was incubated, then poured through a filter that retained only the charged tRNA bound specifically in a ribosome-mRNA-tRNA complex. The binding was measured by counting the radioactivity retained on the filter.

The polynucleotides failed to stimulate binding of leucine tRNA (last column) above control values ("None" means no polynucleotide added). Some phenylalanine tRNA was bound to poly-U and to poly-UG, owing to the UUU codons contained in these polymers; the di- and trinucleotides failed to bind phenylalanine tRNA (center column). Poly-U did not stimulate binding of valine tRNA but poly-UG did (experiment 1, left-most column of figures). In experiment 2, of the three triplets containing 2 U's and 1 G, only GUU stimulated binding of valine tRNA. There was no stimulation of valine tRNA binding in the presence of dinucleotides (experiment 3). From P. Leder and M. W. Nirenberg, Proc. Natl. Acad. Sci. U.S., 52 (1964), 420.

quence at one or the other end. Others include repeating dinucleotide tri- or tetranucleotide sequences. Two examples will suffice. The repeating tetranucleotide poly-UAUC leads to the synthesis of the repeating tetrapeptide Tyr-Leu-Ser-Ile; the repeating tetranucleotide poly-UUAC leads to the synthesis of the repeating tetrapeptide Leu-Leu-Thr-Tyr. Reference to Fig. 8.2 will help you understand why this occurs. As you can see, the first polymer can be read UAU (Tyr) CUA (Leu) UCU (Ser) AUC (Ile) UAU (Tyr) CUA (Leu) . . . .

Figure 8.12 shows amino acid–incorporation results obtained with a series of some synthetic RNA's of repeating sequence. The repeating dinucleotide sequences lead to copolypeptides whose sequence alternates between two amino acids, for example, Ser-Leu-Ser-Leu-Ser-.... Many of the repeating trinucleotides allow incorporation of three amino acids each into a separate homopolymer. Several just allow incorporation of two amino acids. In one case, the failure to stimulate incorporation of a third amino acid can be traced to degradation in the reaction mixture (deamination of asparagine). In the other two cases (poly-GAU and poly-GUA), it appears as if the polymer can be translated only in restricted fashions. The same kind of restriction is observed when certain repeating tetranucleotides are used for amino acid–incorporation studies. These anomalies are attributed to the special triplets UAG, UAA, and UGA, which do not code for amino acid incorporation (Fig. 8.2). As we shall see in Chap. 9, the three special triplets are chain-terminating codons, serving to act as periods during translation of the messenger.

FIG. 8.12. *Amino acids incorporated by some synthetic RNA's with repeating sequences. H. G. Khorana* et al., Cold Spring Harbor Symp. Quant. Biol., 31 *(1966), 39; H. Kössel, A. R. Morgan, and H. G. Khorana.* J. Mol. Biol., 26 *(1967), 449.*

Repeating dinucleotides	Copolymers (alternating sequences)
poly-UC	Ser-Leu
poly-AG	Arg-Glu
poly-UG	Val-Cys
poly-AC	Thr-His

Repeating trinucleotides	Homopolymers
poly-UUC	Phe; Ser; Leu
poly-AAG	Lys; Glu; Arg
poly-UUG	Cys; Leu; Val
poly-CAA	Gln; Thr*
poly-UAC	Tyr; Thr; Leu
poly-AUC	Ile; Ser; His
poly-GAU	Met; Asp
poly-GUA	Val; Ser

Repeating tetranucleotides	Copolymers (alternating sequences)
poly-UAUC	Tyr-Leu-Ser-Ile
poly-UUAC	Leu-Leu-Thr-Tyr
poly-GUAA	none
poly-GAUA	none

* Asparagine is deaminated in amino-acid-incorporating mixture and thus incorporation is not yet realized.

Triplets in DNA

The discussion in this chapter has centered on mRNA triplets. There is every reason to believe from mutation studies and what we know about mRNA that these nucleotide sequences are transcribed from DNA by DNA-dependent RNA polymerase. Since mRNA can anneal with one of the strands of DNA, it is assumed to have the complementary copy of this strand, except that U replaces T and the sugar in the backbone is ribose, not deoxyribose. The Watson-Crick pairing rules for U and T are the same. The template triplet in the DNA is, then, an antipolar complementary copy of the mRNA triplet. This means that the DNA triplet for the phenylalanine codon, UUU in mRNA $(5' \rightarrow 3')$ is AAA $(3' \rightarrow 5')$, which, in the DNA, is base-paired with TTT $(5' \rightarrow 3')$. Mutation studies such as those indicated in the legend to Fig. 8.4 support this view.

In the case of degeneracies, one can sometimes define which of the degenerate codons is operative in a particular situation. The legend to Fig. 8.4 explains why particular codons were selected to represent the arginine and glutamic acid amino acid replacements; these, in turn, limited designation of the glycine codon originally present. A similar type of reasoning was applied to selection of some of the codons in Fig. 8.8 (see the legend).

Thus in vitro studies on the assignment of codons for particular amino acids have supplied the foundation for subsequent genetical verification. The methods of genetics and biochemistry when elegantly combined have established unequivocally the letter order of the triplet code.

Universality

Can we integrate evidence for the code from different organisms? Is the sequence that codes for a particular amino acid in a bacteriophage protein precisely the same sequence that codes for the same amino acid in, let us say, a protein of the human? The answer to these two questions is a tentative yes, with, as we shall see, minor qualifications. The genetic code, as presented in Fig. 8.2, basically applies to all organisms; however, for particular organisms, footnotes of detail would have to be appended to Fig. 8.2 to account for all intricacies of translation.

The best evidence for universality in coding is that the products formed by in vitro ribosomal preparations obtained from different organisms most often reflect the source of the mRNA used. In the last section of Chap. 6 we mentioned that when amino acid–charged tRNA from the bacterium *E. coli* was placed with rabbit reticulocyte mRNA and ribosomes, the product was rabbit hemoglobin. The hemoglobin was shown to be identical in its primary structure with hemoglobin made with reticulocyte tRNA insofar as no differences were noted in tryptic peptide analyses. The bacterial tRNA appears to be able to recognize perfectly the mammalian mRNA for hemoglobin and also to work harmoniously with mammalian ribosomes.

Studies with synthetic messengers and binding studies with tRNA's also give credibility to a universal code. There is, however, an apparent variability in usage of codons among organisms, reflected in quantitative differences in abundance of particular tRNA's and other components of the translational machinery. Organisms with high G/C contents in the DNA appear geared for more frequent reading of degenerate codons ending in C or G, for example. Their proteins also are relatively rich in amino acids coded for by G- and C-rich codons, for example, Ala, Arg, and Gly, whereas their proteins are relatively deficient in Ile, Lys, Phe, and Tyr (check the codons in Fig. 8.2).

Another point in favor of universality in the genetic code is the great uniformity in amino acid sequence of homologous proteins from widely divergent species. For example, a sequence of 11 amino acids (including 8 different amino acids) is identical in the protein cytochrome c prepared from the human, horse, chicken, tuna, yeast, and several bacteria. These proteins have many other similarities in sequence, although genetic divergence between these organisms is thought to have taken place hundreds of millions of years ago. The preservation of some sequences may be essential for cytochrome function, but current evidence indicates that other sequences have been preserved through a long period of evolution and truly reflect common phylogenetic origin (Chap. 11).

Exceptions to absolute universality in genetic coding occur in certain mutants of microorganisms. In Chap. 9 we shall describe mutants that have gained ability to read nonsense triplets. However, the accessory ability is only partial; nonsense triplets are still recognized as nonsense much of the time. Some natural differences also may exist among organisms. There are strong indications that initiation of polypeptide chains, as mentioned in Chap. 9, is encoded differently in bacteria and their viruses as opposed to higher organisms. Also, in mammals, a tRNA for Cys is bound well by the UGA triplet, known to be nonsense in bacteria; the biological significance of this observation remains to be assessed. Such differences do not invalidate the genetic code presented in Fig. 8.2 or the concept of universality; their existence merely tells us that there is more to biology than 64 triplets!

Questions

8.1. In a scientific journal (for example, *Proc. Natl. Acad. Sci. U.S.*; *Science*; *J. Mol. Biol.*), search for a recent article on the genetic code. Write a one-page report in which you compare the observations in the article with the description in this chapter.

8.2. What is the evidence for a triplet code?

8.3. Look back at earlier chapters of this book and outline the reasons for believing that mRNA carries the genetic code.

8.4. List the reasons for believing that the genetic code is degenerate.

8.5. Some workers believe there is some form of life on the planet Mars.

(*a*) If you could visit Mars, what type (or types) of hereditary material, if any, might you expect to find? Why?

(*b*) Do you think the genetic code will be truly universal (or, at least, interplanetary) ? Why?

(*c*) How would you go about testing to find out the chemical nature of the hereditary material in organisms from Mars?

(*d*) Assuming that the genetic material of a Martian organism is found to be DNA, how would you go about testing to see if the genetic code is (or is not) universal?

8.6. List in summary fashion the main methods that have been used in deciphering the genetic code and consider the relative merits and limitations of each approach.

8.7. Using the genetic code diagrammed in Fig. 8.2, list the possible triplet compositions for wild-type TMV protein and for the mutant proteins at those residues listed in the tabular portion of Fig. 3.6. Keep separate lists for each mutagen, and see if you can find a correlation between mutagen and type of base-pair change predicted.

8.8. How many polyribonucleotide sequences could a mRNA coding for the tetrapeptide Ser-Pro-Thr-Ala have?

8.9. Describe four lines of evidence which show that the genetic code is nonoverlapping.

8.10. Define the terms missense, nonsense, wild type, frameshift, codon, and anticodon.

References

Bennett, J. C., and W. J. Dreyer, "Genetic Coding for Protein Structure," *Ann. Rev. Biochem., 33* (1964), 205. Both this and reviews cited at the end of Chap. 7 are directly pertinent to the topic of this chapter.

Bretscher, M. S., and O. W. Jones, "The Biochemistry of the Genetic Code," in *Techniques in Protein Biosynthesis,* Vol. I. New York: Academic Press, Inc., 1967, p. 217.

Cold Spring Harbor Symp. Quant. Biol., 28 (1963) and *31* (1966) . Two excellent symposia that cover many aspects of coding.

Crick, F. H. C., "The Recent Excitement in the Coding Problem," *Progr. Nucleic Acid Res. Mol. Biol., 1* (1963), 164. A critical look at research and ideas on coding as it stood a few years ago. Crick has another interesting essay on coding that forms the introduction for the 1966 Cold Spring Harbor Symposium cited above.

Khorana, H. G., "Polynucleotide Synthesis and the Genetic Code—II," in *Genetic Elements: Properties and Function,* D. Shugar, ed. New York: Academic Press, Inc., 1967, p. 209.

Krieg, D. R., "Specificity of Chemical Mutagenesis," *Progr. Nucleic Acid Res. Mol. Biol., 2* (1963) , 125. An understanding of the specificity of various chemical mutagens is important, for it serves as a cross-check in determination of the genetic code.

Marshall, R. E., C. T. Caskey, and M. Nirenberg, "Fine Structure of RNA Codewords Recognized by Bacterial, Amphibian, and Mammalian Transfer RNA," *Science, 155* (1968), 820. Some observations on tRNA binding pertinent to the question of universality of the genetic code.

Nirenberg, M. W., and J. H. Matthaei, "The Dependence of Cell-Free Protein Synthesis in *E. coli* upon Naturally Occurring or Synthetic Polyribonucleotides," *Proc. Natl. Acad. Sci. U.S., 47* (1961), 1588. The original paper on use of synthetic polyribonucleotides in amino acid—incorporating systems and their applications to analysis of the genetic code. Note that simple innovations in techniques in stabilizing the cell-free system greatly facilitated the experimental research.

Orgel, L. E., "The Chemical Basis of Mutation," *Advan. Enzymol., 27* (1965), 289. An excellent review of chemical mutagenesis.

Speyer, J. F., "The Genetic Code," in *Molecular Genetics,* Part II, J. H. Taylor, ed. New York: Academic Press, Inc., 1967, p. 137. A clearly written presentation that covers much of the material in this chapter.

Streisinger, G., et al., *Cold Spring Harbor Symp. Quant. Biol., 31* (1966), 77; E. Terzaghi et al., *Proc. Natl. Acad. Sci. U.S., 56* (1966), 500; and Y. Okada et al., *Proc. Natl. Acad. Sci. U.S., 56* (1966), 1692. Effect of frameshift mutations on the amino acid sequence of phage T4 lysozyme and their use in confirmation of the genetic code in vivo.

Woese, C. R., "The Present Status of the Genetic Code," *Progr. Nucleic Acid Res. Mol. Biol., 7* (1967), 107.

———, *The Genetic Code.* New York: Harper & Row, 1968.

$\bigwedge\!\!\!\!\!\diagup \mathcal{J}ine$

Guiding Translation

We have stressed the role of the genotype in dictating the phenotype of the cell through control of the *primary structures* of proteins. The genetic code in the DNA is transcribed into an mRNA copy which is translated into the amino acid sequence of the polypeptide chain. Our description has been incomplete in detail, partially for simplicity but also because many facets of these processes presently remain unknown. We are confident, however, that the general outlines presented will stand the tests of time and further research. A sufficiently large body of neatly interlocking evidence from diverse approaches gives us this assurance. We conclude that it is the genetic information that limits *the kinds* of proteins the cell is capable of producing.

The phenotype of a cell, however, is not dictated solely by the *structures* of the proteins encoded in its DNA. There are many secondary consequences of gene mutations (Chap. 5), and many of these may be modified by environmental influences.

Even more important, the *relative numbers* of each type of protein vary; some are abundant, often reflecting their longer half-life relative to other proteins in the cell. Especially in cells of higher organisms, some proteins are quite labile and are constantly undergoing degradation and synthesis ("turnover") in the living cell. There is appreciable breakdown of proteins, also, in micro-

160

organisms, particularly when the cells are not growing rapidly. Furthermore, differential breakdown of various proteins can be influenced by environmental factors that govern the relative stabilities of the proteins themselves.

Other very important determinants act at the level of protein synthesis regulating the relative amount of a particular protein. Some function at the translation step from mRNA to polypeptide chain, whereas other very important controls operate at the level of transcription from DNA to mRNA, determining the relative abundance of different kinds of mRNA's. As we shall see, these two critical steps in the biosynthesis of proteins are interrelated. This makes delineation of factors involved in determining the relative abundance of proteins difficult. It is an area of endeavor which, today, is satiated with ideas but starved of hard facts.

It is the aim of this chapter to focus attention on the translation step, from mRNA to protein, and in the succeeding chapter to the transcription step, from DNA to mRNA. Both qualitative and quantitative control of cellular protein synthesis can be regulated at these stages.

Induction and Repression

In higher organisms, most of the protein in one type of cell may constitute a single protein species that is undetectable in other types of cells from the same organism. Also, a particular protein may be made in abundance at one stage during the development of an organism but appear only in very low quantity, or be undetectable, in other stages. The differential expression of genic activities in higher organisms will be discussed by Markert and Ursprung in *Developmental Genetics*, a companion volume in this series, and will not be discussed extensively here. Instead, we shall focus our attention on well-analyzed phenomena in microorganisms that give some clues to mechanisms regulating gene action.

In microorganisms, a single protein species may be absent under some conditions of cultivation and yet constitute several percent of the total protein of the cell when the microbes are cultured under a different set of conditions. Figure 9.1 illustrates how widely the levels of some proteins may vary. Also note from the figure that there are other proteins that are formed in relatively constant amounts regardless of different conditions of culture.

There are two classes of proteins that fluctuate widely in amounts as a function of changes in the environment of the cell. If the level of a protein *increases* following the addition of a metabolite, it is called an *inducible protein*. If the level *decreases* after addition of a metabolite, it is called a *repressible protein*. When the level of a repressible protein increases after removing a specific metabolite, the phenomenon is termed *derepression*.

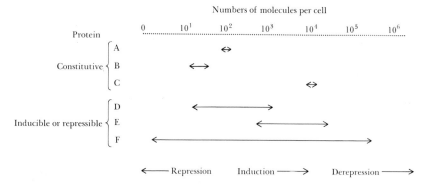

FIG. 9.1. *Numbers of protein molecules in single bacterial cells grown under various conditions. A single bacterial cell can have up to about 10^7 (10 million) protein molecules. If the generation time (time for complete doubling by vegetative reproduction) is 30 min, 10^7 new protein molecules must be made every half-hour to maintain the protein content in the progeny bacteria. Some proteins are present in greater abundance than others. Some proteins vary in concentration but little when the bacteria are grown in different environments (constitutive proteins). Other proteins show wide fluctuations when the bacteria are placed under different environmental conditions (inducible, or repressible, proteins).*

Proteins that do not fluctuate appreciably in amounts under the selected set of growth conditions are termed *constitutive proteins.* It is possible that all protein levels are regulated by metabolites, but that only the synthesis of certain proteins can be regulated by the addition of metabolites to the external environment. The intracellular environment can be altered in living organisms only within relatively narrow limits as compared with the wide variations possible in the surrounding milieu.

Messenger Selection

We shall see in Chapter 10 that a most important component in induction and repression is in the selection of sites on the DNA for transcription to mRNA. Some nucleotide sequences in the DNA are transcribed more frequently than are other nucleotide sequences. Also important in induction and repression is the reading of messages already made. It appears that some mRNA molecules are translated immediately, others stored and then translated at a later time, and still others destroyed without having been fully translated.

The general metabolic fates of mRNA that we may picture are (1) translation or nontranslation, and (2) preservation, partial destruction, or total degradation. Combinations of these different possibilities may exist. It appears that mRNA's for different proteins in the same cell can share different fates.

There is evidence that the synthesis of a particular mRNA does not guarantee its use in protein synthesis. The nuclei of animal cells contain high-molecular-weight RNA's that are rapidly degraded and are not transported to the cytoplasm. Their presence can be detected by permitting incorporation of radioactivity into RNA, extracting the RNA from nuclei, and allowing the RNA to anneal with DNA which has been denatured to single-stranded form (Fig. 6.10*b*). The confinement of this RNA to the nucleus can be demonstrated by adding to the single-stranded DNA a large excess of unlabeled RNA extracted from the cytoplasm. Such RNA does not compete for the same nucleotide sequences on the DNA to which much of the nuclear RNA attaches. Similar annealing competition experiments indicate that RNA's extracted from nuclei of different tissues are much more similar to one another than are the mRNA's found in the cytoplasm. While some protein synthesis does occur in nuclei, it is not yet known if the nuclear-specific RNA's are translated. Differentiation of cells in part may involve selective transport of mRNA's to cytoplasmic sites of protein synthesis.

Other mRNA's in certain cells of higher organisms are made and stored, to be translated at a later date. This is true of messengers located in unfertilized ova of some species. Also, there is evidence that mRNA active in the synthesis of feather proteins in fowl accumulates on polyribosomes, inactive and protected by interaction with some protein component of the cell. Other polyribosomes in the same cell actively synthesize protein. Only at a subsequent period in the life of the cell are these "stored" messages translated into feather proteins. Here again is evidence for selective control of protein synthesis at the level of translation of specific genetic information.

In bacteria, the rapid turnover of mRNA and the fact that only about 2 percent of the total RNA of an *E. coli* cell is mRNA introduces certain experimental problems. If RNA is extracted from a population of *E. coli* and hybridized with *E. coli* DNA, about half of the single-stranded DNA is saturated. This result would be expected if the mRNA were complementary to one of the two DNA strands and if essentially *all* genes present in the bacterial population were transcribed into mRNA. The rapid turnover of mRNA has led to the suggestion that an important control mechanism in bacteria is the differential destruction of untranslated mRNA's. In the case of inducible and repressible proteins in bacteria (Fig. 9.1) (see also Chap. 10), specific low-molecular-weight metabolites can affect the synthesis of specific proteins. Either the withdrawal of the inducer molecules in some cases, or the addition of certain metabolites called *corepressors* in others, can preferentially shut off synthesis of specific proteins. The kinetics of this effect is striking; upon withdrawal of inducer or addition of a corepressor to a bacterial culture, the synthesis of a specific enzyme stops abruptly within 1 or 2 minutes. In the case of mRNA's such cessation of synthesis of a protein cannot be attributed to the destruction of the entire mRNA molecule; the synthesis of one protein may stop, whereas other proteins specified by different regions of the same mRNA molecule may continue to be synthesized for additional times. It is as though the initial binding of ribosomes at the beginning point of the messenger is prevented but those ribosomes already on the messenger continue the translation process until they reach the end of the messenger molecule. Of particular interest in this regard are several experiments which, while complex and difficult to assess, nevertheless suggest that the half-life of a particular mRNA may be prolonged in the presence of its specific inducer.

The single-stranded RNA (mRNA) of phage f2 contains three known cistrons. The cistron for the coat protein of the virus is the only one translated into protein at high frequency in vivo or in vitro. This preferential translation of one cistron stems from the ability of the coat protein to uniquely attach to a specific site or sites on its own RNA. The association of five or six coat protein molecules on the virus RNA blocks translation of two of the phage cistrons but allows continued translation of the coat protein segment at the 5' end of the RNA. This is an unambiguous demonstration of control of protein synthesis exerted at the translational step; whether or not there are parallels in nonviral systems remains to be determined.

The above observations show that controls on protein synthesis sometimes operate at the level of translation. In Chap. 10 we discuss the evidence that very important controls also exist at the level of messenger RNA synthesis. Delineation of control mechanisms in individual systems is an active field of investigation. We need more detailed biochemical studies of the translation process and on the mechanism of mRNA breakdown and stabilization of messenger against breakdown to fully assess the relative importance of translational, as opposed to transcriptional, control in regulation of enzyme levels.

Punctuation on mRNA

We have mentioned that some mRNA's are *polycistronic;* that is, successive segments of a *single* mRNA molecule code for the synthesis of *different* polypeptide chains. How are the syntheses of these separate polypeptide chains effected? Why do we not find a single giant polypeptide chain—a molecular "run-on sentence"? Are there mechanisms for establishing the beginning and end of the sentence? The experiments we shall discuss now show in fact that "signals" are built into mRNA to dictate initiation of polypeptide chains at specific sites on the mRNA and to terminate polypeptide chains at other sites. The nature of these signals, specific nucleotide sequences in the mRNA, may differ in different organisms.

CHAIN INITIATION

Methionine is the most common N-terminal amino acid found in proteins isolated from *E. coli*, although alanine and serine also have been observed in the N-terminal position. It appears that most, if not all, proteins in *E. coli* initially contain *N*-formylmethionine (Fig. 9.2) as the true N-terminal residue. This *N*-formylmethionine subsequently is deformylated in some proteins or entirely removed in others. What evidence do we have for this and what has it to do with the genetic control of protein synthesis?

In one type of experiment, RNA extracted from f2 bacteriophage particles is used as mRNA for in vitro synthesis of virus coat protein (Chaps. 6 and 7). The predominant protein made in this in vitro system is virus coat protein, as shown by comparison of tryptic peptides of the protein made in vitro with peptides obtained from coat protein isolated from intact f2 phage particles. There is a single striking difference between the virus coat proteins synthesized using *E. coli* components, one in vivo and the other in vitro. The protein made in vitro contains *N*-formylmethionine as its N-terminal amino acid in a sequence that we can designate *N*-formyl-Met-Ala-Ser-Asn-Phe-Thr.... In contrast, the same protein made in vivo contains Ala-Ser-Asn-Phe-Thr... as the amino acid sequence at the N-terminal end of the polypeptide chain. One interpretation of these results is that *N*-formylmethionine initiates polypeptide chain formation in *E. coli*, but that in vivo the methionine is hydrolyzed from the N-terminal end of the polypeptide chain. The extent of these changes may be specified in part by the specific amino acid sequence and in part by the accessibility of the N-terminal and adjacent amino acids to hydrolysis as the protein folds into its native configuration.

Note in Fig. 8.2 that only one codon, AUG, is assigned for methionine. However, two different tRNA's, both specific for methionine, have been separated by fractionation techniques. The methionine bound to one of these, the "initiating" tRNA, is enzymatically formylated at the α-amino position in the presence of a folic acid derivative which serves as the donor of the formyl group. *N*-Formylmethionine possesses no free α-amino group, so it cannot react with carboxyl groups of other amino acids to form peptide bonds. Consequently, it cannot be incorporated at internal positions in the polypeptide chain (consult Fig. 7.5). For example, *N*-formylmethionine

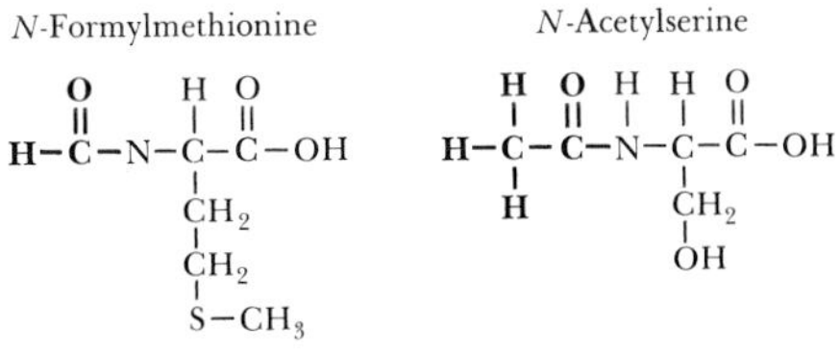

FIG. 9.2. *Formulae of* **N**-*formylmethionine and* **N**-*acetylserine, two amino acids with blocked amino groups.*

is not incorporated into polypeptide when a polymer such as poly-A, terminating in AUG, is used as synthetic mRNA, that is, $A(pA)_n pApUpG$. The noninitiating type of tRNA for methionine also "reads" the AUG triplet, permitting methionine to be inserted at internal and C-terminal positions in the polypeptide. The special initiating formylmethionine tRNA also can bind to AUG triplets that begin or are internal on the mRNA, but, in so doing, they initiate formation of new polypeptide chains with N-formylmethionine occupying the N-terminal position.

The ability of the AUG triplet to lead to rapid and specific chain initiation is demonstrated in vitro with synthetic mRNA's of known sequence (Fig. 9.3). The presence of an AUG triplet in synthetic mRNA predominantly coding for phenylalanine (UUU) greatly stimulates amino acid incorporation, whether the AUG triplet is at the beginning or internal in the polynucleotide (Fig. 9.3). The polypeptide chains have N-terminal formylmethionine residues when the AUG codon is represented in the synthetic mRNA. With slightly more complicated polymers, it can be shown that the AUG triplet sets the phase of reading, the reading frame. For example, in the polymer $ApUpGpG(pU)_{25}$, the GGU triplet (glycine) is not read because it overlaps the AUG triplet that initiates the chains. Instead, the polymer incorporates formylMet (AUG)-Val (GUU)-Phe (UUU)-Phe (UUU)-.... Once the frame is set by the AUG triplet, the mRNA is read sequentially from 5' to 3' until the polypeptide chain is terminated (Chap. 8). In the absence of an AUG triplet, initiation in vitro proceeds more slowly (Fig. 9.3) and requires higher magnesium-ion concentrations. In the latter case, initiation appears to occur more or less randomly along the polymer, an in vitro artifact. In Chap. 7 it was pointed out that in vivo chain initiation is believed to begin by the union of mRNA to the 30S ribosomal component in the presence of "initiating" tRNA. The union of this complex to the 50S subunit gives rise to the active 70S ribosome competent in protein synthesis. Some in vitro experiments suggest that initiating tRNA also can recognize GUG and, weakly, UUG triplets, but the significance of these triplets for chain initiation in vivo remains to be assessed.

It seems that N-formylmethionine is not required for chain initiation in higher plants and animals and by plant viruses. A possible candidate for initiation in these organisms is acetylserine (Fig. 9.2), because this "blocked" amino acid is found N-terminally in some proteins. However, other "blocked" N-terminal amino acids have been found in other proteins. Critical experimentation remains to be done with these systems.

The experiments outlined here and in Chap. 7 indicate that chain initiation in *E. coli* is a specialized event requiring the proper codon, a special initiating tRNA, and possibly several protein-binding factors and enzymes. On polycistronic mRNA, it appears necessary to terminate the first polypeptide chain to initiate the polypeptide chain coded for

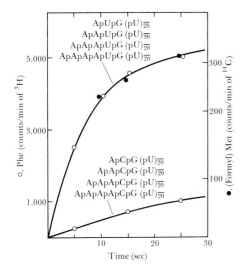

FIG. 9.3. *Kinetics of incorporation of isotopically labeled phenylalanine (^3H) and methionine (^{14}C) with various synthetic polymers.*

The synthetic oligonucleotides were added to an amino acid–incorporating system from **E. coli** *at low magnesium concentrations, where initiation of polypeptide chains is highly dependent upon the AUG triplet. The reaction was stopped after different lengths of time and the incorporation of each amino acid determined. The AUG codon was equally effective in stimulating incorporation when present at the 5' end of the oligonucleotide or when located internally (top curve). The presence of the AUG triplet greatly enhanced the incorporation of phenylalanine* (○) *coded by the UUU triplets at the terminal ends of the polymers. The low incorporation that took place in the absence of the AUG codon (lower curve) probably is due to a small amount of miscoding in the in vitro system. That is, the ACG codon (threonine) is occasionally misread by the formylmethionine-initiating tRNA, leading to aberrant chain initiation. Once started, the chain elongates as the nucleotides are read sequentially in sets of three. Modified from R. E. Thach, T. A. Sundararajan, K. F. Dewey, J. C. Brown, and P. Doty,* Cold Spring Harbor Symp. Quant. Biol., 31 *(1966), 85.*

by the second cistron on the message. Consequently, the chain-initiating triplet AUG may be adjacent to or very near one or more of the codons called *chain-terminating codons.*

CHAIN TERMINATION

Three chain-terminating codons, UAA, UAG, and UGA, have been identified in *E. coli.* They are termed *nonsense codons* (Fig. 8.3). Two of the three nonsense codons, ochre (UAA) and amber (UAG), received pseudonyms to help differentiate them before their actual composition and nucleotide sequence was known; their presence was deduced initially from purely genetic observations made on phage mutants. Subsequently, biochemical studies indicated that certain phage nonsense mutants were, in fact, producing incomplete polypeptide chains instead of normal phage-head protein. These fragments all contained normal amino acid sequences from the N-terminal end of the protein, but lacked different amounts of the C-terminal sequence. Particular suppressor mutations that could reverse the effects of nonsense, but not of missense, codons facilitated the study of nonsense mutants and indicated that different types of nonsense codons must exist, each capable of terminating polypeptide chain synthesis. It also became obvious from biophysical studies that some single large mRNA molecules could code for a number of individual and unique polypeptide chains. Certainly, some punctuation between cistrons on these polycistronic mRNA's is required unless these distinct polypeptide chains are the result of the specific splitting of a giant precursor protein molecule.

The identification of the base sequences in nonsense codons has relied on diverse experimental approaches, ranging from the inability of polymers containing nonsense codons to stimulate amino acid incorporation in vitro to the analysis of amino acid replacements in proteins isolated from revertants of nonsense mutants. The collective mutation data from several *E. coli* and phage systems are outlined in Fig. 9.4.

The assignment of code words in Fig. 9.4 is based largely on the code-word dictionary developed from in vitro amino acid incorporation or tRNA binding studies (Chaps. 7 and 8). This does not detract from the beauty of the in vivo experiments. The agreement between the two is perfect only if the putative nonsense triplets, in fact, *are* the nonsense codons.

Our chapter on coding (Chap. 8) also contains data pertinent to chain termination. Note from Fig. 8.12 that, except in a few cases, amino acid incorporation proceeds as expected for a triplet code when synthetic polymers of known sequence are used. Two polymers of repeating trinucleotide sequence, poly-GUA (which contains the amber codon UAG) and poly-GAU (which contains the UGA codon) code for incorporation of only two amino acids. The products are homopolymers, each polypeptide chain containing but a single repeating amino acid. Two polymers synthesized with repeating tetranucleotides, poly-GUAA (containing the ochre codon UAA) and poly-GAUA (containing the UAG codon), fail to incorporate amino acids into acid-insoluble peptides; whether acid-soluble tripeptides are made between the nonsense codons remains to be determined.

Convincing evidence that nonsense triplets serve to terminate polypeptide chains in vivo has been obtained in analyses of the polypeptide products made by nonsense phage mutants in bacterial hosts. Only the N-terminal part of the protein, discerned by fingerprinting, is found; the part of the protein dictated by the nucleic acid beyond the nonsense triplet is absent in extracts of the infected cells.

FIG. 9.4. *Nonsense codon sequences inferred from reversion studies.*

Nonsense mutations (circled) were elicited in a population of wild-type organisms. Where the amino acid originally present in the wild-type protein is known or can be strongly inferred, an arrow has been indicated pointing from that amino acid with its appropriate codon to the new nonsense codon. Reversions of the nonsense mutants have been obtained and the particular amino acid replacement in each revertant has been determined or inferred from genetic experiments. Revertants are indicated by arrows pointing from the nonsense codons to the respective amino acids. Some reversion tests have utilized chemical mutagens whose mechanism of action is known. For example, HM (hydroxylamine) causes predominantly, if not exclusively, transition mutations from G/C to A/T in the DNA; AP (2-aminopurine) causes only transition mutations from G/C to A/T and from A/T to G/C (see Fig. 10.3).

A check with the genetic-code arrangements derived from in vitro studies (Fig. 8.2) indicates that UAG is the only triplet that can give rise to the seven indicated amino acids (and their triplets) by single-base substitutions. Similarly, UAA can mutate to UAG through a transition mutation and give rise to six different amino acid replacements in revertants. UGA, by transition mutations, gives rise to two types of revertants and by a G → A transition mutates to the ochre triplet UAA. The nonsense mutations are detected and classified by their ability to be corrected by codon-specific suppressor mutations.

Genetic crosses have been carried out between nonsense mutants having base substitutions located within the same triplet. No wild-type recombinants are obtained with ochre (UAA) × amber (UAG) or ochre (UAA) × UGA crosses. Wild-type recombinants are recovered from amber (UAG) × UGA crosses; the amino acid present in the wild-type recombinants is

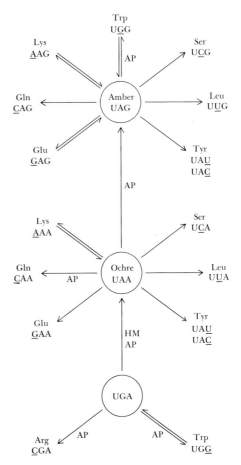

presumed to be tryptophan (UGG), but this has not yet been established.

Assignment of UGA as a nonsense codon completed the assignment of primary functions to the 64 codons in E. coli. Data compiled from A. S. Sarabhai, A. O. W. Stretton, S. Brenner, and E. Bolle, Nature, 201 (1964), 13; M. G. Weigert, E. Gallucci, E. Lanka, and A. Garen, Cold Spring Harbor Symp. Quant. Biol., 31 (1966), 145; A. Sarabhai and S. Brenner, J. Mol. Biol., 26 (1967), 141; S. Brenner, L. Barnett, E. R. Katz, and F. H. C. Crick, Nature, 213 (1967), 449.

The molecular mechanism of chain termination is unclear. One theory proposes that there is a tRNA-like molecule that does not attach amino acid. The entry of this molecule at a nonsense codon terminates the polypeptide chain and stimulates hydrolysis of the chain from the final ribosome-bound tRNA. Such a proposal uses as a model the action of the antibiotic puromycin, a tRNA analogue, which enters the tRNA ribosomal binding sites and is covalently bound to the elongating polypeptide chain. However, the attachment of puromycin to the ribosome is weak, permitting dissociation of the peptidyl–puromycin complex. Another possibility is that the polypeptide chain is cleaved from the tRNA to which it is attached when no additional tRNA molecule, either charged or uncharged, can enter the adjacent open site and pair with the mRNA (Fig. 7.5).

Reinitiation of polypeptide chain synthesis usually does not occur within a single cistron of a polycistronic mRNA if a nonsense codon is introduced into that cistron. However, reinitiation normally is observed at the beginning of the next cistron. The probability of reinitiating polypeptide synthesis seems highest when the reinitiating site is not far removed from the chain-terminating site. Perhaps the most efficient reinitiation takes place only when a terminating and an initiating codon are in sequence. Reinitiation at the beginning of cistrons occurs in phase, and the correct reading frame is subsequently maintained. This leads to the view that termination and initiation of polypeptide chains are interrelated events. If there is a special tRNA or protein involved in termination, perhaps the insertion of this factor potentiates the binding of initiating N-formylmethionyl–tRNA at the proper spot nearby.

These speculations merely point out how much more we have to learn before we can apply our knowledge of the genetic code to the punctuation normally found between genes. The processes outlined here provide clues and hypotheses subject to experimental test. They inform us that chain initiation in *E. coli* requires a specific triplet, AUG, on the mRNA as well as N-formylmethionyl–tRNA and accessory protein factors. The mRNA is then read sequentially by triplets until another special signal, a chain-terminating codon, is encountered. This leads to termination of the polypeptide chain. How are polypeptide chain initiation and termination related? This is one of the more provoking questions current research seeks to answer.

Infidelities in Translation

DNA transcription to mRNA and mRNA translation are amazingly precise processes. This fidelity allows us to write down *the* exact amino acid sequence of a protein (Figs. 2.4 and 3.6) and to infer from these studies *the* nucleotide sequence on mRNA and, by extrapolation, the base pairs in the gene. Transcription and translation are multistep, multimolecular processes in which precise function is requisite for cell survival; we would expect them to be systems well buffered against outside perturbations. Yet, as with all cellular metabolism, transcription and translation can be modified and disrupted to some extent by environmental as well as genetic change.

In Chap. 10 we shall discuss infidelities that occur in the transcription step. Now we shall focus attention on several factors known to affect the extent and nature of infidelities in translation.

AMBIGUITIES

One of the "difficulties" encountered in in vitro tRNA binding studies and, to a lesser extent, in amino acid–incorporation studies has been a certain amount of ambiguity. For example, poly-U leads to incorporation predominantly of phenylalanine. But incorporation of a slight amount of leucine is also noted. The ambiguities are enhanced at high Mg^{2+} or NH_4^+ concentrations. Since these elevated concentrations were used in many of the earlier in vitro studies, occasionally you may see published data that do not comply with the genetic code shown in Fig. 8.2.

Extremely careful investigations of proteins made in vivo have now revealed several cases of heterogeneity in protein primary structure overlooked earlier (Fig. 9.5). This heterogeneity could result from somatic mutations or some other cause of nonisogenicity with respect to the gene(s) concerned. However, it is equally plausible that the changes reflect the existence of certain "ambiguous" codons which may be read at low frequency by more than one type of aminoacyl tRNA. Also, because the levels of various aminoacyl tRNA synthetases vary in different tissues, the extent of ambiguity may be tissue-dependent. For example, a dearth or altered conformation of one type of charged tRNA may allow the binding of an incorrect tRNA charged with an amino acid other than the normal one for that position in the polypeptide chain. Certainly, this is a problem with important implications for studies of gene action in differentiation and in disease.

PHENOTYPIC DISRUPTION AND REPAIR

Ambiguities in amino acid incorporation in vitro are greatly stimulated in the presence of the antibiotic streptomycin. Interaction of streptomycin with the 30S ribosomal subunit is responsible for the increased ambiguity in reading. This is demonstrated by extraction of ribosomes from streptomycin-sensitive and streptomycin-resistant bacteria, dissociation of the subunits in low magnesium, separation of the subunits, and reconstitution of subunits in pairwise mixtures. The reconstituted ribosomes containing a 30S subunit from a sensitive strain permit a high level of misreading in the presence of strepto-

Position	Amino acid	Moles amino acid per mole peptide (approx.)
29	Val	0.6
	Leu	0.4
48–49	Phe-Thr	0.53
	Leu-Ser	0.40
	Phe-Ser	0.04
	Leu-Thr	0.03
70	Val	0.8
	Thr	0.2
76	Leu	0.8
	Val	0.2
80	Ser	0.5
	Leu	0.5

FIG. 9.5. *Alternate amino acids found at particular positions in the α chain of rabbit hemoglobin.*

Analysis of most peptides obtained from rabbit hemoglobin indicated that there is a fixed and discrete content of amino acids. In contrast, some peptides contained nonintegral values of amino acid residues, and these were traced to the residues indicated in the table. Since the various α chains containing different amino acids cannot be separated from one another, the amino acid sequence in one particular class of chain cannot be stated. Thus only the gross composition at each position for the population of polypeptide chains can be listed. The values given in the table are for one sample of hemoglobin. These ratios differed for different animals. Hemoglobin samples from some animals exhibited only a single amino acid at one of these positions but still showed variation at one or more of the other positions.

The Leu at position 48 is known to be positioned by a minor tRNA component which does not respond to UUA or UUG codons. Therefore, this Leu codon presumedly cannot mutate to a Ser codon by a single base-pair change (see Fig. 8.2). Similar reasoning is applied to the Val-Thr alternation at position 70. For these reasons, the amino acid substitutions are not readily explained as engendered by somatic mutations. The ambiguities may be due to events occurring during translation. From G. von Ehrenstein, Cold Spring Harbor Symp. Quant. Biol., **31** *(1966),* 705.

mycin. The other components in the amino acid–incorporating system, including the source of the 50S subunit, do not alter this streptomycin-induced misreading.

The extent of ambiguity can be appreciable. Normal and streptomycin-induced ambiguities found under one set of experimental conditions are shown in Fig. 9.6. The codons for ambiguously incorporated amino acids differ but in one letter from the codon for the "authentic" amino acid. Studies with similar polymers show that

| | Radioactivity incorporated (cpm) | | | |
| | − Poly-U | | + Poly-U | |
14C-Amino acid	− SM	+ SM	− SM	+ SM
Phe	80	99	1035	1270
Leu	25	24	400	763
Ile	13	13	88	925
Ser	20	30	36	140

FIG. 9.6.   *Ambiguities during in vitro amino acid incorporation and their stimulation by streptomycin.*

A dialyzed, preincubated amino acid–incorporating system from a streptomycin-sensitive E. coli was used. The reaction mixture contained 19 cold L-amino acids plus the ¹⁴C-labeled radioactive amino acid listed in the figure; thus four experiments were run in parallel on aliquots of the cell extract. In addition, streptomycin, poly-U, or both were added to samples containing each of the radioactive amino acids. The addition of poly-U greatly stimulated incorporation of Phe and, ambiguously, Leu. Further addition of streptomycin greatly stimulated the ambiguous reading of poly-U for Leu, Ile, and Ser. The codons for these amino acids involved in ambiguities differ but one letter from Phe (see Fig. 8.2). Data from J. Davies, W. Gilbert, and L. Gorini, Proc. Natl. Acad. Sci. U.S., 51 (1964), 883; see also L. Gorini, Federation Proc., 26 (1967), 5; L. Gorini and J. R. Beckwith, Ann. Rev. Microbiol., 20 (1966), 401; T. E. Likover and C. G. Kurland, Proc. Natl. Acad. Sci. U.S., 58 (1967), 2385.

streptomycin induces 5′-terminal or internal U to be misread as A or C, 5′-terminal C as A or U, and internal C as A. From Fig. 8.2 you can determine which triplets will be misread in the presence of streptomycin and which will not.

Misreading of mRNA's in vivo is certainly one major explanation for the inhibition of bacteria by streptomycin; defective proteins are made in the presence of streptomycin. The effects are most severe in the case of multimeric enzymes, in which one defective polypeptide chain in the multimer can inactivate the functioning of the entire subunit complex.

Although superficially contradictory, in vivo streptomycin-induced misreading can be both deleterious and helpful. Normal codons can be incorrectly read to create damaging errors. Certain mutant codons can be read as wild type, thereby acting to reverse the mutant phenotype, for example, in nonsense mutants that carry a 5′-U in the triplet. This type of phenotypic reversal is shown in Fig. 9.7. Where analyses for enzyme activities have been made, the streptomycin-induced appearance of enzyme activity has been found in mutant bacteria. The differential effect of streptomycin on the reading of certain triplets frequently permits repair of a particular mutant triplet to exceed the damaging effects at other triplets critical to the growth of the cell.

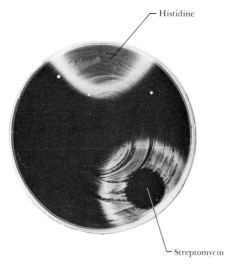

Histidine

Streptomycin

FIG. 9.7. *Phenotypic reversal by streptomycin. A petri plate of glucose-salts-agar medium has been spread with mutant bacteria. The bacteria have a genetic block in biosynthesis of the amino acid L-histidine and thus cannot grow. Crystals of histidine and streptomycin were placed on the agar medium, and the plate was incubated to allow growth. The histidine diffused into the medium, supplied the end product of the blocked pathway, and the bacteria grew. The streptomycin diffused into the medium and killed bacteria at higher concentrations (inhibition zone). The bacteria were able to grow in the absence of histidine where streptomycin was present at low concentrations. The streptomycin allowed some enzymatically active protein to be made.*

These experiments, together with the fact that mRNA is known to bind specifically to the 30S component of the 70S ribosome, provide direct evidence that some structure of the 30S component is critical for correct recognition of the mRNA codon by the tRNA anticodon. The accuracy of this reading can be influenced by environmental factors such as cation concentration or the presence of low molecular-weight compounds of natural origin, such as streptomycin. They also give a clue for the dominance of the gene for streptomycin sensitivity. If half of the ribosomes in a heterozygote are streptomycin-resistant, their presence still would allow the sensitive ribosomes to make translational errors in the presence of streptomycin.

Genetic Modification of Translation

Ordinarily, mutations affecting the steps in protein synthesis are lethal in that such defects usually are irreparable and widespread in action. Nutritional supplementation of the culture medium is of little help. This obstacle to potential genetic probing of the translation machinery of the cell can be circumvented by several means. One is the selection of temperature-sensitive mutants that are defective for some component in the protein-synthesizing system. Temperature-sensitive mutants contain altered proteins that are labile at one temperature but function at another temperature. The cell population thus can be grown and maintained at one temperature. Transfer of the cells to a different temperature causes rapid inactivation of the critical function. Biochemical analysis of cells after a shift in temperature permits dissection of the critical (temperature-sensitive) function, evaluation of its importance and its role in vivo. Most temperature-sensitive mutants so far examined are sensitive to elevated temperatures, but mutants sensitive to low temperatures also are known. We suspect that this latter class will be more widely used in the future. The finding of a temperature-sensitive mutation in a gene is presumptive evidence that the gene specifies the structure of a protein. Such approaches have been used to study temperature-sensitive aminoacyl tRNA synthetases, ribosomes, and so on.

The streptomycin-sensitive and streptomycin-resistant mutants discussed above represent a class of mutants in which translation can be affected under a particular set of conditions. Some of these mutations affect ribosome structure and subsequently the magnitude of streptomycin-induced misreading at certain streptomycin concentrations. Additional mutations that influence ribosomal structure have been found. Some of these mutations suppress, with low efficiency, the effects of ochre chain-terminating mutations. In this respect, the suppressor mutations mimic the effects of streptomycin. They lead to a partial correction of the premature chain termination due to the ochre mutation. The second, correcting mutation is termed a *suppressor mutation* because it suppresses to some extent the mutant phenotype elicited by ochre mutations. Jargon terms it an "ochre suppressor" (suppressor of an ochre mutation). The suppressor mutation presumably acts by modifying ribosomal structure in a way that occasionally allows the ochre UAA triplet to be misread. This allows insertion of an amino acid and subsequent normal elongation of the polypeptide chain instead of its premature termination at the point of the UAA triplet.

Nonsense suppressor mutations involving components of the translation machinery other than the ribosomes have also been detected. These suppressor mutations are codon-specific. One type will suppress only amber (UAG) mutations. Another class suppresses both amber (UAG) and ochre (UAA) mutations. Suppressors specific for the third chain-terminating codon, UGA, also are known. Normal, or nearly normal, proteins are made in vivo by bacteria carrying the suppressor mutation. In several instances, novel new tRNA species have been detected and associated with the nonsense suppressors. The coding sequence of an accessory and dispensible tRNA species is changed so that it recognizes the nonsense triplet. This permits the insertion of a specific amino acid in the polypeptide chain, thereby avoiding premature chain termination. Amino acid analyses of such proteins show that each suppressor gene effects the insertion of the amino acid at exactly the point where the nonsense codon would otherwise terminate the chain. The amino acids detected in each case are given in Fig. 9.8. The efficiency of the suppressor in vivo is also indicated in the figure. Each suppressor functions at about the same efficiency for specific nonsense mutations in any of a number of genes or at any of a number of places within a single gene. In some cases, the wild-type amino acid is inserted ("sense"); in other cases, another amino acid will be inserted ("missense"). This depends upon the codon from which the nonsense triplet was originally derived as well as the specific suppressor mutation. Most of the proteins are active, although serine, glutamine, or tyrosine has been substituted

	Amino acid inserted instead of chain termination, and efficiency of amino acid insertion		
Suppressor gene	Amber UAG	Ochre UAA	UGA
su-1	Serine, 28%	0	0
su-2	Glutamine, 14%	0	0
su-3	Tyrosine, 55%	0	0
su-4	Tyrosine, 16%	Tyrosine, 12%	0
su-5	Basic amino acid, 5%	Basic amino acid, 6%	0
su-UGA	0	0	Unknown amino acid, 55%

FIG. 9.8. *Some* E. coli *suppressor mutations affecting the reading of chain-termi-nating codons. Suppressor gene 1 is active only on UAG codons and leads to serine insertion 28 percent of the time; chain termination still occurs 72 percent of the time. Suppressor genes 4 and 5 are active both on amber and ochre codons. Bac-teria that are wild type except for one of the amber suppressors (su-1 through su-3) or for su-UGA show undiminished growth rates, but bacteria carrying ochre sup-pressors (su-4 and su-5) grow slowly. Compiled from M. G. Weigert, E. Gallucci, E. Lanka, and A. Garen, Cold Spring Harbor Symp. Quant. Biol., 31 (1966), 145; J. F. Sambrook, D. P. Fan, and S. Brenner, Nature, 214 (1967), 452.*

at a given position in the polypeptide chain. This is a further demon-stration of the premise made in Chap. 3—that missense mutations may often remain undetected, because protein function may be relatively unimpaired.

How were tRNA's implicated in suppressor gene action? Although their role in suppression had been suggested by geneticists for some time, experimental proof has become available only recently. RNA ex-tracted from bacteriophage f2 can serve as template in an amino acid–incorporating system for the in vitro synthesis of the virus coat protein. The presence of an amber mutation in the virus RNA results in the formation of incomplete polypeptide chains or fragments of the coat protein. These fragments can be isolated by gradient centrifugation and recognized by tryptic peptide fingerprint analysis and comparison with the peptide profile of the normal coat protein. When extracts of bacteria carrying a suppressor mutation at gene *su-1* (Fig. 9.8) are used, some of the polypeptide chains are completed; that is, normal-sized molecules are made. Fractions from an extract of the suppressor-con-taining bacteria were tested in an amino acid–incorporating system us-ing RNA from the phage amber mutant as mRNA. These tests showed that the active component was a modified or new tRNA. This tRNA was able to insert serine at the position where premature chain termina-tion would otherwise occur. Similarly, a modified tyrosine tRNA has been detected in *su-3* bacteria. This tyrosine tRNA is a minor tRNA species and a "duplicate" of the one primarily used for the insertion of tyrosine at most positions in proteins. Examination of the purified tRNA's shows that the wild-type tRNA contains a coding sequence (anticodon) GUA that can recognize the mRNA triplet UAC by antiparallel pairing:

tRNA
anticodon

←⎯⎯⎯

AUG
UAC

⎯⎯⎯→

mRNA
codon

The tRNA from the mutant is still charged with tyrosine by the appropriate aminoacyl tRNA synthetase, but it contains a single base substitution. It contains a CUA triplet instead of the GUA triplet present in wild type. The CUA can recognize, by antiparallel pairing, the nonsense amber UAG triplet. This is dramatic support for the concept of tRNA as adaptor and its important role in codon recognition; it lends substance and validity to the selection of a particular sequence on tRNA as the anticodon sequence. It also raises questions. For example: What is the *normal function* of the minor, duplicate tyrosine tRNA species? Other cases of nonsense suppression have been pinned down to alterations in tRNA structure. tRNA alterations have been implicated in the case of suppressor genes 1 through 5 in Fig. 9.8.

Note in Fig. 4.3 that tryptophan synthetase mutants *A23* and *A36* contain substitutions of arginine in place of the glycine found at residue position 210 in wild-type protein. A suppressor mutant was selected as a revertant from the *A36* mutant. It contained the original *A36* mutation plus the suppressor permitting it to grow on a medium lacking tryptophan. Extracts were prepared from wild-type and the suppressed mutant. The abilities of these extracts to promote incorporation of radioactive arginine and glycine in response to poly-AG was studied. Figure 9.9 shows that both the wild-type and suppressed mutant extracts incorporate arginine; this incorporation is in the form of a copolypeptide of alternating arginine (triplet AGA) and glutamic acid (triplet GAG) residues (Fig. 8.12). In contrast, the wild-type extract is *inactive* in promoting glycine incorporation, whereas the extract from the suppressor strain elicits this incorporation. The active factor in the mutant extracts was shown to be in the tRNA fraction. Characterization of the product showed that the glycine was incorporated exclusively adjacent to glutamic acid residues. In response to poly-AG, the tRNA fraction from the suppressor-carrying strain (a mixture of tRNA species) had maintained its ability to make an Arg-Glu copolymer while gaining a new ability, that is, the formation of a Gly-Glu copolymer in the absence of arginine.

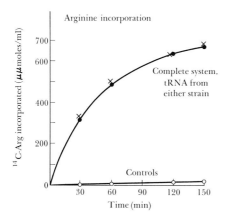
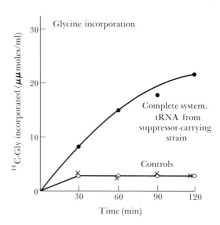

FIG. 9.9. *Ability of tRNA from a suppressor-carrying strain to elicit glycine incorporation in response to poly-AG.*

Poly-AG normally elicits the incorporation of arginine and glutamic acid in a polypeptide of alternating sequence (Fig. 8.12). The experiment depicted at the left shows that significant incorporation of ^{14}C-*arginine occurs in the presence of poly-AG, unlabeled glutamic acid, and the tRNA fraction and ribosomes from either wild-type or suppressor-carrying bacteria (top curve). Only negligible incorporation is obtained when glutamic acid, poly-AG, or ribosomes are omitted from the amino acid–incorporating system (lower curve, controls).*

The experiment depicted at the right shows that significant incorporation of ^{14}C-*glycine occurs only in the presence of poly-AG, unlabeled glutamic acid, and the tRNA fraction from the suppressor-carrying bacteria (top curve). The source of ribosomes can be from either strain. The controls (bottom curve) show only a very slight incorporation when poly-AG is omitted, when glutamic acid is omitted, or when the tRNA fraction is obtained from wild-type bacteria. This slight incorporation is attributed to incorporation of glycine directed by endogenous message and does not occur when ribosomes are omitted from the amino acid–incorporating mixture. Labeled amino acids other than glycine do not show a poly-AG–dependent incorporation in the presence of glutamic acid and tRNA from the suppressor-carrying strain. Thus the incorporation is specific for glycine and for tRNA from the suppressor-carrying strain.*

Note that arginine incorporation is about 30 times more efficient than is glycine incorporation; this gives some indication of the efficiency of action of the suppressor tRNA and, in fact, roughly corresponds to the efficiency of this suppression in vivo.

From J. Carbon, P. Berg, and C. Yanofsky, **Cold Spring Harbor Symp. Quant. Biol., 31 (1966), 487.** *Similar studies have been performed with extracts of a suppressor for mutant A78 that contains a cysteine residue at position 233 in place of the glycine found in wild-type protein. The tRNA's of wild-type bacteria respond to poly-UG only through manufacture of a valine-cysteine copolypeptide (Fig. 8.12). The tRNA's of the suppressor strain also make a valine-glycine copolypeptide when cysteine is absent from the reaction mixture. [See N. K. Gupta and H. G. Khorana,* **Proc. Natl. Acad. Sci. U.S., 56 (1966), 772.**]

Codon-Anticodon Recognition

The above results indicate that tRNA genes can mutate and the resulting tRNA's can "recognize" codons on mRNA which they were previously unable to read. What is the mechanism of this recognition? What forces enter into codon recognition?

We have already mentioned that the ribosome and environment, for example, the cation concentration, participate in the recognition process. Another critical factor, of course, is the precise composition of the coding triplet itself; that is the basis of the genetic code presented in

FIG. 9.10. *Patterns of codon recognition by purified tRNA's from E. coli and from yeast. The tRNA's have been purified until resolved from other species that carry the same amino acid. Several tRNA's have been purified, and the primary structures of a number have been determined. The affinity of the tRNA for a variety of triplets (binding studies to synthetic polynucleotide-ribosome complexes), and, in some cases, its ability to stimulate amino acid incorporation in the presence of particular synthetic polyribonucleic acid polymers were investigated. Some of the tRNA's respond only to a single codon. For example, the tRNA Trp responds only to UGG. Most tRNA's respond to two or more codons, as indicated by the lines joining open and closed circles. The open circles (O) are yeast tRNA's and the closed circles (●) are tRNA's purified from E. coli. Numerous other tRNA's have not yet been purified. Modified after R. M. Bock, D. Söll, and J. D. Cherayil, Progr. Theoret. Biol., 2 (1968), in press; with additions from the recent literature.*

1st letter	2nd letter				3rd letter
	U	C	A	G	
U	●●● Phe O	●● Ser O	●● Tyr OO	Cys	U
	●● Phe O	● Ser O	●● Tyr OO	Cys	C
	─● Leu	Ser O	Ochre O	Nonsense	A
	●●● Leu	● Ser	Amber	● Trp	G
C	Leu	Pro	His	● Arg O	U
	Leu	Pro	His	● Arg O	C
	Leu	● Pro	Gln	● Arg O	A
	● Leu	● Pro	Gln	● Arg	G
A	●● Ile	Thr	Asn	● Ser	U
	●● Ile	Thr	Asn	● Ser	C
	Ile	Thr	●● Lys	Arg O	A
	● ● Met	Thr	●● Lys	Arg O	G
G	●● Val OO	● Ala O	Asp	● Gly O	U
	● Val O	● Ala O	Asp	● Gly O	C
	● Val OO	● Ala O	● Glu	● Gly O	A
	●● Val O	● Ala	● Glu	●● Gly OO	G

Fig. 8.2. At first it was easy to picture the interaction of tRNA with mRNA as due strictly to Watson-Crick base pairing, where the purine adenine (A) pairs with the pyrimidine uracil (U) and where the purine guanine (G) pairs with the pyrimidine cytosine (C) (compare Fig. 1.1). However, studies on the structure of purified tRNA's (Fig. 6.3), studies on the binding of partially purified tRNA's to ribosomes in the presence of various triplets (p. 124), and amino acid–incorporation data with synthetic polyribonucleotides show the interactions to be more complex. Results obtained with 40 partially purified species of tRNA from *E. coli* and from yeast are shown in Fig. 9.10. Although some tRNA's can recognize only a single triplet, others can recognize two or three triplets. The triplets recognized often differ only in the third base.

One model, proposed by F. H. C. Crick, to explain these observations suggests that certain bases can "wobble" and thus form hydrogen bonds effective in pairing of the mRNA codon and the tRNA anticodon when they meet on the ribosome. Another model, proposed by R. M. Bock, D. Söll, and J. D. Cherayil, suggests that the environment on the ribosome can assist particular bases on certain tRNA's to undergo tautomeric shifts that will alter their base-pairing properties. These models attribute special significance to inosine (I), pseudouridine (ψ), and other unusual bases found in tRNA species and thought to reside in some of the anticodons in tRNA (Fig. 9.11). For example, the tRNA shown in Fig. 6.3 contains the presumed anticodon IGC. Since the two pairing RNA strands line up in an antipolar fashion, IGC recognizes GCC as a codon, because I normally forms standard base pairs with C (I behaves like G). However, Fig. 9.10 shows that the purified yeast alanine tRNA can also recognize GCA and GCU. Models of such unusual base pairs (I with A and I with U) have been built and shown to provide feasible explanations for the peculiar affinities of the various tRNA's.

FIG. 9.11. *Current idea of pairing partners involved in tRNA–mRNA recognition: OMG, 2-O-methylguanine; I, inosine; rT, (ribo)thymine; ψ, pseudouridine. Adapted from F. H. C. Crick, J. Mol. Biol., 19 (1966), 548, and R. M. Bock, D. Söll, and J. D. Cherayil, Progr. Theoret. Biol., 2 (1968), in press.*

Base in tRNA anticodon	Recognized bases in mRNA codon(s)
U	A
C	G
G	C or U
OMG	C or U
I	U, C, or A
rT	A or G
ψ	A, G, or (weakly) U

The patterns of codon recognition by increasing numbers of purified tRNA's, along with intimate knowledge of the structures of the tRNA's, indicates that standard Watson-Crick base pairing plays an important role in the translation process. In addition, special pairing rules also must be provided at some locations. The tRNA–mRNA–ribosome aggregate normally allows these complex interactions to occur with high fidelity. The underlying mechanisms allowing this precision remain obscure. However, in view of these events it is not surprising to find that modifications of ribosomal structure and the environment can alter translational fidelity.

Controls on Translation

The experiments outlined in this chapter indicate the importance of genetic and environmental control of protein synthesis. They point to the many levels at which effective regulation of translation can be imposed. They emphasize the importance of the mRNA-tRNA-ribosome complex as the focal point for gene action. Certainly events here can feed back to influence the formation of the next cycle of gene products. They can affect the quantities of proteins formed by the cell, selecting mRNA's for reading and also influencing the ultimate composition of the final polypeptide products.

Chapter 10 presents evidence that controls are exerted at the level of transcription of the master DNA template to RNA. We shall see also that the processes of transcription and translation are intimately related. This presents opportunities for two types of transcriptional control. One may operate directly on the DNA, while translational controls also may influence transcription.

Questions

9.1. What effect does a missense mutation have on synthesis of a protein? A nonsense mutation?

9.2. Read an original paper written during the past year on the mechanism of protein biosynthesis and correlate its salient points with the genetically oriented description in this and earlier chapters.

9.3. By what tests can one pursue an analysis to determine if a partial back mutant is due to a suppressor mutation in a second gene, at a second site in the same gene, or at the same nucleotide pair involved in the first mutation?

9.4. Describe one method which you could use to find out if a suppressor mutation affects tRNA or affects ribosomal structure. Can this method also give you some information on the mutated codon?

9.5. How does an ambiguity differ from a missense mutation?

9.6. Briefly outline how a polypeptide chain is initiated.

9.7. What explanations can you offer for the different efficiencies of nonsense suppressors in restoring function in vivo?

9.8. From your knowledge of protein synthesis and its genetic and environmental control, give four possible explanations for the occurrence of ambiguities in the hemoglobin polypeptide chain. Can you think of any experiments by which you could differentiate between these possibilities?

References

Apirion, D., "Altered Ribosomes in a Suppressor Strain of *E. coli*," *J. Mol. Biol., 16* (1966), 285.

Benzer, S., and S. P. Champe, "A Change from Nonsense to Sense in the Genetic Code," *Proc. Natl. Acad. Sci. U.S., 48* (1962), 1114. Nonsense mutations and nonsense suppressors had a beautiful beginning, herein presented in seven pages.

Capecchi, M. R., "Polypeptide Chain Termination in Vitro: Isolation of a Release Factor," *Proc. Natl. Acad. Sci. U.S., 58* (1967), 1144. Description of a protein component required for polypeptide chain termination, of particular interest from the standpoint of methods used in the analysis (compare with Cuzin et al., below).

————, and G. N. Gussin, "Suppression in Vitro, Identification of a Serine-sRNA as a Nonsense Suppressor," *Science, 149* (1965), 417. A report that presented strong evidence that a suppressor mutation led to synthesis of an altered tRNA.

Church, R., and B. J. McCarthy, "Changes in Nuclear and Cytoplasmic RNA in Regenerating Mouse Liver," *Proc. Natl. Acad. Sci. U.S., 58* (1967), 1548. "It is suggested that selective transport of RNA to the cytoplasm may be an important device for the regulation of translation of potential messengers."

Crick, F. H. C., "The Genetic Code—Yesterday, Today, and Tomorrow," *Cold Spring Harbor Symp. Quant. Biol., 31* (1966), 3. Some cogent comments and ideas on events in translation.

Cuzin, F., N. Kretchmer, R. E. Greenberg, R. Hurwitz, and F. Chapeville, "Enzymatic Hydrolysis of N-substituted Aminoacyl-tRNA," *Proc. Natl. Acad. Sci. U.S., 58* (1967), 2079. An enzyme presumed to be involved in chain termination.

Flaks, J. G., P. S. Leboy, E. A. Birge, and C. G. Kurland, "Mutations and Genetics Concerned with the Ribosome," *Cold Spring Harbor Symp. Quant. Biol., 31* (1966), 623.

Freedman, M. L., M. Hori, and M. Rabinovitz, "Membranes in Polyribosome Formation by Rabbit Reticulocytes," *Science, 157* (1967), 323. A short summary of in vivo evidence that implicates cellular membranes as components in polyribosome formation and translation.

Garen, A., "Sense and Nonsense in the Genetic Code," *Science, 160* (1968), 149. An excellent article to use as a follow-up on the descriptions of nonsense codons found in this chapter.

Gesteland, R. F., W. Salser, and A. Bolle, "In Vitro Synthesis of T4 Lysozyme by Suppression of Amber Mutations," *Proc. Natl. Acad. Sci. U.S., 58* (1967), 2036. A sensitive assay system, in vitro enzyme protein synthesis, and demonstration that the action of some suppressor mutations is mediated through tRNA molecules at the level of translation.

Gorini, L., "Antibiotics and the Genetic Code," *Sci. Am., 214* (April 1966), 102.

———, and J. R. Beckwith, "Suppression," *Ann. Rev. Microbiol., 20* (1966), 401. A review that stresses genetic suppression of nonsense mutants and phenotypic suppression by streptomycin.

———, G. A. Jakoby, and L. Breckenridge, "Ribosomal Ambiguity," *Cold Spring Harbor Symp. Quant. Biol., 31* (1966), 657.

Langridge, J., "Genetic and Enzymatic Experiments Relating to the Tertiary Structure of β-Galactosidase," *J. Bacteriol., 96* (1968), 1711. Suppressors of amber mutations are used in an interesting study that formulates ideas on the folding of the polypeptide chain.

Leboy, P. S., E. C. Cox, and J. G. Flaks, "The Chromosomal Site Specifying a Ribosomal Protein in *E. coli,*" *Proc. Natl. Acad. Sci. U.S., 52* (1964), 1367.

Lee, J. C., and V. M. Ingram, "Erythrocyte Transfer RNA: Change During Chick Development," *Science, 158* (1967), 1330. Embryonic and adult methionyl-, and possibly leucyl-, transfer RNA's may differ.

Lengyel, P., "On Peptide Chain Initiation," in *Molecular Genetics, Part II,* J. H. Taylor, ed. New York: Academic Press, Inc. 1967, p. 193. An area of study that has exploded since 1964.

Neidhardt, F. C., and C. F. Earhart, "Phage-Induced Appearance of a Valyl sRNA Synthetase Activity in *E. coli,*" *Cold Spring Harbor Symp. Quant. Biol., 31* (1966), 557.

Sarabhai, A. S. and S. Brenner, "A Mutant Which Reinitiates the Polypeptide Chain after Chain Termination," *J. Mol. Biol., 27* (1967), 145.

———, A. O. W. Stretton, S. Brenner, and A. Bolle, "Colinearity of Gene with the Polypeptide Chain," *Nature, 201* (1964), 14. Both a demonstration that nonsense codons lead to chain termination in vivo and a demonstration of colinearity.

Strehler, B. L., D. D. Hendley, and G. P. Hirsch, "Evidence on a Codon Restriction Hypothesis of Cellular Differentiation: Multiplicity of Mammalian Leucyl-sRNA-Specific Synthetases and Tissue-Specific Deficiency in an Alanyl-sRNA Synthetase," *Proc. Natl. Acad. Sci. U.S., 57* (1967), 1751. The distribution of activating enzymes for various tRNA's is proposed as an important element in selective translation during ontogeny.

Subak-Sharpe, H., "Virus-Induced Changes in Translation Mechanisms," *Symp. Soc. Gen. Microbiol., 18* (1968), 47. Review of changes observed in tRNA, 5S RNA, activating enzymes, and tRNA methylating enzymes after certain virus infections.

———, W. M. Shepherd, and J. Hay, "Studies on sRNA Coded by Herpes Virus," *Cold Spring Harbor Symp. Quant. Biol., 31* (1966), 583. An indication that some animal virus genes may code for components of the protein-synthesizing machinery to assist in selective translation of virus messages.

Suoeka, N., T. Kano-Sueoka, and W. J. Gartland, "Modification of sRNA and Regulation of Protein Synthesis," *Cold Spring Harbor Symp. Quant. Biol., 31* (1966), 571. Certain bacterial tRNA species are altered in virus infection.

Suskind, S. R., and P. E. Hartman, "Suppressor Genes," *Advan. Genet., 15* (1969), in press.

Control of Transcription

Mechanisms for regulating gene function exist to control RNA synthesis (transcription) as well as to control the synthesis of proteins along mRNA (translation). The latter topic was discussed in Chap. 9. Here we shall examine the regulation of RNA synthesis, particularly as it relates to the temporal control of gene action.

General Regulation of RNA Synthesis

There are three main classes of RNA molecules in the cell: ribosomal RNA, tRNA, and mRNA. The regulation of synthesis of each class of RNA molecules appears to possess some unique features. In addition, controls exist that maintain an overall balance in the synthesis of the different types of RNA molecules. All these regulatory mechanisms are integrated within a metabolic framework, itself subject to control, in which the processes of transcription and translation are maintained in critical balance.

At the present time, general controls exerted on RNA synthesis are little understood. Experiments suggest that the lack of one or more amino acids limits protein synthesis and secondarily decreases RNA synthesis, thereby preventing the accumulation of excessive amounts of cellular RNA. The molecular mechanisms by which these controls are exerted remain to be elucidated. Another factor that may play a general role in regulation of RNA synthesis is the sensitivity of the DNA-dependent RNA polymerase to inhibition by free RNA and by DNA–RNA complexes. An excess of RNA or formation of a DNA–RNA hybrid during transcription might provide a means to inhibit further transcription. Perhaps the binding of ribosomal proteins to ribosomal RNA keeps the RNA from inhibiting further transcription of the ribosomal RNA genes. Similarly, the binding of mRNA to ribosome subunits may allow the synthesis of more mRNA at the same genetic region.

In addition to these admittedly hazy ideas on general regulation of the *overall* rate or RNA synthesis, there are specific regulatory processes that appear to determine *which particular genes in a cell will be copied* —and which will *not* be copied. It is the main purpose of this chapter to examine specific regulatory mechanisms that operate at the level of mRNA synthesis.

Two Strands, One Messenger

Recall from Chap. 6 that DNA-dependent RNA polymerase catalyzes the synthesis of RNA copies of the DNA template by sequential addition of ribonucleotides, with the direction of synthesis being from the 5′ to the 3′ end of the molecule. The polymerase can utilize either single- or double-stranded DNA. When it copies the nucleotide sequences of either type of DNA, it faithfully makes a complementary copy. DNA-RNA hybrid molecules that have been prepared in vitro and studied by X-ray diffraction, possess a double-helical conformation very similar to that of double-stranded DNA. It is plausible that Watson-Crick base pairing is involved in the synthesis of RNA made either on single- or double-stranded DNA templates.

RNA's made from the DNA template by RNA polymerase are single-stranded. If denatured single-stranded or highly damaged double-stranded DNA is used as template in vitro, the RNA polymerase can copy both chains and the RNA products can anneal into a double-stranded RNA product. This is an artifact not found in RNA extracted from cells or in RNA made in vitro on carefully prepared DNA. Such RNA anneals along nucleotide sequences of only one of the two DNA strands at any given position on the DNA. This can be dramatically demonstrated in the case of certain small DNA-containing bacterial viruses, where the two antiparallel DNA strands can be separated and individually used in annealing experiments. The RNA has a base composition and nearest-neighbor frequencies complementary to that of its DNA annealing partner and identical (except that U replaces T) with that of the second DNA strand to which it will not anneal.

The above discussion focuses our attention on the single-stranded nature of cellular RNA's, their polarity of synthesis, and their complementarity to only one of the two DNA strands. This is in keeping with theoretical arguments. It is most difficult to visualize how the complementary base sequence of the nontranscribed DNA strand could code for the *same* protein. That it does not code for a *different* protein is verified by direct biochemical-genetic observation: the one gene–one polypeptide chain relationship. Although one might still argue that the informational content of both strands is required for transcription by a mechanism other than DNA strand separation and Watson-Crick base pairing with one of the strands, several lines of evidence support selective-strand transcription with only a minor role attributed to the complementary DNA strand. The first sort of experiment measures the time of appearance of a new phenotypic character in recipient bacteria after their treatment with DNA prepared from bacteria of different genotype (transforming principle; see Stahl's *The Mechanics of Inheritance* in this series). When the double strands of the donor DNA are dissociated, separated, and each used to transform recipient bacteria, the information in one strand is expressed earlier than that of the second. This observation can be explained readily if only one strand of the DNA duplex contains the genetic information enabling immediate transcription to proceed after integration in the recipient's chromosome. The complementary strand, however, is not initially transcribed but must undergo one cycle of DNA replication to provide the strand essential for transcription. The second type of experiment involves induced messenger mutations and, as you will see shortly, presents further in vivo evidence for the suggestion that only one of the two strands of DNA is transcribed.

If a single-stranded selection mechanism exists during RNA synthesis, it follows that the DNA code (nucleotide sequence) must contain information which "tells" RNA polymerase which strand to copy, that is, where to begin RNA synthesis. Experimental evidence to support this idea has been provided by in vitro studies. A limited number of RNA polymerase molecules bind to DNA, and they serve to protect the adjacent nucleotide sequences of DNA from subsequent digestion by nucleases. This nuclease-resistant region contains the nucleotide sequences from only one of the two DNA strands. The "stickiness" of RNA polymerase is enhanced in the presence of ATP or GTP. This may be related to the fact that during mRNA synthesis (Chap. 6), A and G occur at higher frequency than C and U on the 5' (initiating) end of mRNA chains. In vitro each polymerase molecule synthesizes only one RNA molecule. When synthesis is complete, the RNA polymerase molecule remains attached to the DNA template and the newly synthesized RNA strand. Such DNA–RNA–polymerase complexes are also found in cell extracts. The polymerase is readily dissociated from the complex by agents that denature proteins.

Studies of the types mentioned above, and genetic experiments discussed below, lead to the following general view of the transcription process (Fig. 10.1). RNA polymerase attaches to DNA at certain points

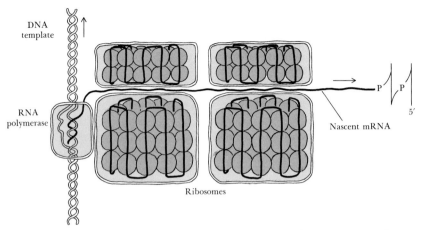

FIG. 10.1. *Highly schematic view of DNA-primed RNA synthesis. From G. S. Stent,* "Genetic Transcription," *Proc. Roy. Soc. (London), B164 (1966), 181;* "Mechanism and Control of Genetic Transcription," *in* The Physiology of Gene and Mutation Expression, *I. Malek, ed., Prague: Publishing House of the Czechoslovak Academy of Sciences, 1966, p. 267;* "Coupled Regulation of Bacterial RNA and Protein Synthesis," *in* Organizational Biosynthesis, *H. J. Vogel, J. O. Lampen, and V. Bryson, eds., New York: Academic Press, Inc., 1967, p. 99.*

and begins transcription in one direction. The details of the orientation mechanism involved in attachment are obscure. Because of the $5' \rightarrow 3'$ direction of RNA synthesis and the rules of base pairing, the proper DNA strand somehow is selected for transcription. The RNA is continually dissociated from the DNA as it is transcribed. Dissociation of the RNA and continuation of transcription may be facilitated in some cases by accessory interactions, such as the attachment and translational movement of ribosomes depicted in Fig. 10.1. Transcription ceases when the RNA polymerase reaches a nucleotide sequence that says "stop."

Messenger Mutations

Errors that occur during mRNA synthesis appear to be rare—just as are the heritable errors, mutations, that take place during DNA replication. Mutations in mRNA are not so important in parent-to-progeny transmission, because they are not replicated and only a relatively few protein molecules out of the total number of that type in the cell may be made along the altered messenger template.

Usually, one cannot recognize small numbers of altered protein molecules in a large population of molecules: thus mRNA mutations are not as readily detectable as are mutations in the genetic material. Only a few biological systems currently are known that offer markers sensitive enough to provide resolution at this level. One example is a colorless mutant of the flowering plant *Delphinium*, where rare single cells show color while the colorless mutation itself persists stably through the germ line. Another example of a uniquely sensitive and useful marker is the motility of bacteria. Among mutant, nonmotile bacteria that lack flagella, rare cells may be found that have transiently gained the ability to produce flagella (Fig. 10.2). They are genotypically nonmotile, and their progeny for the most part lack motility. Nevertheless, the ability to synthesize active flagella can occur as a rare, random event. In one strain, the frequency of such events was found to be about 4×10^{-5} per bacterium per generation.

The above examples suggest that mistakes may be made in the transcription mechanisms involved in protein synthesis. Probably the mistakes occur at the level of mRNA synthesis, for a number of altered protein molecules seem to appear together in a cell in which an event occurs. Only by the all or none property of color, or motility, could such a rare event be detected.

FIG. 10.2. *Rare, spontaneously occurring motile bacteria in large populations of a nonmotile mutant. Parent colonies of 1 to several billion nonmotile bacteria were embedded in soft agar. During the growth of these colonies, a few bacteria acquired motility, although they were genotypically nonmotile. They migrated from the large parent colonies and established the small satellite colonies, also genotypically nonmotile. The number of satellite colonies per parent colony is randomly distributed. From C. Quadling and B. A. D. Stocker,* J. Gen. Microbiol., 17 (1957), 424. *For a review of this subject, consult T. Iino and J. Lederberg, "Genetics of Salmonella," in* The World Problem of Salmonellosis, *E. van Oye, ed., Monogr. Biol., 13 (1964), 111, Hague: W. Junk Publ.*

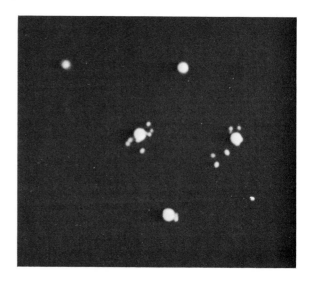

FIG. 10.3. *Predominant mutagenic effects of three compounds on T4 bacteriophage. For detailed information on chemical mutagenesis, see reviews by E. Freese, in* **Molecular Genetics, Part I,** *J. H. Taylor, ed., New York: Academic Press, Inc., 1963; D. R. Krieg,* **Progr. Nucleic Acid Res.,** *2 (1963), 125; L. E. Orgel,* **Advan. Enzymol.,** *27 (1965), 289; E. Freese and E. B. Freese,* **Radiation Res., Suppl.** *6 (1966), 97; or R. M. Herriott,* **Cancer Res.,** *26 Pt. I (1966), 1971.*

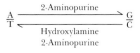

Induced Messenger Mutations

In *The Mechanics of Inheritance* (in this series), Stahl discusses chemical mutagenesis in relation to the structure of DNA. One mechanism of chemical mutagenesis involves the in situ chemical modification of a base in the DNA so that nucleotide pairing on the strand opposite the chemically altered base is changed at the next round of DNA synthesis. Hydroxylamine is an example of a mutagen that causes such transition-type mutations, from a GC base pair to an AT base pair (Fig. 10.3).

A second general mechanism of chemical mutagenesis is the incorporation, during DNA replication, of unusual nucleotides into newly synthesized strands of DNA. Once the base analogues are incorporated into DNA, there is a greatly increased probability that they will pair with the "wrong" complementary base in subsequent replications. The compound 2-aminopurine (Fig. 10.3) is an example of a chemical mutagen that is a base analogue. The action of this mutagen has been used in conjunction with experiments involving codon assignments (for example, Fig. 9.4).

Another base analogue, 5-fluorouracil (5FU), is converted in vivo to the nucleoside triphosphate, and this nucleotide is then built into RNA, replacing up to 40 percent of the uracil in the ribopolynucleotide. Under certain experimental conditions, little or no incorporation of 5FU occurs in tRNA, ribosomal RNA, or DNA. 5FU has properties to suggest that once incorporated into mRNA, it could occasionally attract guanine rather than the more usual complementary base, adenine. In so doing, its positioning in mRNA would exactly counteract a base substitution that previously had occurred in the DNA. This (theoretical) process is shown in Fig. 10.4.

This figure shows a segment of the DNA molecule associated with the synthesis of a segment of an mRNA molecule. During protein synthesis, the mRNA serves as template in attracting particular amino acid-charged tRNA molecules. When the wild-type configuration in the DNA molecule is CG and the mRNA contains C (Fig. 10.4, upper left), a tRNA molecule containing code letter G becomes attached at this site. This fixes the location of amino acid 1. But if, as a consequence of mutation, the CG base pair has been replaced by a TA base pair (Fig.

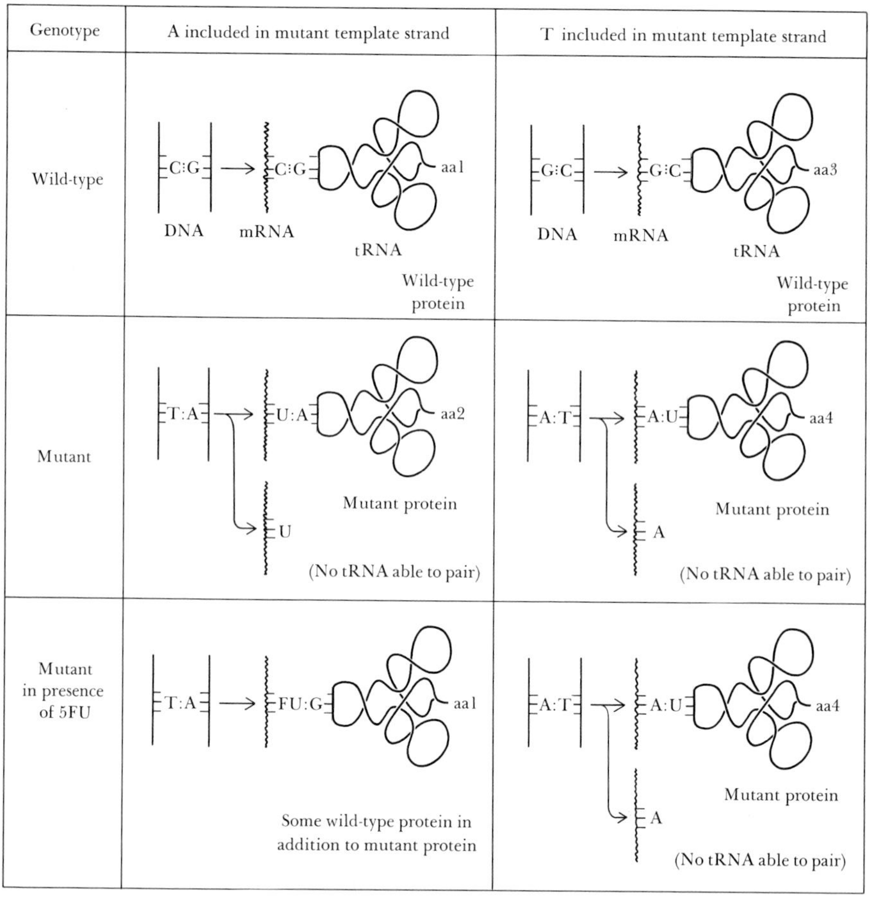

Genotype	A included in mutant template strand	T included in mutant template strand
Wild-type	C:G → C:G → tRNA — aa1 DNA mRNA Wild-type protein	G:C → G:C → tRNA — aa3 DNA mRNA Wild-type protein
Mutant	T:A → U:A — aa2 → U Mutant protein (No tRNA able to pair)	A:T → A:U — aa4 → A Mutant protein (No tRNA able to pair)
Mutant in presence of 5FU	T:A → FU:G — aa1 Some wild-type protein in addition to mutant protein	A:T → A:U — aa4 → A Mutant protein (No tRNA able to pair)

FIG. 10.4. *Theoretical picture of predominant mutagenic effects of 5FU in mRNA synthesis. A group of mutants is selected that shows an increased rate of reversion to wild type in the presence of 2-aminopurine but no appreciable increase in the presence of 5-bromodeoxyuridine or after treatment with hydroxylamine. Mutant genes of this class are assumed to carry an adenine-thymine (AT) base pair in place of the guanine-cytosine (GC) pair characteristic of wild type. The AT base pair may be arranged in the DNA either so the strand carrying A serves as mRNA template or so the strand carrying T serves as mRNA template. If A is included in the mutant template, incorporation of 5FU into mRNA allows occasional pairing with G in tRNA and partially phenotypically reverses the effect of the mutation in the DNA. If T is included in the mutant template strand, FU has no effect. Approximately half of the total number of mutants in the group fall into each category: FU-reversible and FU-nonreversible.*

10.4, middle left), the mRNA molecule containing U as part of its codon may base-pair with a tRNA molecule having an A in the anti-codon and a mutant protein may be synthesized. Alternatively, the mRNA may be incapable of base-pairing with any tRNA. However, if 5FU replaces U in the mRNA (Fig. 10.4, lower left), pairing will still be possible with a tRNA carrying amino acid 1, the amino acid present in the wild-type protein.

Note the consequences when the wild-type CG base pair is reversed, so that the functional base, in mRNA biosynthesis, is C (Fig. 10.4, right). The mutant mRNA copied from T of the mutant DNA now contains A. 5FU does not replace A and so is not incorporated at this position in the mRNA; thus the mutational alteration in the DNA is not counteracted.

According to the rules of chemical mutagenesis, a group of mutants can be selected that represent changes from GC to AT base pairs in the DNA. These are mutants that are caused to back-mutate to wild type by incorporation of 2-aminopurine but are not appreciably reverted by hydroxylamine (Fig. 10.3). When such mutants are examined for the phenotypic-reversing effect of 5FU incorporation, *approximately half* are found to be reversed. This fraction of the mutants is assumed to contain the mutant base pair in the orientation TA, whereas the other half is unaffected by 5FU and is assumed to have the AT orientation. That only half the selected class of mutants are phenotypically reversed by 5FU is support for the idea that only one of the two strands of DNA functions in mRNA synthesis.

Genetic Systems of Regulation

In 1961 F. Jacob and J. Monod collaborated in writing a classic paper in biology on genetic regulatory mechanisms, culminating in the synthesis of a unified hypothesis based on many ideas and observations from their own and other laboratories. This paper and several other pertinent references are cited in the legend to Fig. 10.5. The 1961 article dramatically focused attention on mechanisms underlying induction and repression of protein synthesis. It provided a central theme of contemporary research in this area and continues to stimulate new experimental programs.

Biochemical and genetic studies now extended to numerous gene-regulatory systems in microorganisms have implicated four key components in the control of gene function (Fig. 10.5). They are (1) a gene for specification of a regulator protein, (2) the regulator protein, (3) a gene or gene cluster whose activity is regulated, and (4) an operator region, at one end of the gene, or gene cluster, that is sensitive to the regulator protein or that produces a regulator-sensitive molecule. It should be emphasized that the model shown in Fig. 10.5 is, in broad outline, substantiated by experiment; however, gaps in knowledge are considerable and many of the details of the model are still speculative.

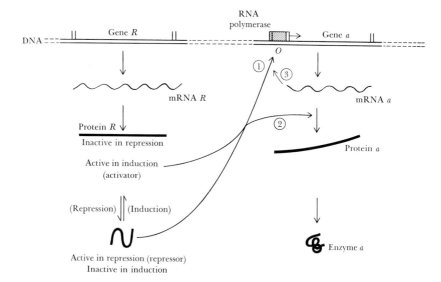

FIG. 10.5. *A general model for induction and repression of specific protein bio-synthesis. The figure shows some of the major components that are presumed to take part in the regulation of genic activity and some possible sites of interaction by the components.*

A gene, R, is responsible for the synthesis of a regulator protein that can exist in two conformations. In one conformation the protein is inactive as a repressor. In the second configuration (bottom) the protein has affinity for a chromosomal location, O (step 1). When the repressor protein is complexed to O, RNA polymerase is unable to synthesize mRNA along gene a. When repressor protein is absent from O, RNA polymerase initiates synthesis of mRNA. A modification of this general scheme is diagrammed as reactions 2 and 3. In this modified model, the repressor acts at the level of mRNA, causing it to remain complexed with the structural gene and to halt further mRNA synthesis at this site on the chromosome.

Since the repressor protein shuts off enzyme synthesis, it is part of a negative control system. Positive control systems are also known. In these, the regulator protein serves as an activator for mRNA synthesis at site O. The inducer in some inducible systems merely serves to change a repressor to an inactive configuration; the inducer in other inducible systems serves to change an inactive protein into an activator.

Adapted with some modification from F. Jacob and J. Monod, "Genetic Regulatory Mechanisms in the Synthesis of Proteins," J. Mol. Biol., 3 *(1961), 318 and* "On the Regulation of Gene Activity," Cold Spring Harbor Symp. Quant. Biol., 26 *(1961), 193. See also F. Jacob and J. Monod, in* Cytodifferentiation and Macromolecular Synthesis, *New York: Academic Press, Inc., 1963, p. 30; F. Jacob,* Science, 152 *(1966), 1470; J. Monod,* Science, 154 *(1966), 475. For discussion of positive control consult E. Englesberg,* J. Mol. Biol., 25 *(1967), 443.*

THE R GENE AND THE REGULATOR

The regulator molecule, currently thought to be a protein, is pictured as existing in two alternative and specific conformations, one active in regulation and the other inactive. The primary structure of the regulator protein presumably dictates to a large extent which of these two forms will be favored. Because the primary structure of the regulator molecule is subject to alteration by mutations in gene R, the proportion of the protein that is active as regulator is under the control of gene R.

There are two general types of regulation, each operating under a particular set of circumstances. In one case, the active form of the R protein exerts a positive control; it activates mRNA synthesis and is thus termed an *activator*. In the other type of regulation, the active form of the protein reduces or represses mRNA formation, and the protein is termed a *repressor* (Fig. 10.5). In each case, metabolites of small molecular weight are visualized as affecting the ratio of the active and inactive conformations of the regulator protein by complexing with one of them. The metabolite that increases the concentration of the active repressor increases enzymic repression and is called a *corepressor*. Another group of low-molecular-weight regulatory molecules are called *inducers*. These are metabolites that either increase the proportion of the inactive R protein or repressor and thus decrease repression, or they may combine with inactive R protein to change it to an activator.

If the R gene is the structural gene for a repressor protein, mutations in the R gene, such as nonsense, frameshift, and deletion mutations, that lead to the loss of regulator protein formation lead to a concomitant loss of repression. These mutations *allow* constitutive enzyme production by gene a (Fig. 10.5). Missense mutations in the R gene that also lead to constitutive enzyme production may elicit formation of a structurally altered repressor protein with a greatly decreased ability to attain the active conformation essential for interaction with the operator site. The mutationally altered repressor protein may fail to bind the corepressor readily or may not undergo the proper conformational change to active repressor after the binding of corepressor. Finally, other missense mutations in repressor genes lead to a hyperrepressed condition in which enzyme production at gene a is reduced below normal. Such hyperrepressed mutations are postulated to act by eliciting the production of active repressor protein that has a very high affinity for the sensitive operator site or that more readily assumes the active repressor configuration.

If the R gene is an activator gene, a situation opposite to that found above will ensue. The mutations that more drastically affect phenotype, for example nonsense, framshift, and deletion mutations, lead to a loss of activator. These shut off enzyme production, as do missense mutations that modify the ability of the protein to function as an activator. Other missense mutations may allow the protein to achieve an active conformation in the absence of inducer, thus leading to constitutive enzyme production.

The characterization of a gene as a repressor or activator gene does not imply that its product protein may not also have an additional catalytic function. Perhaps regulator proteins are simply those enzymes that possess ancillary roles in metabolic control. Many mysteries still surround the nature and mode of action of regulator proteins.

The current view of the relationship between the R gene and the regulator molecule coincides with the classical one gene–one polypeptide concept presented in our earlier discussion of mutant proteins (Chap. 3). An important genetic attribute of an active regulator gene is its dominance. As seen in Fig. 10.6*a*, the R gene functions in the *trans* configuration in the *cis-trans* test, suggesting that the regulator protein exists extrachromosomally. The unique feature of the R gene is its dictation of the structure of a regulatory protein that can interact in a highly specific manner with the operator site or with some product of the operator, and in this manner influences the transcription of mRNA from the structural gene adjacent to the operator.

THE OPERATOR

Operators, as the chromosomal component of the genetic regulatory system, have been proposed to serve as the initiating points for RNA polymerase synthesis of mRNA along one of the DNA strands (*"promotor"* sites), and as sites for interaction, directly or indirectly, with specific regulator proteins that control mRNA synthesis. Mutations in an operator, then, might be expected to affect one or both of these functions.

Mutations in an operator region that reduce mRNA synthesis can be due to one of four causes: (1) loss of binding sites for RNA polymerase; (2) increased affinity of the operator or its product for the specific regulator (repressor) protein or decreased affinity for the regulator protein (activator); (3) newly acquired affinity for a repressor molecule that ordinarily has little or no affinity for the wild-type operator or its product; or (4) an alteration in nucleotide sequence that affects the efficiency of transcription (for example, through changes in the secondary structure of the nucleic acid) or affects the rate of translation of the messenger into protein. The operator mutations that shut off or greatly decrease mRNA synthesis are termed O^0 (operator zero or operator negative) mutations. Mutations in operator that lead to somewhat increased or to completely constitutive enzyme production are termed O^c (operator constitutive). The latter mutations presumably lessen or eliminate completely the affinity of operator or its product for the specific repressor molecule.

Noteworthy is the fact that O^0 and O^c mutations affect only those genes located *cis* to the mutant operator (that is, only those genes contained on the same DNA molecule). Failure of operator mutations to

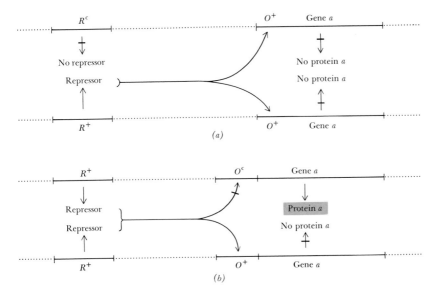

FIG. 10.6. *Dominance relationships of repressor and operator genes.*
Symbols:
R⁺ = wild-type repressor gene   *Oᶜ = constitutive mutant*
Rᶜ = constitutive mutant   *O⁰ = operator zero (operator*
O⁺ = wild-type operator region   *negative) mutant*

   (a) *Production of repressor is dominant in the* **trans** *configuration. When two sets of genes are in the same cell, the functioning of a single repressor gene dictates the formation of an extrachromosomal product capable of affecting (repressing) any susceptible operator region, thus decreasing enzyme production. The active (constitutive) form of an activator gene is also dominant in the* **trans** *configuration.*

   (b) *Operator mutations (Oᶜ and O⁰) do not affect the functioning of genes on the second (trans) element; they affect only those genes cis to operator. In operator constitutive mutants (Oᶜ), protein production continues in the presence of repressor.*

function in the *trans* configuration is taken as evidence that the operator serves as a receptor site and does not exert its effect through the production of an independent cytoplasmic product (Fig. 10.6*b*). Constitutive protein synthesis continues in a cell that contains an *O*ᶜ mutation on one chromosome and a normal repressor-susceptible operator on the homologous chromosome.

THE OPERON

   In the preceding sections we have considered, as a theoretical example of an operator, one that affects the production of only one enzyme, protein A. However, in many bacterial systems, several genes that code the structure of several different proteins may be controlled

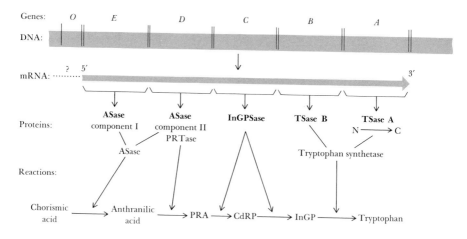

FIG. 10.7. *The tryptophan operon in* E. coli.

by a single operator. Such genes are closely linked on the chromosome. The segment of genetic material that bears the functionally coordinated complex of operator and structural gene (s) is called an *operon*.

One example of an operon is the cluster of genes that determine the structure of the enzymes necessary for tryptophan biosynthesis in *E. coli* (Fig. 10.7). The tryptophan operon dictates the structures of the enzymes depicted in Fig. 2.15, which catalyze one of the final sequences of reactions in the biosynthesis of aromatic amino acids and vitamins shown in Fig. 5.6. The operon contains a beginning point, or operator (*O*), and five adjacent genes, *A* through *E*, that dictate the structures of enzymes involved in tryptophan biosynthesis from chorismic acid.

Production of the tryptophan enzymes is *coordinately* controlled (Fig. 10.8). When tryptophan is withdrawn from the medium, the enzymes become derepressed. Most important, there is the *same* amount of derepression for each of the enzymes.

Under conditions where one enzyme has increased 5-fold, the others also have increased 5-fold in specific activity. A 10-fold increase in one enzyme is reflected in a 10-fold increase in each of the others; and so on. Coordinate derepression can be achieved in two other ways. Endogenously formed tryptophan may be limited through addition to the culture of 3-methylanthranilate. 3-Methylanthranilate blocks conversion of PRA to InGP (Fig. 10.7). In its presence, the enzymes before the analogue-sensitive reaction (ASase and PRTase), the enzyme inhibited (InGPSase), and the last two proteins (the A and B proteins of tryptophan synthetase) are coordinately derepressed. A second way the tryptophan enzymes may become coordinately derepressed is through mutations in one of the regulator genes specific for the tryptophan

FIG. 10.8. (a)–(d) *Coordinate variation of ASase, PRTase, InGPSase, and B protein with respect to A protein. Different enzyme levels were obtained as follows. E. coli was grown in a minimal medium plus 0.2 percent glucose, 20 μg per ml of L-tryptophan, and 0.1 percent acid-hydrolyzed casein at 37° C for 4 hr on a rotary shaker. The exponentially grown culture was cooled rapidly and centifuged in the cold. Cells were washed once with a cold minimal medium and resuspended in the same medium. The washed cells were then transferred to prewarmed minimal medium containing 0.2 percent glucose and 0.1 percent acid-hydrolyzed casein. A 1.5-liter culture was shaken in a 4-liter flask at 37°C. At various times during the subsequent 50 min, 50-ml aliquots of the bacterial culture were harvested, cooled rapidly, and centrifuged in the cold. Extracts were prepared from the bacteria, and protein and enzyme activities were assayed. (Figure 10.7a) Specific activity of ASase plotted against specific activity of A protein. (Figure 10.7b) Specific activity of PRTase plotted against specific activity of A protein. (Figure 10.7c) Specific activity of InGPSase plotted against specific activity of A protein. (Figure 10.7d) Specific activity of B protein plotted against specific activity of A protein. From J. Ito and I. P. Crawford, Genetics, 52 (1965), 1303.*

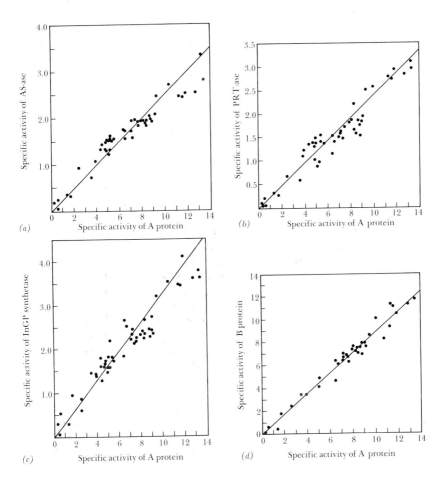

operon, *trpR*. Mutations in *trpR* lead to constitutive, coordinate production of all five proteins of the tryptophan operon.

In addition, deletion of the operator portion of the operon can lead either to loss of synthesis of all the tryptophan enzymes or to enzyme synthesis at a constitutive rate; the rate is uninfluenced by the presence or absence of the *R* gene or of tryptophan. The enzymes whose structures are dictated by the genes in such an operon are produced coordinately; an operator for an adjacent cluster of genes on the chromosome presumably has assumed control in these deletion mutants.

The best available data indicate that the regulation of mRNA formation, one mRNA per operon, underlies all of these coordinate control systems.

One Operon, One mRNA

In several systems it has been shown that each operon serves as the template for the transcription of a specific type of mRNA molecule. The mRNA population is uniform in size for a given wild-type operon, implying the presence of a mechanism for determining initiation and termination sites for transcription of each operon.

The sizes of mRNA molecules have been estimated by several approaches. These include the following:

1. Analyses of the sedimentation properties of polyribosomes prepared from cells to give an estimate of the number of ribosomes bound to one mRNA. Assumptions are made for the spacing of the ribosomes on the mRNA and mRNA size can be approximated (see Fig. 7.2 for an example).

2. The use of two radioactive tracers to detect a specific type of mRNA made in one bacterial culture but not in another. This differential labeling technique involves growing one culture for a brief period of time in the presence of a *tritium-labeled* RNA precursor under conditions where synthesis of specific enzymes are repressed. The second culture is grown in the presence of RNA precursor labeled with ^{14}C, but under conditions permitting enzyme synthesis (derepression or induction). The two populations of bacteria are mixed, and the RNA's are quickly extracted and analyzed for size and distribution by column chromatography and preparative ultracentrifugation. By calculating the tritium/^{14}C ratio of the fractions, a unique mRNA species, synthesized in derepressed or induced cells, can be detected and its molecular weight estimated (even though this mRNA may constitute less than 1 percent of the total RNA synthesized during the time the cells were exposed to the radioactive pulse).

3. The ability of specific mRNA to hybridize in vitro with a particular nucleotide sequence on the DNA and its inability to hybridize with mutant DNA lacking those nucleotide sequences (deletions) permits purification of a specific mRNA. After hybridizing wild-type mRNA

and mutant DNA, the specific unhybridized mRNA can be recognized and characterized by its capacity to hybridize with wild-type DNA (see Chap. 6) . A refined and reliable method based on this rationale is depicted in Fig. 10.9. Special virus particles, transducing phages, can be obtained from bacteria. These phage have lost some of their own genetic material and incorporated in its place genetic material from their host. The phage can be grown in high numbers and purified before the DNA is extracted. This amounts to genetic dissection and subsequent enrichment of specific nucleotide sequences of bacterial DNA because the 0.5 to 2 percent of the host DNA trapped in the viral genome is replicated many times. DNA extracted from such phage particles provides a source of highly purified bacterial tryptophan genes for hybridizing with bacterial mRNA transcribed from the tryptophan operon. Obviously, critical control experiments must be included to correct for nonspecific reactions with phage DNA and other bacterial genes.

In the case of the tryptophan operon, a giant mRNA molecule with a sedimentation coefficient of 33S is synthesized by wild-type bacteria. This is a mRNA molecule of several million molecular weight. Mutants that have deletions of some of the tryptophan genes synthesize smaller mRNA molecules, which represent the transcription of only a portion of the intact operon. As predicted from genetic recombination tests, a mutant deleted for the "right" half of the operon, lacking genes *C, B,* and *A* makes mRNA that anneals only with *ptC-E* and *ptA-E;* the mRNA does not anneal with *ptAB* (Fig. 10.9) .

Hybridization also has been used to monitor mRNA synthesis during

Fig. 10.9. **Tryptophan operon segments in various transducing derivatives of φ80 bacteriophage. The tryptophan operon of E. coli is shown at the top. Bacteriophage φ80 contains no sequences strictly homologous to the host tryptophan operon (thin line). However, transducing derivatives of φ80 contain various segments of the tryptophan operon. One clone, ptAB, carries genes A and B and perhaps a small segment of gene C. An independent isolate, ptC-E, carries part of gene C and the entirety of genes D and E. A third independently isolated transducing derivative, ptA-E, carries the entire tryptophan operon. For details consult papers by A. Matsushiro and F. Imamoto and their collaborators, Virology, 19 (1963), 475; J. Mol. Biol., 11 (1965), 54; ibid., 13 (1965), 157, 169; Cold Spring Harbor Symp. Quant. Biol., 31 (1966), 235.**

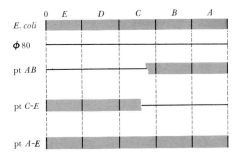

derepression of enzyme formation. The time sequence and the orientation of transcription of the genes in the tryptophan operon has been studied. mRNA was labeled by feeding bacteria radioactive uridine for short periods of time during derepression. Early in derepression, small mRNA molecules were detected that anneal preferentially with *ptC-E*. Subsequently larger labeled mRNA molecules were detected which anneal both to *ptC-E* and to *ptAB*. Thus, transcription starts at *O* and proceeds in sequence through genes *E* to *A*.

Modulation and Polarity

As pointed out in Chap. 9, the messages contained in polycistronic mRNA's are punctuated. Where several polypeptide chains are translated from a single mRNA, there are nucleotide sequences that dictate the end of one polypeptide chain and the beginning of another. In the case of f2 bacteriophage RNA, and some other mRNA's, not all the sequences along the polynucleotide chain are translated with equal frequency. The nucleotide sequence in f2 RNA that codes for coat protein is translated more times than are other genes, for example, the gene for the RNA polymerase or replicase involved in virus RNA propagation. A possible role of the coat protein in this modulation was mentioned briefly in Chap. 9. Similarly, more molecules of the polypeptide subunit of β-galactosidase are synthesized in *E. coli* than are polypeptide chains of transacetylase, another protein whose structure is dictated by the same operon, the "lac" operon. Here enzyme levels are strictly coordinate. Most conditions that change the level of one protein alter the levels of the other proteins the same relative amount. However, in absolute terms, there is more of one kind of polypeptide chain made than the other (*modulation*). Not all normal operons in *E. coli* show modulation; the tryptophan operon in wild-type *E. coli* produces equal numbers of each of the five polypeptide chains.

Modulations in enzyme levels can be elicited by mutation of a structural gene in an operon. Such mutations generally terminate normal protein synthesis dictated by the mutant gene and reduce the levels of enzymes coded for by genes more distal from the operator. This is called *polarity,* and the mutants are called *polar mutants.* For example, polar mutations in gene *B* (Fig. 10.7) lower production of A protein; polar mutations in gene *D* lower production of proteins coded by genes *C, B,* and *A;* and so on. Protein formation that occurs distal to the point of mutation remains coordinately controlled, but the levels of protein synthesis are much lower than normal. Most of the mutations effective in polarity are chain-terminating nonsense mutations or frameshift mutations which lead to chain-terminating triplets within the region where the genetic message has become scrambled. In bacteria, most missense mutations do not have this polarity effect. In higher organisms, there is evidence that some missense mutations may have polarity effects.

When mutations occur in the first gene of an operon, the degree of polarity is also a function of the position of the mutation within the gene. Figure 10.10 shows that mutations in the proximal portion of gene *E* produce only about 5 percent of the normal amount of tryptophan synthetase A protein [and each of the other proteins, except that no ASase is produced because the mutation is contained within that structural gene (see Fig. 10.7)]. Mutations located near the end of gene *E* produce about 60 percent of the normal A protein. Clearly, premature chain-termination leads to a decrease in enzyme production by genes distal to the site of mutation.

The severity of polarity appears to be due to two factors. One factor may be the affinity of the subsequent chain initiator for components that start the new polypeptide chain. A second factor, in gene *E* as cited above and in some but not all other genes, is the distance of the non-sense mutation to the next chain-initiating nucleotide sequence on the mRNA. This second factor appears important only in genes near the operator.

It is possible that some of the polar effect occurs during translation, for example by the disengagement of ribosomes from the messenger. However, annealing experiments with mRNA extracted from polar tryptophan mutants shows that much of the polar effect in *E* mutants occurs during transcription. Polar mutants produce two types of messengers, normal long mRNA and short mRNA that terminates prematurely, at or near the chain-terminating codon (Fig. 10.11).

FIG. 10.10. *Polarity effect of mutations leading to premature chain termination in the tryptophan* **E** *gene on the level of tryptophan synthetase A protein.*

The map order of mutant sites within the gene E *is given. All are nonsense mutations except 9803 and 9887, which are frameshift (fs) mutations. The* E *gene is the first gene in the tryptophan operon (Fig. 10.7). The A protein polarity value is the percent of tryptophan synthetase A protein detected in extracts of the mutant as compared with extracts of wild-type bacteria. Thus mutant 9802 synthesizes only 5 percent of the normal amount of A protein, whereas mutant 5972 synthesizes 60 percent of the normal amount of A protein. No E activity is present in the mutants because the chain-terminating mutations are located in the* E *gene. The levels of D, C, and B proteins are reduced below normal and coordinate with the level of A protein. From F. Imamoto, J. Ito, and C. Yanofsky,* **Cold Spring Harbor Symp. Quant. Biol.,** *31 (1966), 235. See also C. Yanofsky and J. Ito,* **J. Mol. Biol.,** *21 (1966), 313; ibid., 24 (1967), 143.*

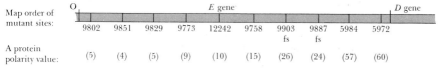

Map order of mutant sites:	O	E gene									D gene
		9802	9851	9829	9773	12242	9758	9903 fs	9887 fs	5984	5972
A protein polarity value:		(5)	(4)	(5)	(9)	(10)	(15)	(26)	(24)	(57)	(60)

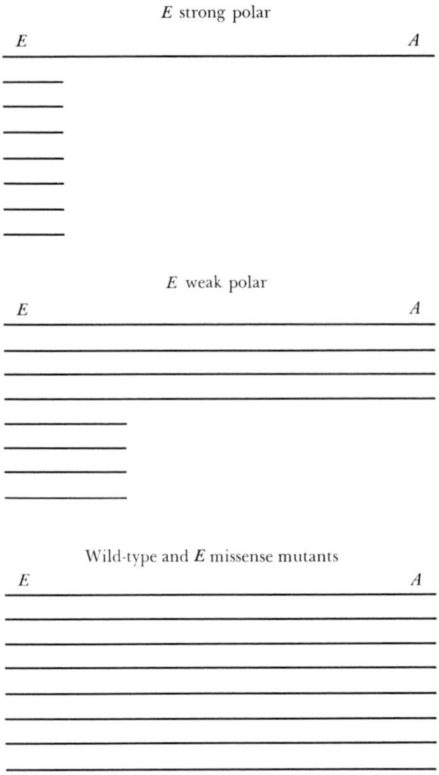

FIG. 10.11. *Schematic diagram of the mRNA molecules made in wild-type and various E mutants of the tryptophan operon of E. coli. The molecular heterogeneity of tryptophan mRNA produced in various E polar mutants is indicated. The normal, full-length mRNA molecules produced by wild-type bacteria and missense mutants are shown at the bottom. Modified from F. Imamoto, J. Ito, and C. Yanofsky,* Cold Spring Harbor Symp. Quant. Biol., 31 (1966), *235.*

Wild-type and missense mutants produce only one detectable kind of mRNA for the tryptophan operon.

Observation of polarity again reminds us of the asymmetry of the operon. Polarity mutants lead us to consider seriously a model of transcription dependent, at least in its initial phases, on concomitant translation (Fig. 10.1). Once it is acknowledged that transcription and translation are interrelated, one can see the obstacles facing in vivo experiments designed to pinpoint the precise site of action of activators and repressors. Does the repressor or the activator function at the level of the DNA (circled 1 in Fig. 10.5)? At the level of the mRNA-DNA complex (circled 3)? At the level of translation (circled 2)? Can mRNA be translated in the cytoplasm of bacterial cells, or is it translated only during its synthesis?

The Cell and the Test Tube

Some of the main components involved in bacterial control mechanisms have been outlined and some evidence for their existence has been presented in this chapter. The molecular interactions that actually effect the control remain enigmatic. What is an operator? How much, if any, of the operator is transcribed into mRNA? Translated into protein? The proteins produced by genes adjacent to the operator in several operator-constitutive strains are known to be identical to wild type in their gross properties, but comparisons of primary structure are lacking. On the other hand, mutations are known in the structural gene ASase (gene *E* in Fig. 10.7) that affect ability to derepress. Is this due to the conformation of the nascent protein in process of synthesis? To an interaction of this protein with another, for example, the repressor protein? What bearing do studies on repression and gene activation in bacteria have for control mechanisms in higher organisms?

Although in vivo studies with microorganisms, supplemented by the powerful tool of genetics, can divulge and define important problems, more penetrating probes at the molecular level will be possible when biochemically resolved systems are available. Certainly the resolution of the genetic code is a case in point. Purification and manipulation in the test-tube complement and greatly extend in vivo experimentation. As discussed in Chap. 6, biologically active mRNA can be synthesized in vitro from DNA with RNA polymerase. Virus protein has been synthesized in vitro from viral RNA messages. Increased understanding of these types of systems, in vitro, will eventually allow refined analyses of cellular control mechanisms. It is the job of genetics to supply tools that facilitate the in vitro analysis and allow extrapolation of these observations back to living systems.

Questions

10.1. What types of punctuation are necessary in mRNA synthesis? In translation?

10.2. What is the evidence indicating that modulation occurs in normal, wild-type bacteria?

10.3. Describe three methods that can be used for the *detection* of mRNA specific for a particular gene or operon.

10.4. Why are operator mutations dominant in the *cis* configuration whereas repressor gene mutations are dominant in the *trans* configuration?

10.5. What level of tryptophan synthetase (constitutive level or repressed level) would you expect to find in an *E. coli* partial diploid carrying mutations O^cA^- in one genetic element and O^+B^- in the second genetic element? Why?

10.6. Why do *trpR* mutants, with high enzyme levels, fail to excrete large amounts of tryptophan?

10.7. Name three ways that derepression of the tryptophan operon may be brought about.

10.8. Look in the literature and see if you can find some evidence for, or against, the existence of operons in metazoans.

10.9. Cite the evidence indicating that only one of the two DNA strands is directly involved in mRNA synthesis.

10.10. From the information in both this and in earlier chapters, describe three molecular explanations for *intra*genic suppression.

10.11. From the information in both this and in earlier chapters, describe three molecular mechanisms for *inter*genic suppression.

References

Ames, B. N., and R. A. Martin, "Biochemical Aspects of Genetics: The Operon," *Ann. Rev. Biochem., 33* (1964), 235. An excellent summary.

Ames, B. N., et al., *Proc. Natl. Acad. Sci. U.S., 45* (1959), 1453; *J. Mol. Biol., 7* (1963), 23; *ibid., 22* (1966), 325; and D. Antón, *ibid., 33* (1968), 533. Studies on the histidine operon that outline the role of operator. The studies also demonstrate that some "regulatory" genes are involved in metabolism of one compound to an effective corepressor and thence are only indirectly involved in repression. Also see the Goldberger reference below.

Baker, R. F., and C. Yanofsky, "The Periodicity of RNA-polymerase Initiations: A New Regulatory Feature of Transcription," *Proc. Natl. Acad. Sci. U.S., 60* (1968), 313; "Direction of *in vivo* Degradation of a Messenger RNA," *Nature, 219* (1968), 26. Two new and important papers on the *E. coli* tryptophan system that supplement observations reported in this book.

Beckwith, J. R., "Regulation of the Lac Operon," *Science, 156* (1967), 597. This review can lead you to the wealth of information regarding the lactose operon in *E. coli;* the article presents the case for the viewpoint that regulation of protein synthesis occurs predominantly at the level of DNA.

Bonner, D. M., ed., *Control Mechanisms in Cellular Processes.* New York: The Ronald Press Company, 1961.

Bonner, J., M. E. Dahmus, D. Fambrough, R. C. Huang, K. Marushige, and D. Y. H. Tuan, "The Biology of Isolated Chromatin," *Science, 159* (1968), 47.

Brenner, S., "Theories of Gene Regulation," *Brit. Med. Bull., 21* (1965), 244. A short, cogent survey of problems still pertinent today.

Bretscher, M. S., "How Repressor Molecules Function," *Nature, 217* (1968), 509.

Campbell, A., "Regulation in Viruses," in *Molecular Genetics, Part II,* J. H. Taylor, ed. New York: Academic Press, Inc., 1967, p. 323.

Clever, U., "Regulation of Chromosome Function," *Ann. Rev. Genet., 2* (1968), 11.

Cohen, N. R., "The Control of Protein Biosynthesis," *Biol. Rev., 41* (1966), 503. A 57-page review with numerous references to the original literature; the emphasis is on the years 1962–1966 and on mammalian systems, including descriptions of the effects of hormones on enzyme levels.

Cold Spring Harbor Symp. Quant. Biol., 26 (1961), *28* (1963), and *31* (1966). Symposium volumes containing reviews and original contributions toward analysis of control mechanisms with emphasis on systems in microorganisms.

Englesberg, E., et al., *Virology, 9* (1959), 314; *Genetics, 47* (1962), 417; *J. Bacteriol., 84* (1962), 137; *Proc. Natl. Acad. Sci. U.S., 48* (1962) 137; *Genetics, 49* (1963), 95; *Proc. Natl. Acad. Sci. U.S., 50* (1963), 696; *J. Bacteriol., 90* (1965), 946; *J. Mol. Biol., 25* (1967), 443. Progressive description of the *E. coli* arabinose operon and its definition as a system involving positive control mechanisms.

Epstein, W., and J. R. Beckwith, "Regulation of Gene Expression," *Ann. Rev. Biochem., 37* (1968), 411.

Geiduschek, E. P., L. Snyder, A. J. E. Colvill, and M. Sarnat, "Selective Synthesis of T-Even Bacteriophage Early Messenger in Vitro," *J. Mol. Biol., 19* (1966), 541. One of several papers now available in the literature that point toward selective transcription by RNA polymerase in vitro.

Gilbert, W., and B. Müller-Hill, "Isolation of the *Lac* Repressor," *Proc. Natl. Acad. Sci. U.S., 56* (1966), 1891; "The *Lac* Operator Is DNA," *ibid., 58* (1967), 2415. First description of the isolation of a repressor protein and description of some of its properties.

Goldberger, R. F., and M. A. Berberich, in *Organizational Biosynthesis,* H. J. Vogel, J. O. Lampen, and V. Bryson, eds., New York: Academic Press, Inc., 1967, p. 199. Kinetic studies on repression and on derepression of the histidine operon.

Hamilton, T. H., "Control by Estrogen of Genetic Transcription and Translation," *Science, 161* (1968), 649.

Ippen, K., J. H. Miller, J. Scaife, and J. Beckwith, "New Controlling Element in the *Lac* Operon of *E. coli,*" *Nature, 217* (1968), 825. RNA polymerase binds to "promoter" but transcription is blocked if repressor is bound to operator; a companion paper to those by Gilbert and Müller-Hill cited above.

Jacob, F., A. Ullmann, and J. Monod, "Deletions fusionnant l'operon lactose et un operon purine chez *E. coli,*" *J. Mol. Biol., 13* (1965), 704. A direct demonstration of the role of operator in control of genetic material located adjacent to it.

Koningsberger, V. V., and L. Bosch, eds., *Regulation of Nucleic Acid and Protein Biosynthesis,* Biochimica Biophysica Acta Library, Vol. 10. New York: American Elsevier Publishing Company, 1967. Articles from a June 1966 symposium.

Korner, A., "Ribonucleic Acid and Hormonal Control of Protein Synthesis," *Progr. Biophys. & Mol. Biol., 17* (1967), 149. An annotated bibliography to the literature arranged according to hormone.

Martin, R. G., et al., *J. Mol. Biol., 21* (1966), 357; *Cold Spring Harbor Symp. Quant. Biol., 31* (1966), 215; *J. Mol. Biol., 26* (1967), 311. Studies on polarity in the histidine operon.

McFall, E., and W. K. Maas, "Regulation of Enzyme Synthesis in Microorganisms," *Molecular Genetics,* Part II, J. H. Taylor, ed. New York: Academic Press, Inc., 1967, p. 255.

Morse, D. E., R. F. Baker, and C. Yanofsky, "Translation of the Tryptophan Messenger RNA of *Escherichia coli,*" *Proc. Natl. Acad. Sci. U.S., 60* (1968), 1428. "Several features of the temporal relationship between transcription and translation are elucidated."

Neidhardt, F. C., "The Regulation of RNA Synthesis in Bacteria," *Progr. Nucleic Acid Res. Mol. Biol., 3* (1963), 145. A thorough critique to 1963 on regulation of tRNA, ribosomal RNA, and mRNA synthesis.

Pitot, H. C., "Metabolic Regulation in Metazoan Systems," in *Molecular Genetics*, Part II, J. H. Taylor, ed. New York: Academic Press, Inc., 1967, p. 383.

Shin, A., J. Eisenstadt, and P. Lengyel, "On the Relation between Ribonucleic Acid Synthesis and Peptide Chain Initiation in *E. coli*," *Proc. Natl. Acad. Sci. U.S., 56* (1966), 1599.

Shin, D. H., and K. Moldave, "Effect of Ribosomes on the Biosynthesis of Ribonucleic Acid in Vitro," *J. Mol. Biol., 21* (1966), 231. One of several papers that show a stimulation of in vitro RNA polymerase activity by the addition of ribosomes, an observation whose significance is unclear.

Tomkins, G. M., and B. N. Ames, "The Operon Concept in Bacteria and in Higher Organisms," *Natl. Cancer Inst. Monogr., 27* (1967), 221. Included in this short discussion are some facets of regulation not emphasized elsewhere.

Vogel, H. J., and R. H. Vogel, "Regulation of Protein Synthesis," *Ann. Rev. Biochem., 36* (1967), 519. Some views on regulation of mRNA synthesis, including some involving the translational machinery, and a review of some recent literature.

Vogel, H. J., V. Bryson, and J. O. Lampen, eds., *Informational Macromolecules*. New York: Academic Press, Inc., 1963.

Zubay, G., M. Lederman, and J. K. DeVries, "DNA-directed Peptide Synthesis. III. Repression of β-galactosidase Synthesis and Inhibition of Repressor by Inducer in a Cell-Free System," *Proc. Natl. Acad. Sci. U.S., 58* (1967), 1669. Studies indicating that regulation of protein synthesis can be achieved in the test-tube; detailed analyses seem only to await purification of the components involved.

$\mathcal{E}leven$

Gene Action and Evolution

Evolution is a continuing process. Through studies of populations living today we can extrapolate into the past and set the theoretical framework for developments that took place many years ago. Most of our knowledge of the evolutionary process derives from studies of the relationships of individuals—individuals within different populations of a single interbreeding species that shares a common gene pool. In a companion volume in this series, Mettler and Gregg's *Population Genetics and Evolution*, current ideas and methodology in the study of populations and the application of this knowledge to evolutionary concepts are cogently summarized. You will find from their presentation that diverse techniques are used in the study of evolution. The relatedness of organisms can be examined in genetic breeding tests, on morphological-anatomical grounds, in behavior, by resort to chromosome morphology, by immunological tests, chemical composition, and so on. Such taxonomic features form the basis for the systematic classification of the approximately 2 million species of plants and animals that inhabit the world today (Fig. 11.1). They also give us some insight into mechanisms of speciation by providing clues of ancestral relationships.

In recent years, studies at the level of gene action have developed to an extent where new approaches may be brought to bear in clarifying our knowledge of evolution.

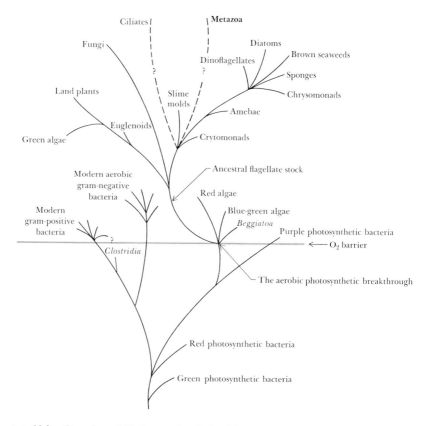

FIG. 11.1. *One view of phylogenetic relationships among organisms. The usual textbook diagram emphasizes relationships of the phyla of the animal kingdom, or of the plant kingdom, or both, neglecting microorganisms. The view presented in this figure by a protozoologist pictures these as mere branches in a much larger tree whose branch points could extend back as far as 3 billion years. Molecular approaches can contribute both in the realm of the small branches and in the realm of the branch points that took place in the more distant past. From S. H. Hutner, in* This Is Life: Essays in Modern Biology, *W. H. Johnson and W. C. Steere, eds., New York: Holt, Rinehart and Winston, Inc., 1962.*

This chapter outlines several examples of these approaches. Our focus here will be on what we might term "the mainstream of evolution," the development of the biotic world during earth's history. Like the more classic methodology, the new approaches require extrapolation into the past from phenomena observed in the present. In this light, all such studies share common pitfalls. For example, almost all the methods are based on studies of the relatedness of living organisms, their similarities and their differences, and the true nature of their predecessors is only inferred. Similarly, "explanations" offered for mechanisms responsible for divergence and continuity during the evolutionary process in the past again rely on extrapolation into the past.

The most recent departures from classical techniques of studying evolution rest in the analyses of relationships probed at the molecular level. These departures afford tremendous resolving power and in some cases have disclosed clear distinctions not apparent earlier. For example, the usual classification of microorganisms, especially bacteria, is largely empirical. It provides little insight into the biochemical usefulness of the relationships in the evolutionary sense, that is, to true phylogenetic relationships. The more classical approaches should not be overlooked, however. Our emerging concepts of contemporary and historic evolution must be based on the harmony of a vast number of observations and approaches, including molecular studies. In the evolution of man's knowledge, as well as his person, the new adds to the old.

The Early World

The earth is thought to be some 4 to $4\frac{1}{2}$ billion years old, that is, 4,000 to 4,500 million years old. This contrasts with the presence on earth of mammals for about 180 million years and of vertebrates for about 500 million years, as determined from the fossil record (Fig. 11.2). In recent years more intensive study of the fossil records has helped to forge a strong link with primordial organismal life on our planet; bacteria-like organisms about 3,000 million years old have been detected, providing a significant clue about the types of organisms that inhabited the earth at this early time. Perhaps developments in methodology can extend further the fossil record and allow detection of even more primitive forms.

Realistically speaking, we are faced with a void in our knowledge of biological evolution during the first quarter or third of the earth's history. No experimentation and little speculation about this period was available until the publication of a book on the subject in 1936 by A. I. Oparin. In 1953 a pioneering experiment was performed by S. L. Miller and H. C. Urey. They demonstrated the synthesis of organic compounds, including some amino acids, in a spark-discharge apparatus containing water and a reducing environment of gases (hydrogen, methane, and ammonia) presumed to resemble the composition of the primordial atmosphere. This type of experimental approach has suggested that the early evolution of organic molecules, and possibly also the early organization of systems of molecules, has followed a narrow, highly probable course from which few deviations are possible. That is, certain molecular subunits, the building blocks from which all living things are made today, can be synthesized from those raw materials thought to be available on earth during its primitive molecular-oxygen-free and carbon-dioxide-free periods of evolution.

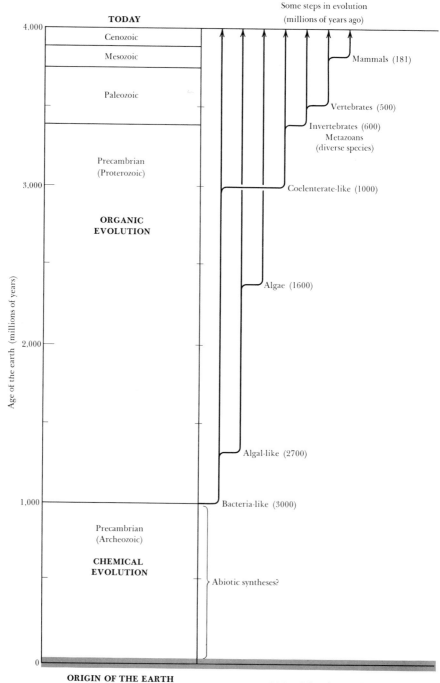

FIG. 11.2.   *The time scale of evolution.*

Such considerations lead many scientists to speculate that organic molecules and even reproducing organisms could exist on other planets. This makes it critical to determine not merely whether there are organic molecules elsewhere, for example, on Mars, but to look for other properties of such molecules, like enzymic activity or the ability to grow and replicate. The possibility certainly exists that similar primordial "organisms" capable of replication may have appeared many times during the long history of earth. On the other hand, perhaps once selection was applied only a single "species" predominated and survived. At present we cannot be sure if life on our planet had but a single origin or stemmed from multiple events of a similar, yet unique, nature.

Extensions of studies on abiotic syntheses may give us some guidelines for filling in an enormous gap in our knowledge: the nature of the first organism(s). One can find interesting speculation and disagreement in the current literature about the sequence and role of events such as replication and the genetic code in determining the course of evolution. Hopefully, these fascinating discussions soon will be documented by experimentation and observation—even to analysis of a Martian genetic code, should one exist.

Metabolic Patterns

Comparative biochemistry has provided experimental proof of many similarities in the biochemical pathways of various organisms. There is also considerable diversity. In fact, the greater diversity among pathways of aerobic than anaerobic metabolism led J. S. B. Haldane in the 1920s to suggest that the first organisms were anaerobes, a conjecture in keeping with later ideas about the reducing nature of the primitive earth atmosphere. It is also possible that uniformity in anaerobic pathways has been selected later in evolution during competition for survival.

The possession of a particular metabolic pathway is often accompanied by some phenotypic property that bestows a selective advantage, for instance, the possession of a particular kind of cell wall. Although of obvious value in taxonomy, exploitation of the significance of such factors in problems of evolution even today remains quite restricted. Most recently, studies have uncovered additional biochemical correlations that may assist in the tracking of branch points in the evolutionary past. "Biochemical fossils" can be detected by analyzing distinctive biochemical pathways leading to the *same* essential end product in different organisms or by examining a *single biochemical pathway* that responds to quite *different control mechanisms* in diverse organisms.

DISTINCTIVE PATHWAYS

Studies on the metabolism of radioactive compounds by various organisms have led to the discovery of two pathways used in the biosynthesis of the amino acid L-lysine (Fig. 11.3). The DAP-lysine pathway

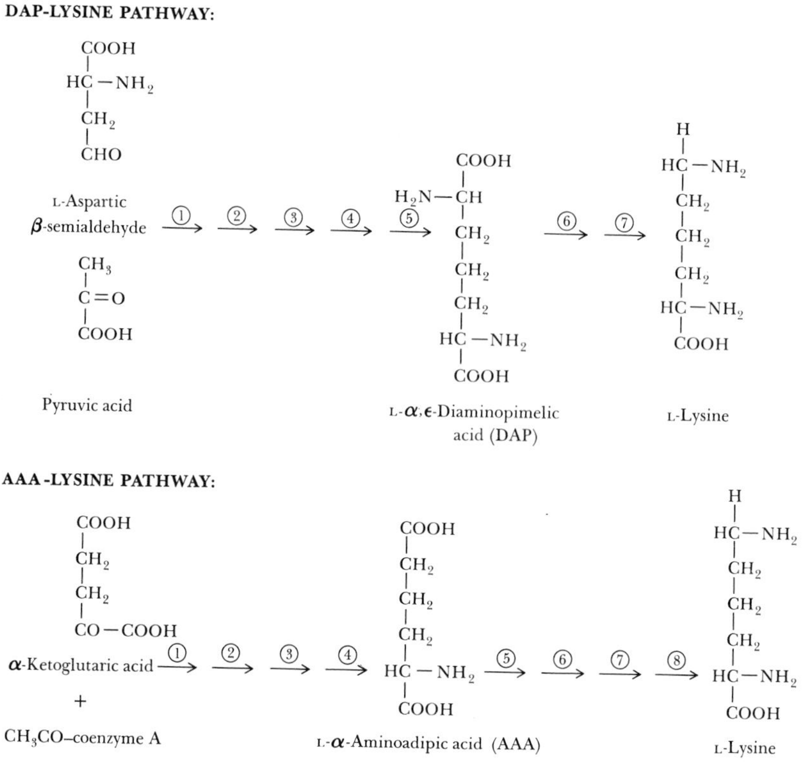

DAP-LYSINE PATHWAY:

```
COOH
|
HC—NH₂
|
CH₂
|
CHO
```

L-Aspartic
β-semialdehyde   →(1) →(2) →(3) →(4) →(5)

```
CH₃
|
C=O
|
COOH
```

Pyruvic acid

```
COOH
|
H₂N—CH
|
CH₂
|
CH₂
|
CH₂
|
HC—NH₂
|
COOH
```

L-α,ε-Diaminopimelic
acid (DAP)

→(6) →(7)

```
H
|
HC—NH₂
|
CH₂
|
CH₂
|
CH₂
|
HC—NH₂
|
COOH
```

L-Lysine

AAA-LYSINE PATHWAY:

```
COOH
|
CH₂
|
CH₂
|
CO—COOH
```

α-Ketoglutaric acid   →(1) →(2) →(3) →(4)

+

CH₃CO–coenzyme A

```
COOH
|
CH₂
|
CH₂
|
CH₂
|
HC—NH₂
|
COOH
```

L-α-Aminoadipic acid (AAA)

→(5) →(6) →(7) →(8)

```
H
|
HC—NH₂
|
CH₂
|
CH₂
|
CH₂
|
HC—NH₂
|
COOH
```

L-Lysine

FIG. 11.3. *Two distinctive pathways of lysine biosynthesis found in different organisms. Abbreviated from H. J. Vogel, "Lysine Biosynthesis and Evolution," in* Evolving Genes and Proteins, *V. Bryson and H. J. Vogel, eds., New York: Academic Press, Inc., 1965, pp. 25–40.*

progresses by a series of seven reactions from the substrates aspartic-semialdehyde and pyruvic acid. The AAA-lysine pathway is comprised of eight reactions, whereby four carbons are derived from α-ketoglutarate and two from acetate. None of the steps in the DAP pathway is duplicated in the AAA pathway. Studies on the pathways in a wide variety of species show very clear and consistent distributions, suggesting that each pathway arose just once during evolution. This idea is reinforced by the large number of distinctive reaction steps involved in each pathway. Placement of the various groups of organisms into a hypothetical evolutionary scheme of descent (Fig. 11.4) also relies upon considerations of other features of relatedness and ideas on the early evolution of biosynthetic capabilities.

Although just one of many possible ways of probing events of the past, the distribution of the two lysine pathways illustrates the potential of this type of analysis.

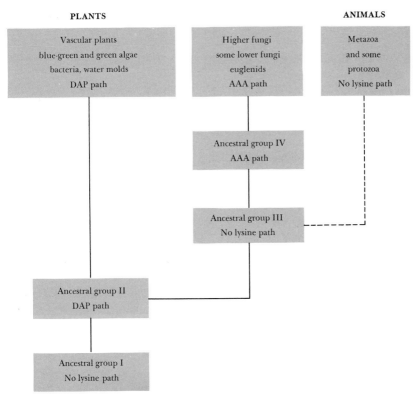

PLANTS

ANIMALS

Vascular plants
blue-green and green algae
bacteria, water molds
DAP path

Higher fungi
some lower fungi
euglenids
AAA path

Metazoa
and some
protozoa
No lysine path

Ancestral group IV
AAA path

Ancestral group III
No lysine path

Ancestral group II
DAP path

Ancestral group I
No lysine path

FIG. 11.4. *Distribution of the two lysine biosynthetic pathways in different living organisms (top boxes) and some possible lines of descent that correlate with major lines of evolution. The paths are characteristic for assemblages, some members of which may have lost the ability to produce lysine. The DAP path is associated with bacteria and plants; the inability of all members to produce lysine is associated with animals. The AAA path is a feature of organisms that have veered from the mainstream of evolution of the plant kingdom in the direction of animality. This clearly divides the phycomycetes into two evolutionarily quite separate groups ("water molds" and "some lower fungi" in the figure), a property that correlates with mode of spore flagellation. The two groups are presumed to have converged toward similar gross phenotypes during evolution, but their different ancestry is imprinted in their distinctive biochemical pathways. Figure and description after H. J. Vogel, "Lysine Biosynthesis and Evolution," in* Evolving Genes and Proteins, *V. Bryson and H. J. Vogel, eds., New York: Academic Press, Inc., 1965, pp. 25–40.*

DISTINCTIVE CONTROL MECHANISMS

Recent studies show that biochemical fossils may lie hidden in many metabolic pathways that are currently thought of as *alike* in different organisms. The *reaction steps* are the same in these cases. It is the metabolic control mechanisms exerted on the pathways that are distinctive. Both types of control have been discussed in this book. One involves feedback inhibition of enzyme *activity* (Chap. 5) and the second involves repression of enzyme *synthesis* (Chaps. 9 and 10). Observations show that different organisms exert distinctive sets of controls on similar metabolic sequences.

The pathway of aromatic amino acid biosynthesis is a case in point. Figure 5.6 shows this metabolic pathway. The figure and its legend describe the control mechanisms operating in one species of bacterium, *E. coli*. The legend also points out the contrasting control mechanisms as currently understood to operate in an unrelated bacterial species, *Bacillus subtilis*. The metabolites involved and the reaction steps they influence by feedback inhibition differ in the two organisms: *E. coli* has three different PKDH synthetases (enzyme 1 in Fig. 5.6), whereas *B. subtilis* has but one. In addition to these features, controls exerted by repression of enzyme formation differ in the two types of bacteria.

It is not clear at the present time if the quite different modes of regulation possessed by these bacteria is a consequence of divergence during evolution or reflects independent origin. Further studies on these and other organisms may serve to shed some light on this point. In any event, the contrasting metabolic patterns at the level of regulation in enzyme activity and in enzyme synthesis provides a powerful new tool for analyses of relatedness.

Subunits and Enzyme Activities

It is now apparent in the case of the aromatic pathway discussed above (Fig. 5.6), as well as in others, that basic differences in enzyme structure underlie what otherwise might be considered subtle differences in control mechanisms. This situation has been studied on a comparative basis in the biosynthesis of tryptophan (reactions 8 through 12 in Fig. 5.6). The sequence of five reactions depicted in Figs. 2.16 and 5.6 are shown again in Fig. 10.7. The reaction steps are identical in many organisms, but the quaternary structure of the enzyme catalyzing the same reaction may be different in diverse species. This is outlined in Fig. 11.5. The figure indicates the subunit structures of the enzymes involved in tryptophan biosynthesis from aromatic precursors in five microbes, using the letters or numbers of their respective genes. (The numbers and letters are genetic symbols which happen to have been used by various scientists and are unrelated to any genetic homologies that may exist among the species shown.) For *E. coli*, the products are individual polypeptide chains, as outlined in Fig. 2.16; *E. coli* differs from *B. subtilis* in the utilization of PRTase as a component essential for ASase activity. *E. coli* also contains a bifunctional enzyme, enzyme C, present as two distinct proteins in *B. subtilis*. The patterns of both *E. coli* and *B. subtilis* differ from the members of the three orders of fungi shown. Only *A. nidulans* and *N. crassa,* members of

Reaction step	1	2	3	4	5	
Enzyme	Anthranilate synthetase (ASase)	PR-transferase (PRTase)	PRA-isomerase (PRAIase)	InGP synthetase (InGPSase)	Tryptophan synthetase (TSase)	Genetic organization
Bacteria						
Escherichia coli	E–D	D	C	C	A–B	Clustered; E–D–C–B–A
Bacillus subtilis	1	2	3	4	5a–5b	Clustered; 1–2–4–3–5a–5b
Fungi						
Saccharomyces cerevisiae	2–3	4	1	3	5	Unlinked
Aspergillus nidulans	A–C	D	C	C	B	Only A and D linked (15 units apart)
Neurospora crassa	1–2	4	1	1	3	Unlinked

FIG. 11.5. Neurospora TSase is composed of two pairs of nonidentical polypeptide chains whose structures are dictated by the trp-3 locus (see Fig. 4.3). The TSase of the trp-5 gene in Saccharomyces and the trp-B gene of Aspergillus have not been thoroughly characterized as to their subunit structure. Compiled in part from D. M. Bonner et al., in Evolving Genes and Proteins, V. Bryson and J. H. Vogel, eds., New York: Academic Press, Inc., 1965, p. 305; J. Wegman and J. A. DeMoss, J. Biol. Chem., 240 (1965), 3781; M. Carsiotis et al., Biochem. Biophys. Res. Commun., 18 (1965), 877; T. R. Manney, Genetics, 50 (1964), 109; R. K. Mortimer and D. C. Hawthorne, Genetics, 53 (1966), 165; C. F. Roberts, Genetics, 55 (1967), 233; R. Hütter and J. A. DeMoss, Genetics, 55 (1967), 241; B. C. Carlton, J. Bacteriol., 94 (1967), 600; J. A. DeMoss et al., Genetics, 56 (1967), 413; R. Hütter and J. A. DeMoss, J. Bacteriol., 94 (1967), 1896.

Organism	Enzyme readily dissociable into dissimilar enzymatically active subunits, A and B	Component B activity (Ind-to-Trp) enhancement by component A	Form enzymatically active with:		Inhibited by antiserum to:	
			E. coli A protein	E. coli B protein	S. typhimurium B	N. crassa TSase
Gram-negative bacteria						
Escherichia coli	+	++	+++	++	++	0
Salmonella typhimurium	+	++	++	++	++	0
Serratia marcescens	+	++	−	−	++	−
Gram-positive bacterium						
Bacillus subtilis	+	0	−	−	−	−
Blue-green alga						
Anabaena variabilis	+	0	+	0	+ (weak)	0
Green alga						
Chlorella ellipsoides	+	0	+	0	0	+ (weak)
Fungi						
Saccharomyces cerevisiae	0	−	−	−	0	++
Neurospora crassa	0	−	0	0	0	++

FIG. 11.6. *Properties of tryptophan synthetases of various organisms. Adapted from D. M. Bonner, J. A. DeMoss, and S. E. Mills, "The Evolution of an Enzyme," in* Evolving Genes and Proteins, *V. Bryson and H. J. Vogel, eds., New York: Academic Press, Inc, 1965, p. 305; E. Balbinder, Biochem. Biophys. Res. Commun., 17 (1964), 770; see also T. E. Creighton, D.R. Helinski, R. L. Somerville, and C. Yanofsky, J. Bacteriol, 91 (1966), 1819, for peptide patterns of several bacterial A proteins. (+ = positive; 0 = no effect; − = not determined.)*

the two orders that are considered closely related by other criteria, show similar gene–polypeptide chain relationships.

Information about the evolution of a protein has also been gained from comparative studies of tryptophan synthetase found in several microorganisms. The survey summarized in Fig. 11.6 indicates striking similarities among organisms that seem somewhat related in a gross taxonomic sense, yet may be widely divergent in origin. Homologies of this and other types may allow the myriad of organisms in the microbial world to be studied from the point of view of their evolutionary relationships. It is obvious that a very potent probe into the relatedness of organisms is now just beginning to be exploited.

Homologous Polypeptide Chains

Comparative studies of the primary structure of proteins with similar function in different organisms provide sequence information with many genetic implications and offer strong support for evolutionary concepts developed in classical biology. They afford the means to probe fine-structure relationships between organisms and to retrace the evolutionary process. From analyses of this sort, the probable structures of ancestral proteins of organisms long extinct may be conjectured, and in conjunction with the physicochemical and functional properties of the proteins, molecular functions as they were carried out in the distant evolutionary past may some day be deduced. In addition, primary sequence analyses can define the extent of homology between "duplicate proteins" in a single organism. Although different genes now dictate the structure of "duplicate proteins," these genes are thought to have originated by duplication and mutation from a single gene present in an ancestral species. The myoglobins and hemoglobins are contemporary examples of such "duplicate proteins" controlled by separate genes.

Hemoglobin in red blood cells and myoglobin in muscle are conjugated proteins that contain a protein, globin, to which a particular iron-containing porphyrin, heme, is attached as the prosthetic group. Hemoglobin and myoglobin are but two of a wide array of heme-containing proteins that deserve wider attention in studies of evolutionary biology. For example, one heme enzyme, involved in an important type of detoxication reaction is found in the livers of mammals, birds, and reptiles but not found in fishes or certain amphibians. The appearance of this type of reaction may have been an important step in the migration of animals from a marine to a terrestrial environment some 400 million years ago. Interestingly, there are many common reactions in the pathways leading to the formation of heme and chlorophyll. These homologies in reaction sequence again exemplify the types of correlations now available to the student of evolution.

Now to return to the evolution of the globin molecule as an example of the trends in evolution that have taken place in "recent history," that is, the last few hundred million years. Hemoglobin can be prepared by lysis of blood cells, and over 95 percent of the soluble protein so obtained from mammalian red cells is hemoglobin. The heme is identical in all hemoglobins examined, but variations occur in the globin component. The hemoglobins are tetramers, normally composed of two different classes of polypeptide chain, that is, two pairs of identical monomers. Mammals synthesize different types of hemoglobin based on the types of monomers comprising the tetramer. Hemoglobin A_1 is about 90 percent of the total hemoglobin in adult humans, although a number of other minor components have been detected. The various types of hemoglobin, obtained from a single individual or from populations of individuals, have been separated and their quaternary structures determined. There are various tetramers present and these are designated $\alpha_2\beta_2$ for the two α- and the two β-polypeptide chains of hemoglobin A_1. Human fetal hemoglobin is designated $\alpha_2\gamma_2$, and a minor hemoglobin found in adults, hemoglobin A_2, is designated $\alpha_2\delta_2$. Four separate genes control the production of the four types of polypeptide chains. The structure of myoglobin, a monomer, is dictated by a fifth gene.

The five types of polypeptide chains are about the same length. They form similar secondary and tertiary structures, but, as mentioned above, myoglobin differs in quaternary structure, existing as a monomer rather than a tetramer. Consideration of the amino acid sequences of these different globins has led to speculation on their evolutionary origin (Fig. 11.7). The amino acid sequences are lined up and compared by matching up the 23 positions occupied by the same amino acid residue in all five human globins. The basis for this speculative scheme is summarized in Fig. 11.8, along with "guesstimates" of mutational changes that have led to these alterations.

FIG. 11.7. *Scheme for evolution of human hemoglobin genes. After gene duplication* (—●—), *the polypeptide products of the hemoglobin genes acquire characteristics advantageous to the organism to form dimers, for example, α_2, and later tetramers, for example, $\alpha_2\beta_2$. The numbers at the points of divergence are crude estimates of time of occurrence given in millions of years; these values may be compared with the presentation in Fig. 11.2. After V. M. Ingram, "The Evolution of a Protein," Federation Proc., 21 (1962), 1053; E. Zuckerkandl, "The Evolution of Hemoglobin," Sci. Am., 212 (May, 1965), 110; E. Zuckerkandl and L. Pauling, in Evolving Genes and Proteins, V. Bryson and H. J. Vogel, eds., New York: Academic Press, Inc., 1965 p. 97.*

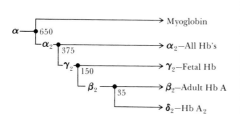

	M/α	M/β	M/γ	a/β	a/γ	β/γ	β/δ	a/h	β/h	M/W
Variable amino acid residues	119	123	123	118	118	125	125	121	125	132
Apparent base pair changes										
None	14	15	15	43	38	85	115	105	99	116
One-base	57	53	57	53	55	30	9	12	18	11
Two-base	47	54	49	22	25	10	1	5	8	5
Three-base	1	1	2	0	0	0	0	0	0	0
Transitions	45	60	61	30	41	22	2	8	8	8
Transversions	109	104	100	67	65	28	9	14	26	13
Average per variable amino acid residue										
Base changes	0.43	0.44	0.44	0.28	0.30	0.13	0.029	0.060	0.090	0.053
Amino acid changes	0.88	0.88	0.88	0.64	0.68	0.31	0.08	0.14	0.21	0.12

FIG. 11.8. *Base changes and amino acid changes in the relationship between human α, β, γ, and δ hemoglobins and myoglobin (M), between human and horse hemoglobins (α/h, β/h), and between human and whale myoglobin (M/W). The number of amino acid residues that differ among the hemoglobins and are present in the pair of proteins being compared are indicated as "Variable amino acid residues"; 23 other residues are regarded as invariable. Beneath this are shown the minimal number of base-pair changes that can account for the amino acid differences, based on the current genetic code (Fig. 8.2). These base-pair changes are sorted into "Transitions" (where a purine/pyrimidine base pair has been substituted for the other purine/pyrimidine base pair) and "Transversions" (where a purine/pyrimidine base pair has been substituted by a pyrimidine/purine base pair, or vice versa. The last two lines indicate the average number of base-pair changes and amino acid changes per variable amino acid residue. The schemes shown in Figs. 11.7 and 11.9 are based on data such as these. After T. H. Jukes, Molecules and Evolution, New York: Columbia University Press, 1966.*

Figure 11.8 also compares the amino acid sequences of globin from humans and several from other species. Extensive examination of these and of globins from other animals lead to evolutionary schemes such as that shown in Fig. 11.9. The gene duplication that gave rise to primordial α and β chains is thought to have occurred about 375 million years ago, before the ancestral divergence of man, horse, and cattle. Obviously some structural features have been conserved, presumably because they are required for the function of the molecule. Examination of homologous proteins from widely divergent species allows an estimate of "evolutionarily allowable," amino acid substitutions at specific sites; there are about 117 of these variable amino acid residues in the case of hemoglobins. The data so far obtained with hemoglobin indicate that an allowable substitution will occur at a particular residue on the average about once in 800 million years. This strongly implies, as indicated in Fig. 11.9, that all the hemoglobins and myoglobins share a common ancestry, although from a highly branched mainstream of evolution. One big question mark in these extrapolations, however, is the *rate* of evolution of a particular polypeptide chain. This may well vary from chain to chain and vary at different times during the evolution of one species of polypeptide chain.

Convergences also may occur. For example, the hemoglobins of various lamprey eels appear to be monomers when oxygen is bound to them and to aggregate into multimers under other conditions. What is known of the primary structures of some lamprey hemoglobins leads to the conjecture that they have followed a different course of evolution from the hemoglobins shown in Fig. 11.9. Thus the possibility is suggested that hemoglobins may have made more than one appearance during evolution, derived from a common or similar archetypical protein by separate events. More intensive studies on the hemoglobins of different species could resolve this point.

What were the amino acid sequences of the primordial "protoglobins" that have given rise to the hemoglobins? The codons for a

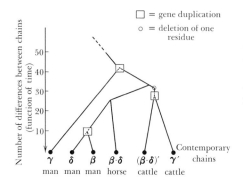

□ = gene duplication

o = deletion of one residue

FIG. 11.9. *Probable evolutionary relationship of some mammalian hemoglobin chains. Modified from E. Zuckerkandl and L. Pauling, in* Evolving Genes and Proteins, *V. Bryson and H. J. Vogel, eds., New York: Academic Press, Inc., 1965, p. 97.*

particular residue? It may one day be possible with some degree of assurance to ascertain the sequences in these proteins, to synthesize such proteins through techniques in solid-state chemistry, and to determine their properties. Also, one day we may be able to trace the divergence in structure and function of proteins currently thought to be unrelated but actually stemming from a common progenitor protein and still bearing traces of this ancestry. At the moment, there are wide differences in speculations proposed by scientists, but common agreement exists on the continuing need for meaningful experimental data and novel experimental approaches.

Origin of Cytoplasmic Organelles

In recent years, chloroplasts and mitochondria have been shown to contain DNA of the size found in bacteria. Like bacterial DNA, the organelle DNA appears to be circular in structure and to lack histones present in the nuclear DNA's of higher organisms. These organelles also contain ribosomes of the 70S type, characteristic of bacteria, rather than of the 80S type, characteristic of animal, plant, yeast, and fungal cytoplasm. The organelles also have been cited as containing tRNA's and aminoacyl tRNA synthetases that interact with bacterial systems, for example, from *E. coli*, to a much greater extent than do their cytoplasmic counterparts. Are these vestiges of evolution, or do they represent convergent processses in evolution? Through application of some of the techniques outlined in this book, perhaps ultimately we can make a decision on this point.

Nucleic Acid Hybridization and Evolution

Comparison of DNA base composition is being used as an additional criterion in modern taxonomy. Although closely related organisms do have very nearly similar DNA base compositions, unfortunately, distantly related organisms are not always significantly different. Determination of nearest-neighbor frequences in DNA's provides much greater resolving power, but the procedure is considerably more laborious. In another approach, the frequencies of mono-, di-, tri-, and so on, nucleotides in hydrolysates of DNA can be compared. A more sensitive method for detection of polynucleotide sequence similarities is the ability of one strand of a DNA molecule to hybridize with a complementary strand of DNA or RNA. This annealing reaction provides a potent tool for the determination of genetic relatedness.

Hybridization studies are performed in a variety of ways. (Recall the discussion in Chap. 6.) Two different single-stranded (in the case of DNA, denatured) nucleic acids can be mixed in solution and the extent of hybrid formation compared to the homologous control. If one of the component nucleic acids is labeled with a density label, presence of the hybrid can be detected by means of its different buoyant density in a CsCl gradient centrifugation experiment. This type of experiment may be complicated by the ability of the opposite strand of homologous origin to competitively inhibit base pairing with the strand of heterologous origin. Another method utilizes denatured labeled heterologous nucleic acid and measures specific hybridization with unlabeled or differentially labeled denatured nucleic acid that is embedded in a matrix such as agar.

The labeled nucleic acid can be synthesized in vivo and then extracted, or it can be made in vitro with the proper polymerase and template. In general, much greater labeling with radioisotope can be achieved by synthesis in vitro. Radioisotope also may be introduced directly into nucleic acid in vitro by methylation with radioactive dimethyl sulfate.

The amount of homology that one detects by the above methods is a function of the experimental conditions. One may use rather lax conditions of lower temperature, higher ionic strength, and long-term incubation to perceive relatively indiscriminate combinations involving a low order of homology at the level of nucleotide sequence. More stringent conditions select for longer stretches or greater exactness in "homologous" sequence. Thus by adjusting the conditions for annealling one can adjust for the span of polynucleotide similarities, and thereby the evolutionary time scale, examined in a particular experiment. The abilities of unlabeled nucleic acids from various sources to compete for base-pairing sites have been examined, but these experiments are difficult to interpret. A useful and very sensitive method measures the melting profile of the hybrid, to obtain the quantity of label converted to a single-stranded form as the temperature is gradually increased. Again, the stability of the double-stranded polynucleotide with increased temperature is taken as further evidence of homology between the strands.

Results from experiments of this type are just beginning to be evaluated. Final interpretations require additional experimental comparisons and better knowledge of the forces that act in the "zipping" together of double-stranded complexes. Nevertheless, there are already indications that these approaches will be extremely valuable in studies of evolution. Figure 11.10 diagrams observations made in competition experiments between various DNA's. Clearly, a large cross section of the evolutionary spectrum can be scrutinized in this fashion, ranging from instances of relatedness between races or strains only recently separated to the relatedness of orders and classes of organisms. Eventually, one would hope that these studies also will tell us something about the *rates* of evolutionary change as they occurred in the past and are taking place in the present.

FIG. 11.10. *Relationship between polynu-cleotide similarity and time of evolution-ary divergence. The times since divergence, determined by more classic methods, are shown as bars reflecting the uncertainty of precise timing. The percent of simi-larity in polynucleotide sequences was determined by competition in DNA-DNA annealing experiments.* Consult B. H. Hoyer, B. J. McCarthy, and E. T. Bol-ton, "A Molecular Approach in the Sys-tematics of Higher Organisms," Science, 144 (1964), 959; B. J. McCarthy, "The Evolution of Base Sequences in Polynu-cleotides," Progr. Nucleic Acid Res. Mol. Biol., 4 (1965), 129; B. H. Hoyer, E. T. Bolton, B. J. McCarthy, and R. B. Roberts, "The Evolution of Poly-nucleotides," in Evolving Genes and Pro-teins, V. Bryson and H. J. Vogel, eds., New York: Academic Press, Inc., 1965, p. 581; B. H. Hoyer and R. B. Roberts, "Studies of Nucleic Acid Interactions Using DNA-Agar," in Molecular Genetics, Part II, J. H. Taylor, ed., New York: Academic Press, Inc., 1967, p. 425.

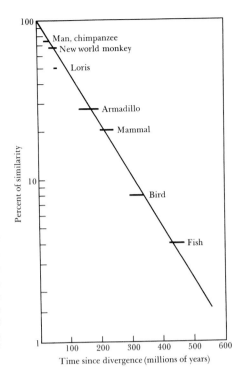

Questions

11.1. Select one organism and, after library research, describe the basis for its current classification in relation to other organisms.

11.2. Of the three organisms man, *Euglena* (a protozoan), and *E. coli* (a bacterium), which do you suspect are the most closely related phylogenetically? State your arguments.

11.3. Some scientists believe that there are thousands, if not millions, of other planets on which physical evolution has progressed similarly to the earth's history. Would you expect to find living creatures on these planets? What kind of organisms? Why?

11.4. Although a scheme of evolution still cannot be based upon the use of a single method, which one of the wide variety of approaches do you find the most informative? Defend your choice.

11.5. How can one distinguish evolutionary convergence from common origin?

11.6. What properties do you feel should be possessed by a "primordial molecule"? What would constitute experimental proof of the "cre-ation of life?" What criteria can be applied to establish the aggre-gate property we call "life"?

11.7. Pick out a biochemical sequence of four or more reactions that is present in some organisms but not in others and attempt to trace, through library research, its phylogenetic distribution.

11.8. Some specialized species have lost or gained during evolution a large quantity of the DNA contained in otherwise closely related organisms [see B. J. McCarthy, *Bact. Rev., 31* (1967), 226; G. L. Stebbins, *Science, 152* (1966), 1463]. What methods could you use to determine if this difference in DNA content is due to redundant genes (duplicate genes) as compared with unique genes? What methods could you use to determine if this difference in DNA content involves genes which function, or fail to function, in the organism that possesses them?

11.9. Suggest some reasons why evolutionary relationships derived from the various methods discussed in this chapter (and other methods) might not be entirely consistent in some cases.

11.10. What important practical applications can be derived from a firm knowledge of true phylogenetic relationships among, for example, microorganisms?

11.11. Tell how you would carry out an experiment designed to provide knowledge of the types of control mechanisms operating in a series of organisms with an otherwise identical biochemical pathway.

References

Berlyn, M. G., "Gene-Enzyme Relationships in Histidine Biosynthesis in *Aspergillus nidulans,*" *Genetics, 57* (1967), 561. Comparative aspects of the genetics and enzymology of histidine biosynthesis in several bacteria and fungi are discussed.

Bernal, J. D., *The Origin of Life,* Cleveland: World, 1967.

Britten, R. J., and D. E. Kohne, "Repeated Sequences in DNA," *Science, 161* (1968), 529. About half of the DNA of higher organisms contains sequences that are repeated thousands of times; these sequences diverge from one another during evolution, but redundancy is replenished by occasional extensive reduplication.

Brookhaven Symposium in Biology, 21, "Structure, Function, and Evolution in Proteins," 1968. Hydrolytic enzymes, immunoglobulins, and cytochrome c receive particular attention in this series of papers.

Bryson, V., and H. J. Vogel, eds., *Evolving Genes and Proteins.* New York: Academic Press, Inc., 1965. A well-organized symposium that contains contributions quite relevant to the main themes and topics covered in this chapter.

Calvin, M., "Chemical Evolution," *Progr. Theoret. Biol., 1* (1967), 1.

Canovas, J. L., L. N. Ornston, and R. Y. Stanier, "Evolutionary Significance of Metabolic Control Systems," *Science, 156* (1967), 1695. A comparative study of β-ketoadipate biosynthesis and its regulation in several genera of bacteria leads to interesting evolutionary interpretations.

Cohen, S. S., "On Biochemical Variability and Innovation," *Science, 139* (1963), 1017. "A growing interest has . . . developed in the definition of origin as well as in the definition of function. The advances of the past decade have clarified genetic problems to the degree that many problems of evolution, phylogeny, and embryology are now ripe for study by biochemists."

Crawford, I. P., and I. C. Gunsalus, "Inducibility of Tryptophan Synthetase in *Pseudomonas putida*," *Proc. Natl. Acad. Sci. U.S., 56* (1966), 717. In *E. coli* and *B. subtilis,* tryptophan represses tryptophan synthetase formation. In *Pseudomonas,* tryptophan does not act in repression of tryptophan synthetase; rather, indole glycerol phosphate acts as an inducer. Feedback inhibition of anthranilate synthetase activity is exerted by tryptophan in all three genera. PRAIase and InGPase may be separate enzymes in *Pseudomonas,* in contrast to the bifunctional enzyme of another Gram-negative bacterium, *E. coli* (see Fig. 11.4). See also *J. Bacteriol., 95* (1968), 107.

Dixon, G. H., "Mechanisms of Protein Evolution," in *Essays in Biochemistry,* P. N. Campbell and G. D. Greville, eds., Vol. II, New York: Academic Press, Inc., 1966, p. 147. A useful discussion of results and ideas deriving from recent comparative studies of protein structure.

Dobzhansky, T., M. K. Hecht, and W. C. Steere, eds., *Evolutionary Biology,* Vol. 2. New York: Appleton-Century-Crofts, 1968. One of a series of volumes with collections of review articles on evolution including some on molecular aspects.

Dutta, S. K., N. Richman, V. W. Woodward, and M. Mandel, "Relatedness among Species of Fungi and Higher Plants Measured by DNA Hybridization and Base Ratios," *Genetics, 57* (1967), 719.

Edelman, M., D. Swinton, J. A. Schiff, H. T. Epstein, and B. Zeldin, "Deoxyribonucleic Acid of the Blue-Green Algae *(Cyanophyta)*," *Bacteriol. Rev., 31* (1967), 315. A survey with implications for phylogenetic taxonomy.

Fischer, A. G., "Fossils, Early Life and Atmospheric History," *Proc. Natl. Acad. Sci. U.S., 53* (1965), 1205. An overall view that focuses on the environment as a critical factor in determining the rate of evolution.

Florkin, M., *Biochemical Evolution,* S. Margulis, transl. New York: Academic Press, Inc., 1949. Discussion of evolution from the point of view of the presence of classes of molecules.

Fox, S. W., ed., *The Origins of Prebiological Systems and of Their Molecular Matrices.* New York: Academic Press, Inc., 1965. Proceedings of a carefully edited 1963 conference emphasizing experimental studies and speculation on the synthesis of organic molecules under primitive earth conditions and containing some lucid discussions on points of interest.

Giles, N. H., M. E. Case, C. W. H. Partridge, and S. I. Ahmed, "A Gene Cluster in *Neurospora crassa* Coding for an Aggregate of Five Aromatic Synthetic Enzymes," *Proc. Natl. Acad. Sci. U.S., 58* (1967), 1453. Comparative aspects of the aromatic amino acid biosynthetic pathway, outlined in Chap. 5 and discussed further in the current chapter, are extended in this paper.

Goldberg, A. L., and R. E. Wittes, "Genetic Code: Aspects of Organization," *Science, 153* (1966), 420. This paper can serve as a companion to one by T. M. Sonneborn, in *Evolving Genes and Proteins,* Bryson, V. and Vogel, H., eds., New York: Academic Press, Inc., 1965, concerning teleological aspects of the genetic code and its evolution.

Hütter, R., and J. A. DeMoss, "Organization of the Tryptophan Pathway: A Phylogenetic Study of the Fungi," *J. Bacteriol., 94* (1967), 1896.

Enzyme associations and activities in otherwise similar biochemical pathways are used as a phylogenetic tool; the legend to Fig. 5.6 gives additional references to this same theme.

Ingram, V. M., *The Hemoglobins in Genetics and Evolution,* New York: Columbia University Press, 1963. A thorough treatment by the scientist whose work has been a primary stimulus for developments in this area.

Jensen, R. A., D. S. Nasser, and E. W. Nester, "Comparative Control of a Branch-Point Enzyme in Microorganisms," *J. Bacteriol., 94* (1967), 1582. Controls exerted on the reaction shown as step 1 in Fig. 5.6 is the focal point for a survey of biochemical relatedness. See also *J. Bacteriol., 95* (1968), 197.

Jukes, T. H., *Molecules and Evolution.* New York: Columbia University Press, 1966. Some molecular trends in the study of evolution are outlined in the last half of this book along with references to the original literature. The book also contains some typical speculations on the "evolution" of the genetic code.

Kaplan, R. W., "Probleme der Lebensentstehung und der frühesten Evolution," in *Evolution der Organismen,* G. Heberer, ed. Jena: Gustav Fischer Verlagbuchhandlung, 1966.

Keosian, J., *The Origin of Life.* New York: Reinhold Publishing Corporation, 1964. A fine little paperback.

Kornberg, H. L., "The Co-ordination of Metabolic Routes," *Symp. Soc. Gen. Microbiol., 15* (1965), 8. Both this article and one by the same author that appears as a companion essay to the one by Dixon cited above discuss the comparative biochemistry and control of metabolic flow with special emphasis on carbohydrate metabolism.

Marmur, J., S. Falkow, and M. Mandel, "New Approaches to Bacterial Taxonomy," *Ann. Rev. Microbiol., 17* (1963), 329. A thorough review of genetic and molecular methods as applied to the classification of bacteria.

Matthews, C. N., and R. E. Moser, "Prebiological Protein Synthesis," *Proc. Natl. Acad. Sci. U.S., 56* (1966), 1087. A recent paper typical of experimental work in progress.

McCarthy, B. J., "Arrangement of Base Sequences in Deoxyribonucleic Acid," *Bacteriol. Rev., 31* (1967), 215. A review of in vitro hybridization experiments with nucleic acids and their application to current problems in biology, including evolution.

Neurath, H., K. A. Walsh, and W. P. Winter, "Evolution of Structure and Function of Proteases," *Science, 158* (1967), 1638.

Nolan, C., and E. Margoliash, "Comparative Aspects of Primary Structure of Proteins," *Ann. Rev. Biochem., 37* (1968), 727.

Oparin, A. I., *The Origin of Life.* New York: Dover Publications, Inc., reprinted in 1953. A paperback reprint of a classic book, first published in 1936 and translated in 1938, which presents a modern theory for the origin of organic substances and their evolution into the earth's primordial organisms.

———, *The Origin of Life on the Earth,* 3rd ed. London: Oliver and Boyd Limited, 1957. Translation by Ann Synge of a revised and enlarged edition of Oparin's classic book cited above.

Pollock, M. R., "Origin and Function of Penicillinase: A Problem in Biochemical Evolution," *Brit. Med. J., 4* (1967), 71. Interesting speculations on the molecular ancestry of a highly improbable, but nevertheless extant, enzyme.

Reissig, J. L., A. S. Issaly, and I. M. deIssaly, "Arginine-Pyrimidine Pathways in Microorganisms," *Natl. Cancer Inst. Monogr., 27* (1967), 259.

Shneour, E. A., and E. A. Ottesen, eds., *Extraterrestrial Life: An Anthology and Bibliography.* Washington, D.C.: National Academy of Sciences, 1966, Publication 1296A. Includes a number of articles on the primitive earth.

Smith, R. T., P. Miescher, and R. A. Good, eds., *Phylogeny of Immunity.* Gainesville: University of Florida Press, 1966.

The Origin of Life on the Earth, Proceedings of the First International Symposium, Moscow, 1957, International Union of Biochemistry Symposium Series, Vol. I. Oxford, England: Pergamon Press, Ltd., 1959. A collection of papers relating to the generation and evolution of organic molecules and metabolic pathways. Some selections from this volume have been published, in 1960, by the same publisher and edited by M. Florkin under the title *Aspects of the Origin of Life.*

Vogel, H. J., "Lysine Biosynthesis and Evolution," in *Evolving Genes and Proteins,* V. Bryson and H. J. Vogel, eds. New York: Academic Press, Inc., 1965. p. 25. Note particularly the last section of this paper, "Protozoan-Bacterium Complex," along with the references to literature on additional complexes of a similar nature; possibly significant from the standpoint of the origin of organelles of higher organisms.

Wald, G., "The Origins of Life," *Proc. Natl. Acad. Sci. U.S., 52* (1964), 595. A stimulating short discussion that covers a lot of ground in a simple, understandable fashion.

Twelve

Perspectives and Horizons

In the past, our ideas of the nature of the hereditary material and how it controls the characteristics of the organism have continually undergone revision. Certainly, our present concepts will similarly be tested and changed as more experimental information becomes available. The preceding chapters, then, have merely "frozen" within the confines of the printed page our comprehension of genic activities at the time of writing. Our documentation, while very incomplete, exemplifies the kinds of experimental evidence that have been obtained by biologists in support of the principles that underlie our current concepts. Some principles are thoroughly proved, but others require extensive further investigation before they can be accepted without reservation by either the reader or the authors.

In our discussions thus far, we have posed questions that we hope future research will answer but more often our approach has been didactic rather than inquisitive. This chapter is set aside to explore with you some of the important problems in the biology of the future and how genetics may play an important experimental or conceptual role in their solution. We have confidence that molecular biology, as now developed, needs but little refinement and adaptation to attack these areas of the unknown.

Vitalism versus Chemical Reactions

We are far from understanding many critical biological phenomena. Yet, through advances in biochemical genetics and nucleic acid and protein chemistry, a comprehension of two important properties of life, heretofore puzzling and mysterious, appears within our reach. In the past, the utter lack of understanding of these properties of life had been a major factor leading to the view that living organisms possess an inherent, vitalistic "something," perhaps akin to a "spirit." The ability to define this "something" in physical and chemical terms was thought to be unattainable.

One property is the expression and transmission of heritable traits. The broad outlines of DNA replication and gene action via mRNA synthesis are helping greatly to bring this property to precise definition. Another property is the control of cellular structures. Recent experiments support the view that the folding and interactions of structural proteins and many of the properties of the fully formed protein are attributable to the primary structure of the molecule. The amino acid sequence certainly limits the number of useful configurations that can be attained in a given intra- and extracellular environment. Consequently, protein primary structure contributes substantially to the architecture of the living cell.

Two areas of research that require extensive and immediate investigation before other related problems can be solved concern questions of "cellular organization" and "cellular interaction."

CELLULAR ORGANIZATION

We have pointed out examples of multiple enzyme activities which are found associated in macromolecular aggregates rather than in homogeneous proteins possessing a single activity in the usual sense. There is every reason to believe that associations of this type reflect the in vivo state of these proteins. What is the significance of such specific high-molecular-weight aggregates in cellular metabolism? Are there further associations present in vivo that have escaped our notice in vitro? How important is enzyme localization and how are enzymes compartmentalized within certain regions of the cell's ultrastructure?

The general pathways of amino acid biosynthesis appear reasonably well defined. And we can provide some details for several of the biochemical sequences leading to the incorporation of amino acids into proteins. We know something about the assembly of polypeptide chains into a three-dimensional protein structure. But how about more complex protein multimers and other protein-containing macromolecular structures such as membranes, mitochondria, ribosomes, and cell walls? New techniques as well as modifications of basic approaches that have been successful in unraveling simpler systems now are being brought to bear on these more complex problems.

It appears that the phenotype of the cell is not merely the sum of its heredity and its environment. The past history of the cell also is important. Why? Is there present in a particular cell a "primer," essential for the functioning of an enzyme or complex of enzymes otherwise not expressed? An activator or an inhibitor of enzyme activity? It is a matter of scientific history that superficially complex biological problems can be dissected effectively by rephrasing the problem in terms of a series of relatively simple biochemical questions. Genetics has and will continue to supply unique and important technical and conceptual probes.

CELLULAR INTERACTIONS

In multicellular organisms cells can "recognize" one another to selectively associate into tissues and organs. There is a wealth of excellent descriptive literature on such phenomena, and it is our feeling that this area of research will soon see extensive penetration and illumination by biochemistry and the techniques of molecular biology.

A second type of intercellular event involves the passage of molecules from one cell to another. In some cases these appear to be simple molecules; we have emphasized in this book the role of environment on genic expression and the ultimate development of phenotype. Low-molecular-weight metabolites manufactured by one cell type may be taken up from the environment by another cell type, altering some aspect of the recipient's metabolism. But more complex interactions are possible in animal cells. For example, there may be unidirectional transfer, or reciprocal exchange, of hormones and even macromolecules through transient intercellular bridges. What methodology may be applied in the search for events of this type, and what role may they play in the fate of the cell and its progeny?

Regulation of Gene Expression

We can expect to see rapid advances in the area of regulation of gene expression in macroorganisms, because the elegant studies of the genetics of control mechanisms using in vivo systems has provided a firm foundation for crucial in vitro analyses. Not many years will elapse before the pathway from DNA to inducible enzyme is achieved in the test tube—in experiments meaningful to interpretation of intracellular phenomena. The molecular basis for regulation of gene expression in higher organisms and its undoubtedly important role in growth and development remains a keystone in our future understanding of normal growth processes and neoplasia.

Growth and Development

One of the major areas of biology now being infused with contemporary molecular genetic thought is the growth and development of higher organisms. How does the single fertilized egg become differentiated during subsequent cell divisions into the diverse specialized tissues that constitute the adult organism?

A vast amount of *descriptive* knowledge is available about the changes exhibited by organisms during development, and now, in addition, biochemical and genetical data are being applied to the problem (see Markert and Ursprung's *Developmental Genetics* in this series and the companion Foundations of Developmental Biology Series).

A critical aspect of growth and development appears to involve the turning on and turning off of certain genes in particular groups of cells at very specific times. The techniques and approaches worked out for microorganisms, and described in the preceding chapters, are now being employed to determine whether this is so. For example, certain cells seem to contain a unique assortment of mRNA's during a particular stage of development. There also seem to be selective control mechanisms at other levels, such as in the rate of mRNA destruction, the availability of ribosomes, and the quantity, function, and specificity of certain types of tRNA and activating enzymes. We know relatively little about cellular regulatory mechanisms in microorganisms; the major facets have been mentioned in earlier chapters of this book. We do not know whether these mechanisms will apply to higher organisms. And, once a parallel is found, one still must ask whether the mechanism is important in differentiation and how it operates.

In *The Mechanics of Inheritance,* Stahl mentions the structural differences between the chromosomes of bacteria (procaryotes) and viruses and the chromosomes of higher organisms (eucaryotes). Chromosomes of the former are essentially naked DNA molecules, not surrounded by a nuclear membrane or associated with the types of protein components associated with the latter. Do these proteins of chromosomes (histones and nonhistone proteins) play general or specific roles in gene action? What is the meaning and function of the nucleolus, an intranuclear structure rich in RNA and associated with gene loci that have been implicated in synthesis of ribosomes of higher organisms?

Intuition tells us that some similarities will be found between regulatory systems in microorganisms and those in higher organisms and that such systems will be found to be important in guiding differentiation. But science relies upon experimental demonstration, not on intuition. It is logical to assume that controlling mechanisms peculiar to higher organisms will be discovered. We do not yet have a detailed picture of the structure of chromosomes of higher organisms; and without this, our understanding of how genic expression can be influenced and regulated is limited. For instance, the two genetical phenomena discussed below present characteristic enigmas. Neither phenomenon is understood, although many examples have been recorded.

GENE-DOSAGE COMPENSATION

In Chapter 4 it was stated that gene products are present in proportion to gene dosage; the heterozygote produces one-half normal protein and one-half mutant protein. This is generally true of autosomal genes and their products, although exceptions to the rule constitute cases for conjecture. The rule often does not apply to sex chromosomes. The human female has two X chromosomes; the male has only one X chromosome, along with a Y chromosome bearing relatively few functional genes (see McKusick's *Human Genetics* in this series). Yet, where certain genes on the X chromosome are lacking on the Y chromosome, equal amounts of the proteins coded by those genes appear to be synthesized by males and by females. This is called *dosage compensation*.

In somatic cells of human females, one of the two X chromosomes seems to remain in a functional, extended state during interphase. The second X chromosome clumps, is relatively afunctional, and forms a darkly staining chromatin body at the periphery of the nucleus (Fig. 12.1). Which X chromosome clumps is usually random, although, occasionally, heterozygous females are found in which only a particular one of the two X chromosomes functions in the vast majority of cells. Thus the human female is normally a cellular mosaic, some cells possessing a functional X chromosome derived from the father, while others possess a functional X chromosome derived from the mother. The mechanism by which one of the two chromosomes becomes clumped is unknown. Whatever the mechanism, only one X chromosome can function in a single cell except in the germinal cell line where both may function.

Dosage compensation is known also in *Drosophila*, although outright clumping of X chromosomes has not been described. Furthermore, in *Drosophila*, genetic evidence indicates that the function of the entire X chromosome is not turned off. This is illustrated by the lack of variegation of most sex-linked traits on the cellular level.

VARIEGATED POSITION EFFECTS

A gene adjacent to a region of the chromosome where breakage has occurred is sometimes stably mutant. This might be expected if the break has occurred within the polydeoxyribonucleotide segment of that gene, thus disrupting the base sequence requisite for normal func-

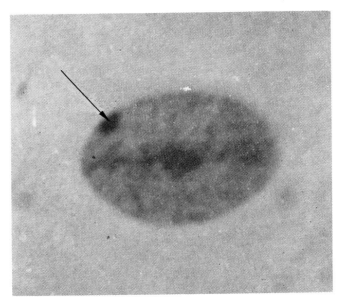

FIG. 12.1. *Interphase nucleus from a cell of a normal human female, showing the peripheral body of chromatin that is presumed to represent a condensed X chromosome.*

tion. This behavior is characteristic of chromosome breakage in higher organisms where the broken end is often rejoined to a lightly staining (euchromatic) portion of the same or of a different chromosome (*264–48, –53,* and *–63* in Fig. 12.2). Only occasionally is a discrepancy found. In *Drosophila* strain *264–34* (see Fig. 12.2), a stable mutation is produced even though the chromosome break has occurred some distance away from band 3C7, where the facet-Notch gene (*fa*) is supposedly located.

A contrasting behavior is exhibited when the end of a chromosome broken in a presumedly similar manner is rejoined to the darkly staining, basophilic sections of the chromosome (the heterochromatic regions, upper portion of Fig. 12.3). Now the genes over relatively long segments of the chromosome function only sporadically. The organism is a mosaic of phenotypically normal and mutant portions—it is variegated. Figure 12.3 (lower portion) is an illustration of this variegated position effect.

The genes influenced by this position effect are not themselves structurely defective. They still are able to function in some cells of the organism, and they become stable wild-type genes once they are removed from the heterochromatic region, either by recombination or by a second chromosomal aberration. These observations indicate that

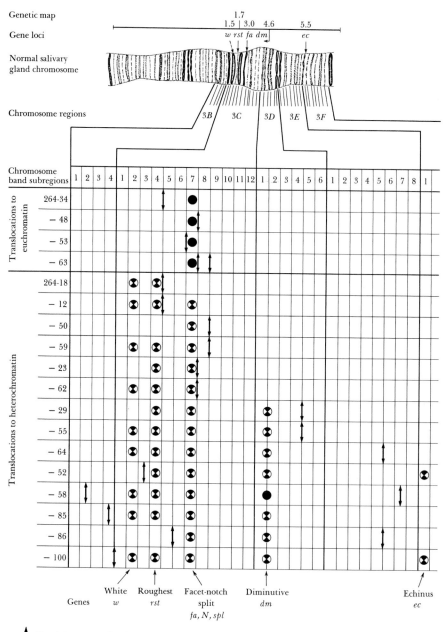

the lack of activity of the genes is due to their position next to heterochromatin and not to structural defects within the genes themselves. Some blocks of heterochromatin appear to exert strong position effects, while others exert weak effects. In addition, there is a clonal distribution of the phenotypes of cells in the mosaic individuals (Fig. 12.3) ; that is, the different types of cells occur in discrete groups.

Many speculations have been advanced to explain these observations; for the most part, they are inadequately supported by experimental evidence. Perhaps an inquisitive reader may someday furnish the answer to this or to other unanswered problems in the genetics of growth and development. What is the organization of the chromosome of higher organisms? What is heterochromatin? How does juxtaposition with heterochromatin elicit such striking instability in expression of the function of the gene?

FIG. 12.2. *Variegated position effects in* Drosophila melanogaster *caused by aberrations involving the X chromosome. The positions at which five gene loci have been mapped are indicated at the top of the figure. The correlation of these gene loci with positions on the banded salivary gland choromosome is indicated beneath the genetic map (for methods, see C. P. Swanson, Timothy Merz, and W. J. Young's* Cytogenetics *in this series). Cytologists have agreed upon nomenclature, dividing the cytological structure into regions, and subregions, a few of which (3B1 through 3F8) are indicated beneath the drawing of the normal salivary gland chromosome structure. A large number of translocations, inversions, and other chromosomal aberrations are known that involve this region of the X chromosome. The positions of the breaks that have given rise to these aberrations have been located by cytological analysis of the salivary gland chromosomes and are indicated by the vertical arrows. Other breaks, occurring outside the indicated region, are not shown in the figure.*

When the chromosome segment is translocated to a lightly staining, banded euchromatic portion of the X chromosome (or to a similarly staining region of another chromosome), the gene adjacent to the position of the break is sometimes stably mutant (● in the top section). Rarely, a gene several bands distant from the break is stably mutant (for example, in mutant 264-34).

When a chromosome segment is translocated to a heterochromatic portion of the chromosome, genes quite distant from the position of the break cause a variegated phenotype by turning on and off during growth and development (⊗ in the lower section). The number of genes affected depends upon the particular heterochromatic region to which the chromosome segment has been translocated. The gene nearest the heterochromatin (nearest the break) is turned off more frequently than are those further distant. Whenever a more distal gene is turned off, all the intervening genes are also turned off.

When the giant salivary chromosomes of variegated flies are examined, the bands containing the genes undergoing variegation are sometimes clumped in the heterochromatic chromocenter rather than in their normal distended and banded form. Based in part on M. Demerec, Genetics, 25 (1940), 618, and Proc. 7th Intern. Congr. Genet. (1941), 100. Also see G. Lefevre, Jr., and M. D. Wilkins, Genetics, 53 (1966), 175, and E. S. Gersh, Genetics, 56 (1967), 309.

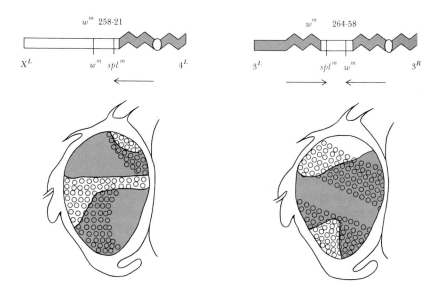

FIG. 12.3. *The upper portion shows two translocations 258-21 and 264-58, which give rise to mottled eye color (w^m) in* Drosophila. *In 258-21, part of the left arm of the X chromosome, shown in white (X^L), has been translocated to the fourth chromosome, and in 264-58 a smaller fragment has been translocated to the third chromosome. The positions of the chromosome breaks and genes affected in 264-58 are shown in Fig. 12.2.*

The lower portion of the figure shows examples of the eyes of flies carrying one of the two translocations. The circles indicate the areas of rough-eye phenotype caused by the split gene; shaded areas indicate pigment, and white areas represent no pigment. Note that in translocation 258-21 the white areas are always rough. The position effect is exerted in one direction, from the position of the break (arrow above eye). In translocation 264-58 note that the white areas may or may not be rough and that the rough areas may or may not have pigment. The position effect is exerted independently from either side, because heterochromatic material is now present on both sides of the short translocated fragment. Redrawn from W. K. Baker, Am. Zoologist, 3 (1963), 57.

Enzyme Structure and Function

In spite of considerable knowledge about the structure of proteins, we know relatively little about the molecular mechanisms and structural requirements underlying the catalytic activities of enzymes. Chemists have made some progress in structurally modifying proteins, but, undoubedly, genetic modification—that is, the use of mutant proteins—offers a new and almost inexhaustible source of enzymes that are modified specifically at various positions in the primary structure. Such precise alteration in structure, without the attendant problems of denaturation and secondary modification characteristic of chemical or physical treatment, should provide a wealth of information. The relationship between protein structure and function and also on the exact structural requirements for the maintenance and evolution of catalytic activities are amenable to such analyses.

We foresee important uses of mutant proteins in this type of study during the next few years. Later on, however, improved methods for the in vitro synthesis of polypeptide chains should allow the test-tube manufacture of tailor-made proteins of known amino acid sequence. Even at that time, studies on naturally occurring mutant proteins will continue to be valuable for purposes of extrapolation to in vivo situations as opposed to test-tube assays.

For some time proteins have been placed into categories such as fibrous, globular, and so on. A tremendously wide diversity of function has been demonstrated among globular proteins, and this does reflect large differences in primary structure. Nevertheless, complementation patterns (Chap. 4) suggest that certain structural restrictions may be placed on the molecule in terms of "protein survival." For example, certain sequences may recur near proline residues in a variety of proteins, and this could severely limit the number of possibilities for the correct folding of the polypeptide chain. Do the overall, three-dimensional models of various globular proteins also fall into classes? If so, is this due to selection at diverse times during evolution (convergent evolution) or to common ancestry once a unique and efficient sequence was obtained?

Memory and Aging

A friend once stated that "Loss of memory is one of the three important criteria of aging, and I forget the other two." What mechanisms underlie memory? Aging? Neurophysiology and gerontology are two areas now beckoning present-day workers in the field of gene action. There is an optimistic belief that these important aspects of biology soon will be attacked vigorously by the methods of genetics and biochemistry. For some time it was tacitly accepted that the use of microbial mutants would not contribute to our basic knowledge of essential or irreparable functions, that is, those which could not be supplied from the environment, such as the mutations affecting the mechanism of DNA replication, protein biosynthesis, and so on. Now, through the use of conditional lethal mutants (dependent upon the presence of suppressor genes for survival or temperature-sensitive mutants), penetrations into new areas already are evident. The same will hold true for other problems, seemingly inaccessible to the investigator at present. Breakthroughs in the past have come from two main sources: innovations in technique and the introduction of new types of biological material. Certainly we can note the importance of isotopes, chromatography, and density-gradient centrifugation, to mention but a few, as well as the selection of *Drosophila, Neurospora,* and finally bacteriophage for appropriate genetic studies.

What *techniques* will crack apparently complex problems into more simple systems amenable to experimental analysis? What *is* the organism of the future? We don't have answers to these questions, but to the query, "What horizons exist for molecular genetics?" we can confidently reply, "Unlimited!"

Synthetic Messages, Programmed Cells, and Programmed Evolution

Bacteriophage RNA, biologically active in terms of infectivity and subsequent replication, has been enzymatically synthesized in vitro using isolated and purified phage RNA as the template. Recently (Fig. 12.4) the test-tube synthesis of infectious DNA has been accomplished using single stranded DNA from the bacteriophage ϕX174 as the template. This achievement has been popularized as the "creation of life in a test tube," not quite true because a master template molecule had to be present. However, several polynucleotides of known

FIG. 12.4. *In vitro synthesis of viral DNA. φx single-stranded circular DNA molecules (plus chain) were separated and used as template for the synthesis of DNA by DNA polymerase in the presence of the three usual deoxynucleoside triphosphates and deoxybromouridine triphosphate (BrU) indicated by the dotted circle. The addition of a joining enzyme closed the circle. The new minus strands containing BrU were separated from the template plus strands. The newly synthesized BrU DNA was used as template for the synthesis of new plus strands. The newly synthesized molecules were shown to be infectious for the same E. coli bacteria that are sensitive to the original DNA. After M. Goulian, A. Kornberg, and R. L. Sinsheimer, Proc. Natl. Acad. Sci. U.S., 58 (1967), 2321.*

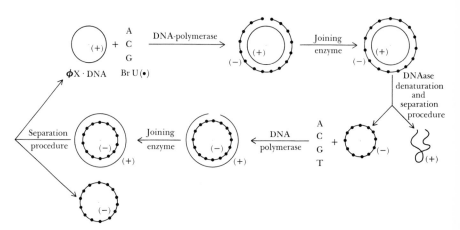

sequence have been synthesized using combined organic chemical and enzymatic methods (see Chap. 8). Furthermore, techniques for successfully sequencing large polynucleotides are available and in use. It takes little clairvoyance to realize that before very long similar approaches and refined techniques will result in the *total synthesis* of meaningful biologically active genetic messages. This can be predicted, for most of the predominant features of the genetic language are known, and the code appears to be universal. The fact that the methods for insertion and excision of genetic messages are routine procedures in microbial genetics assures us that the programming of metazoan cells hereditarily (using DNA messages) or transiently (using RNA messages) will not be far off, perhaps even within the next decade or two. Hence the possibility exists that human engineering with its attending moral and ethical problems will soon be a serious concern to scientists and to society in general. If somatic cells can be programmed and development altered (euphenics), then no doubt germ cells will be similarly amenable to change. Thus eugenics, or programmed evolution, may become an experimental reality. Many outstanding scientists envisage an impact of this on society even greater than that caused by developments in nuclear physics.

Genetics—Man's Health and Welfare

As our society has evolved, with its strong emphasis on control of infectious disease, starvation, and so on, it has become apparent that the frequency of detection of illness and mortality due to genetic cause is increasing. More examples are recognized of disorders due to chromosomal aberrations, to inherited metabolic disorders resulting from single gene mutations, and to malignancies of possible genetic origin. Problems of aging, hypertension, and behavior are being viewed now through genetically tinted glasses. Similarly, worldwide concern with problems related to population control, food production, social welfare, and education have inherent genetic components that must be understood and evaluated by those given the responsibility for decision making.

How will you view and react to such challenges of the future?

References

Abercrombie, M., "Contact-Dependent Behavior of Normal Cells and the Possible Significance of Surface Changes in Virus-Induced Transformation," *Cold Spring Harbor Symp. Quant. Biol.,* 27 (1962), 427. A subject of intense interest and promise in the field of cancer research at the present time.

Ambrose, E. J., and F. J. C. Roe, eds., *The Biology of Cancer.* Princeton, N.J.: D. Van Nostrand, Inc. 1966. Many articles, here and elsewhere, describe the properties of tumor cells and view the transformation of normal cells into tumor cells as changes in gene action.

Baker, W. K., "Position-Effect Variegation," *Advan. Genet., 14* (1968), 133. A well-written review that includes recent experimental studies on variegated position effects.

Bell, E., *Molecular and Cellular Aspects of Development.* New York: Harper & Row, Publishers, 1965. A collection of reprints with introductions and additional references grouped according to topics.

Bonner, J., and P. Ts'o, eds., *The Nucleohistones.* San Francisco: Holden-Day, Inc., 1964; H. Busch, *Histones and Other Nuclear Proteins.* New York: Academic Press, Inc., 1965; A. V. S. de Reuck and J. Knight, eds., *Histones.* London: J. & A. Churchill Ltd., 1966. An area in which careful chemical analyses and biochemical experimentation will assist advances in biology.

———, M. E. Dahmus, D. Fambrough, R. C. Huang, K. Marushige, and D. Y. H. Tuan, "The Biology of Isolated Chromatin," *Science, 159* (1968), 47.

Brachet, J., *Chemical Embryology.* New York: John Wiley & Sons, Inc. (Interscience Division), 1950.

Brink, R. A., ed., *Heritage from Mendel.* Madison: University of Wisconsin Press, 1967. Contains an excellent section of four papers on gene action in microorganisms and metazoans.

Brown, D. D., and I. B. Dawid, "Specific Gene Amplification in Oocytes," *Science, 160* (1968), 272. A discussion of oocyte nuclei that contain extrachromosomal replicas of the genes for ribosomal RNA.

Brown, D. D., and J. B. Gurdon, "Absence of Ribosomal RNA Synthesis in the Anucleolate Mutant of *Xenopus laevis,*" *Proc. Natl. Acad. Sci. U.S., 51* (1964), 139. An excellent example of how new techniques, utilized in work with microorganisms, may be fruitfully applied to investigation of higher organisms.

Brown, F. A., Jr., "Living Clocks," *Science, 130* (1959), 1535, and *Cold Spring Harbor Symp. Quant. Biol., 25* (1960), symposium on "Biological Clocks." Oscillation is a fundamental property of all living things, but the basic mechanisms underlying biological rhythms remain to be elucidated.

Brown, S. W., "Heterochromatin," *Science, 151* (1966), 417. Perhaps there is an "importance of doing nothing."

Bucher, N. L. R., "Experimental Aspects of Hepatic Regeneration," *New Engl. J. Med., 277* (1967), 686, 738.

Caspari, E., "Genetic Basis of Behavior," in *Behavior and Evolution,* A. Roe and G. G. Simpson, eds. New Haven: Yale University Press, 1958, p. 103.

———, "The Problem of Development," Brookhaven National Laboratory Lecture Series 35. Upton, N.Y.: Brookhaven National Laboratory, 1964. "The fundamental mechanisms may well turn out to be simple. . . ."

Cohen, E. P., "On the Mechanism of Immunity—In Defense of Evolution," *Ann. Rev. Microbiol., 22* (1968), 283.

Cohen, S., and C. Milstein, "Structure and Biological Properties of Immunoglobulins," *Advan. Immunol., 7* (1967), 1.

Cold Spring Harbor Symp. Quant. Biol., 29 (1964); *32* (1967). The first volume contains articles on human proteins and on somatic cell genetics; the second volume is on antibodies.

Crick, F. H. C., *Of Molecules and Men.* Seattle: University of Washington Press, 1966. A Nobel-prize winner thinks out loud about vitalism and the prospect before us in a short and lucid volume.

Curtis, A. S. G., "Cell Contact and Adhesion," *Biol. Rev., 37* (1962), 82. Review of the contact behavior of cells.

Davis, B. D., and L. Warren, eds., *The Specificity of Cell Surfaces.* Englewood Cliffs, N. J.: Prentice-Hall, Inc., 1967. The emphasis is on bacteria and on animal cells in this 1965 symposium.

Denis, H., "Role of Messenger Ribonucleic Acid in Embryonic Development." *Advan. Morphogenesis, 7* (1968), 115.

Dutton, R. W., "In Vitro Studies of Immunological Responses of Lymphoid Cells," *Advan. Immunol., 6* (1967), 253.

Finch, B. W., and B. Ephrussi, "Retention of Multiple Developmental Potentialities by Cells of a Mouse Testicular Teratocarcinoma during Prolonged Culture in Vitro and Their Extinction upon Hybridization with Cells of Permanent Lines," *Proc. Natl. Acad. Sci. U.S., 57* (1967), 615.

Fuller, J. L., and W. R. Thompson, *Behavior Genetics.* New York: John Wiley & Sons, Inc., 1960. Probably the best place to go to find out how little we really know, genetically and otherwise, concerning behavior.

Gartler, S. M., and D. A. Pious, "Genetics of Mammalian Cell Cultures," *Humangenetik, 2* (1966), 83.

Green, H., and G. J. Todaro, "The Mammalian Cell as Differentiated Microorganism," *Ann. Rev. Microbiol., 21* (1967), 573. A review of cell culture methods in the study of differentiation.

Greenwalt, T. J., ed., *Advances in Immunogenetics.* Philadelphia: J. B. Lippincott Company, 1967. Genetic variations in human immunoglobulins and other blood proteins and antigens are reviewed.

Gross, P. R., "Biochemistry of Differentiation," *Ann. Rev. Biochem. 37* (1968), 631.

———, "RNA Metabolism in Embryonic Development and Differentiation," *New Engl. J. Med., 276* (1967), 1239, 1297.

Herzenberg, L. A., H. O. McDevitt, and L. A. Herzenberg, "Genetics of Antibodies," *Ann. Rev. Genet., 2* (1968), 209.

Heslop-Harrison, J., "Differentiation," *Ann. Rev. Plant Physiol. 18* (1967), 325. A look at developmental mechanisms in plants.

Hirsch, J. (ed.), *Behavior-Genetic Analysis.* New York: McGraw-Hill Book Company, 1967. A source book that concentrates on basic biology and methods.

Krohn, P. L., ed., *Topics in the Biology of Aging.* New York: John Wiley & Sons, Inc. (Interscience Division), 1966.

Krooth, R. S., "The Future of Mammalian Cell Genetics," *Birth Defects Orig. Article Ser., 1* (1965), No. 2, 21.

Lennox, E. S., and M. Cohn, "Immunoglobulins," *Ann. Rev. Biochem., 35,* Pt. I (1967), 365.

Locke, M., ed., *Cytodifferentiation and Macromolecular Synthesis* (1963) and *Major Problems in Developmental Biology* (1967) —Symp. Soc. Study of Development and Growth. New York: Academic Press,

Inc. These and other symposia in the series form good introductions to modern experimentation in developmental biology.

Lyon, M., "Chromosomal and Subchromosomal Inactivation," *Ann. Rev. Genet., 2* (1968), 31.

Nemer, M., "Transfer of Genetic Information During Embryogenesis," *Progr. Nucleic Acid Res. Mol. Biol., 7* (1967), 243.

Makinodan, T., and J. F. Albright, "Proliferative and Differentiative Manifestations of Cellular Immune Potential," *Progr. in Allergy, 10* (1967), 1. An advanced critique of experiments bearing on the cellular mechanisms underlying antibody formation.

Plescia, O. J., and W. Braun, eds., *Nucleic Acids in Immunology.* New York: Academic Press, Inc., 1968. A symposium including original papers on the role of nucleic acids in antibody formation.

Reiner, J. M., *The Organism as an Adaptive Control System,* Englewood Cliffs, N.J.: Prentice-Hall, Inc., 1968. Chapter 6 in this book discusses "the organism as a whole" in a manner that points out well important questions facing students of gene action.

Rothfield, L., and A. Finkelstein, "Membrane Biochemistry," *Ann. Rev. Biochem., 37* (1968), 463. Membrane structure and function are amenable to analyses heretofore reserved for the more simple biochemical pathways.

Rous, P., "The Challenge to Man of the Neoplastic Cell," *Science, 157* (1967), 24.

Sonneborn, T. M., "Implications of the New Genetics for Biology and Man," *Am. Inst. Biol. Sci. Bull., 13,* No. 2 (1963), 22. Both biological and biochemical approaches are indispensable for mutual progress; one of the few analyses written without a chip on the shoulder.

———, "Does Preformed Cell Structure Play an Essential Role in Cell Heredity?" in *The Nature of Biological Diversity.* J. M. Allen, ed. New York: McGraw-Hill, Inc., 1963, p. 165. The answer is as stimulating as the question posed, and extensions are to be found on page 375 of the book, cited above, edited by R. A. Brink.

Spuhler, J. N. (ed.), *Genetic Diversity and Human Behavior.* Chicago: Aldine, 1967. A series of advanced reviews of a not-so-far advanced area of endeavor.

Steinberg, M. S., "Reconstruction of Tissues by Dissociated Cells," *Science, 141* (1963), 401. The adhesion and motility of cells as they spread out in specific patterns.

Stoker, M., "Contact and Short-range Interactions Affecting Growth of Animal Cells in Culture," *Current Topics in Developmental Biol., 2* (1967), 107.

Strehler, B. L., ed., *Biology of Aging.* Washington, D.C.: American Institute of Biological Sciences, 1960. A symposium on an age-old, old-age problem.

Swanson, C. P., *Cytology and Cytogenetics.* Englewood Cliffs, N.J.: Prentice-Hall, Inc., 1957. A thorough, advanced textbook that treats position effects and gene dosage and gives numerous references to the original literature.

"Symposium on Differentiation and Growth of Hemoglobin- and Immunoglobin-Synthesizing Cells," published as Suppl. 1 of *J. Cellular Physiol., 67* (1966). Articles that examine the structure, synthesis, and evolution of two important classes of proteins.

Ursprung, H., "Genetic Control of Differentiation in Higher Organisms," *Federation Proc., 23* (1964), 990, and "Genes and Development," in *Organogenesis,* R. L. DeHaan and H. Ursprung, eds. New York: Holt, Rinehart and Winston, Inc., 1965, p. 3. The latter article is an extension of the former; both attempt to extrapolate ideas from microbial systems into the less well-defined realm of developmental processes in higher organisms.

———, "Developmental Genetics," *Ann. Rev. Genet., 1* (1967), 139. A concise picture of results obtained in various approaches in the elucidation of animal development that may be broadly classified as genetical.

Wilson, E. B., *The Cell in Development and Heredity,* 3rd ed., with corrections. New York: The Macmillan Company, 1925. This and Brachet's *Chemical Embryology,* classics of the eras in which they were written, call attention to many interesting problems that current concepts and techniques in molecular biology appear capable of solving in the future.

Wright, B. E., "Multiple Causes and Controls in Differentiation," *Science, 153* (1966), 830.

Subject Index

Suppressor:
  action in vitro, 175–178
  action in vivo, 175–178
  amber, 175
  anticodon, 176–177
  intragenic, 50–52, 146–149
  joining of channeled pathways, 92–93
  of missense, 175
  of nonsense, 168–169, 175
  ochre, 175
  relation to tRNA, 175–178
  tRNA primary structure, 177
  UGA, 175
Synthetase:
  aminoacyl tRNA, 98–100
  polypeptide, 129
Synthetic polynucleotides (*see* Ribopoly-
    nucleotides, synthetic)
Syntrophism (crossfeeding), 80–81, 83

Temperature-sensitive mutants, 41–42,
    174–178
Template, DNA, 2
  in mRNA synthesis, 112–116, 131–132
Terminal amino acid:
  C-terminal, 12
  N-terminal, 12, 20, 124–125, 165–167
Terminal CCA in tRNA, 101–102
Terminal purines in mRNA, 113
Termination:
  effect on transcription, 201–202
  polypeptide chain, 130, 167–170
  and suppressor mutations, 168–169
Tertiary structure, proteins, 9, 22–25
Thr (*see* Threonine)
Threonine, structure, 10
Thymine:
  ribothymidine in tRNA, 101, 180
  structure, 3
TMV (tobacco mosaic virus):
  amino acid replacements, 47–50
  amino acid sequence, 48
  electron micrograph, 26
  lesions, 47
  monomers, 74
  multimers, 27, 74
  structure, 25–27
Trans configuration, definition, 60
Transcription, 4
  control of, 161–162, 184–203
  definition, 3
  direction, 112–116
  initiation complex, 186–187, 194
  mRNA, 108–112
  relation to translation, 186, 196–202
Transduction, 58–59, 199

Transfer RNA (*see* tRNA)
Transition mutation, 144
Translation, 160–181:
  amino acid incorporation, 120–121
  artifacts, 124, 125, 171
  chain initiation, 124–125, 165–167
  chain termination, 130, 167–170, 201–
    202
  controls, summary, 181
  definition, 3
  direction in vitro, 130–133
  direction in vivo, 126–130, 133, 148–
    149
  fidelity, 99–100, 170–174
  genetic modification, 174–178
  infidelities, 170–174
  initiation, 124–125, 165–167
  relation to transcription, 196–202
  role of ribosomes, 107, 187
  in vivo, model, 127–129, 134–135
Translocase, 129
Transversion mutation, 144
Trinucleotides, binding to ribosomes,
    125
Tripeptide, definition, 11
Triplet code, definition, 141
tRNA, 100–103:
  acceptor activity, 98–100
  anticodon, 103
  attachment site of amino acid, 102
  binding and genetic code, 140, 153–
    156
  binding to ribosomes, 124–125
  codon-anticodon recognition, 177, 179–
    180
  esterification, 102
  genetic control, 100
  molecular weight, 102
  nucleotide sequence, 101–102
  periodate treatment, 102
  references, 117–119, 182–183
  specificity, 103
  structure, 101–102
  in suppressor mutants, 174–178
  synthetase, 98–100
  unusual nucleotides, 101–102, 180
  wobble hypothesis, 180
Trp (*see* Tryptophan)
Trypsin, specificity, 13–14
Tryptic peptides, 16–17, 126–127
Tryptophan:
  biosynthesis:
    and aromatic pathway, 89–90
    detailed pathway, 38–39
    diagram, 30, 39, 90, 196
    Neurospora, 40–41
  mutants, crossfeeding, 80–81

Author Index